Orwell and the Left

Orwell and the Left

Alex Zwerdling

New Haven and London, Yale University Press

Library of Congress catalog card number: 74-75951
International standard book number: 0-300-01686-7

Designed by John O. C. McCrillis
and set in Baskerville type.
Printed in the United States of America by
The Alpine Press, Inc., South Braintree, Massachusetts.

Published in Great Britain, Europe, Africa, and Asia
(except Japan) by Yale University Press, Ltd., London.
Distributed in Australia and New Zealand by Book &
Film Services, Artarmon, N.S.W., Australia; and in
Japan by Harper & Row, Publishers, Tokyo Office.

To Florence

Contents

Abbreviations

Quotations from Orwell's books are taken from the Uniform Edition of his work published by Secker and Warburg. Abbreviations used in the citations refer to the following texts:

AF	*Animal Farm: A Fairy Story* (London, 1962)
BD	*Burmese Days: A Novel* (London, 1949)
CD	*A Clergyman's Daughter* (London, 1960)
CEJL	*The Collected Essays, Journalism and Letters*, ed. Sonia Orwell and Ian Angus (London, 1968), 4 vols.
CUA	*Coming Up for Air* (London, 1948)
DOPL	*Down and Out in Paris and London* (London, 1949)
HC	*Homage to Catalonia* (London, 1951)
KAF	*Keep the Aspidistra Flying* (London, 1954)
NEF	*Nineteen Eighty-Four: A Novel* (London, 1950)
RWP	*The Road to Wigan Pier* (London, 1959)

Other quotations, from Orwell's uncollected pieces and from other writers, are identified in the notes.

Acknowledgments

I began to think about this book during a year as a fellow of the Center for Advanced Study in the Behavioral Sciences in Palo Alto, California. I am deeply grateful to the staff of that exemplary institution for the readiness with which they seemed to provide for every need: quiet and leisure, excellent secretarial help, and a distinguished group of colleagues with whom to discuss one's work. I particularly want to thank Robert C. Tucker of Princeton and Yosal Rogat of Stanford, from whom I learned a great deal during that year. I am also grateful to the American Council of Learned Societies and to the University of California Humanities Research Committee for fellowships that allowed me to complete the book.

The Orwell Archive at University College, London, proved invaluable; I am indebted to its director, Ian Angus, and to its former assistant librarian, Margaret Skerl, for their help. Dr. Lola Szladits, Curator of the Henry W. and Albert A. Berg Collection of the New York Public Library (Astor, Lenox, and Tilden Foundations), permitted me to use the important collection of Orwell letters there.

A number of people have read all or parts of the book in manuscript and have offered valuable suggestions for improvement: Paul Alpers, Richard Bridgman, Frederick Crews, Allen Guttmann, Samuel Hynes, Martha Meisel, Martin Meisel, Leonard Michaels, and Florence Zwerdling. I am greatly indebted to them, and to my patient and scrupulous editor, Barbara Folsom, for helping to make this a better book.

Orwell's works are quoted by permission of Mrs. Sonia Brownell Orwell, Martin Secker and Warburg, Ltd., and Harcourt Brace Jovanovich, Inc. Copyright © 1952, 1968 by Sonia Brownell Orwell. *Burmese Days*, Harcourt Brace Jovanovich, Inc., copyright © 1934 by George Orwell, copyright renewed 1962 by Sonia Pitt-Rivers. *Coming Up for Air*, copyright © 1950 by Harcourt Brace Jovanovich, Inc. *Down and Out in Paris and London*,

Part I

Taking a Stand

1

The Left's Loyal Opposition

i

One of the constant temptations of the intellectual historian is to see pattern or unity where once there was chaos or opposition. As the near past recedes from us, its quarrels, once sculpted in high relief, flatten out; we discover an overarching unity in its diversity; we invent the generalizations by which we characterize a decade, an age, and finally a civilization. Something like this process has begun to affect our view of the 1930s. The "personality" of the decade has become sharper and more easily identifiable—like a telling caricature. In literary history it is identified as a period in which the writer was under great internal and external pressure to write with a political purpose. He was told that art could only be justified as an instrument for the transformation of society, or at any rate for the molding of consciousness. The practice of writing to satisfy a private rather than a public need was widely discredited. A writer anxious to remain politically neutral had to resist an extraordinary barrage of criticism. Western civilization was in peril and Olympian detachment was considered an act of treachery.

Yet the response of writers to this pressure was far from uniform. Some resisted it entirely or produced works that were more hermetic than anything they had written previously. It is worth remembering that both *Finnegans Wake* and Yeats's final version of *A Vision* were published in the "political decade." The pressure of events created as many partisans of the Right as of the Left, although the gravitation from the political center to the poles of commitment—fascism and communism—was unmistakable. The attraction toward the two extremist movements "bore all the signs of inexorable fatality," as Arthur Koestler later wrote:

"There was no 'third force' and no third choice." [1]

The association of certain writers with these two political movements has fostered a sense of them as moving in groups and producing works characteristic of the period rather than of the author. Books like the influential collection of writers' confessions, *The God That Failed*, have succeeded in creating a stock figure of the left-wing writer in the 1930s: the religious convert to communism and the cult of Russia who became disillusioned at the end of the decade and moved toward the Right or political quietism. The danger is that the individual writer becomes lost in this group identity.

George Orwell's is a case in point. The books by which most readers know him, *Animal Farm* (1945) and *Nineteen Eighty-Four* (1949) seem to be products of the last stage of disillusionment with the Left, from which one might well deduce the first steps of the familiar process: the infatuation with communism, the growing doubts, the inevitable break. Even Lionel Trilling's fine essay on Orwell interprets the earlier *Homage to Catalonia* in this way, as an example of "a whole literary genre with which we have become familiar in the last decade, the personal confession of involvement and then of disillusionment with Communism." [2] Nevertheless, neither the interpretation of the last works as right-wing documents nor the inference of a prior conversion and apostasy has any basis in fact. For Orwell was never either a true believer or a turncoat: his political beliefs developed rather than changed in the course of his career. He identified himself with the Left from the mid-thirties until his death in 1950. As he says in the late essay "Why I Write," "Every line of serious work that I have written since 1936 has been written, directly or indirectly, *against* totalitarianism and *for* democratic Socialism, as I understand it" (*CEJL* 1: 5). And when his work, after the publication of *Animal Farm*, became popular with a conservative audience, he refused to associate himself with his new readers. When he was asked in 1945 to address a meeting protesting Soviet pressure on Yugoslavia, sponsored by what Orwell took to be "an essentially

1. *Arrow in the Blue: An Autobiography* (New York, 1961), p. 258.
2. *The Opposing Self* (New York, 1959), p. 152.

Conservative body," he declined, even though he shared their indignation. "I belong to the Left and must work inside it," he insisted. "It seems to me that one can only denounce the crimes now being committed in Poland, Jugoslavia, etc if one is equally insistent on ending Britain's unwanted rule in India" (*CEJL* 4: 30).

Conor Cruise O'Brien has argued that Orwell "shook the confidence of the English left, perhaps permanently," that his effect on it "might be compared to that of Voltaire on the French nobility: he weakened their belief in their own ideology, made them ashamed of their clichés, left them intellectually more scrupulous and more defenceless."[3] Though all of this may be true, not all of it was Orwell's intention. He was interested in attacking the complacency of the Left, not its confidence; in making it more scrupulous, not more defenseless. Essentially he thought of himself as a diagnostician of the Left's ills. His aim was to reform and strengthen, not to discredit the world to which he had pledged his loyalty: he was the Left's loyal opposition. His critique of socialism could be savage, particularly in *The Road to Wigan Pier*, which Richard Rovere has called "perhaps the most rigorous examination that any doctrine has ever received at the hands of an adherent."[4] Yet his criticism was always designed as internal; it was precisely Orwell's unquestioning fidelity to the ideals of the movement that, in his mind, justified his uncompromising criticism of some of its theories, tactics, and leaders.

In following this policy, Orwell was in effect dissociating himself from the powerful propagandistic pressures of his time. He was widely accused of turning the weapon of his art against his own side, of being a Judas of the Left. A writer's political criticism was supposed to be external, not internal; otherwise he was "objectively" helping the enemy. This attitude toward literature, which was to influence so many writers on the Left in the 1930s, originated in its modern form in the Soviet Union and was popularized in Western countries by the Communist Party. It has

3. "Orwell Looks at the World," *Writers and Politics* (New York, 1965), pp. 32–33.
4. "Introduction," *The Orwell Reader: Fiction, Essays, and Reportage* (New York, 1956), p. xv.

its roots in Marx's theory that culture and ideology are ultimately determined by the economic conditions of the society that creates them. "It is not the consciousness of men that determines their being, but, on the contrary, their social being that determines their consciousness," as Marx put it in a well-known formula.[5] The idea clearly undermines the importance of the arts; far from shaping their society, they are its products, its commodities. Marx thinks of this process as indirect, subtle, and unwilled. In the Soviet state, the idea was significantly altered. Marx thought that art was an unconscious product of political and economic necessity; Lenin and Stalin attempted to turn it into a conscious one. Thus literature became a recognized part of the official ideology, and its manipulation and control became one of the tasks of the state. "Down with non-partisan writers! Down with literary supermen!" Lenin wrote in his *Party Organization and Party Literature.* "Literature must become *part* of the common cause of the proletariat, 'cog and wheel' of a single, great Social-Democratic mechanism brought into motion by the entire politically-conscious vanguard of the entire working class. Literature must become a component of organized, planned and integrated Social-Democratic party work." [6] When Lenin became the leader of the new Soviet state, he put this policy into practice. The language of coercion ("must") became the language of literary criticism. Furthermore, the new Soviet leader established a clear hierarchy in artistic matters: the Communist Party set tasks for the Commissariat of Education; the Commissariat did the same for the various artistic organizations; and those organizations in turn passed the word along to their individual members. He established the chain of command which was later to be called the "Party line." [7] Although Lenin himself made little use of this centralized control of culture, his successors have not hesitated to do so.

5. Preface to *A Contribution to the Critique of Political Economy*, reprinted in Karl Marx and Frederick Engels, *Selected Works in Two Volumes* (Moscow, 1962), 1: 363.

6. V. I. Lenin, *Where to Begin? Party Organization and Party Literature; The Working Class and Its Press* (Moscow, n.d.), pp. 21–22.

7. See the resolution he sent to the Proletcult Congress in 1920, reprinted in V. I. Lenin, *Selected Works in Three Volumes* (Moscow, 1960–61), 3: 518–19.

The metaphors used in communist directives concerning the arts are frequently mechanical. Lenin called literature the "cog and wheel" of a machine. Stalin referred to writers as "engineers of human souls." [8] The importance of these images lies in their assumption that literature can be manufactured and is strictly comparable to the product of any other factory. Orwell satirizes the whole process in *Nineteen Eighty-Four* by making his heroine an operator of a novel-writing machine in the Fiction Department:

> She enjoyed her work, which consisted chiefly in running and servicing a powerful but tricky electric motor. She was "not clever", but was fond of using her hands and felt at home with machinery. She could describe the whole process of composing a novel, from the general directive issued by the Planning Committee down to the final touching-up by the Rewrite Squad. But she was not interested in the finished product. She "didn't much care for reading", she said. Books were just a commodity that had to be produced, like jam or bootlaces. [*NEF*, p. 134]

The ideal is that of a service literature that exists to satisfy the needs of a society or a political movement as they are determined, not by the writer, but by his hierarchical superiors. It casts the artist in the role of a disseminator rather than a discoverer of truth, and it implies a good deal of self-confidence on the part of those who control him. For they are the real artists of their society, in the sense that they create its values and ideas; the writers are only, in effect, their publishers. So Lenin could say that the socialist movement needs writers who can convey the "already known and already evaluated policy." [9] The phrase occurs in his essay "The Character of Our Newspapers" (1918); but this early Soviet formula for journalism eventually became a policy for literary creation as well. In the words of Andrei Sinyavsky, the subjects of Soviet literature "all develop in one direction, and a direction well known in advance." [10] Literature must not move

8. Quoted in A. Zhdanov et al., *Problems of Soviet Literature: Reports and Speeches at the First Soviet Writers' Congress* (New York, n.d.), p. 21.

9. "The Character of Our Newspapers," in Lenin, *Where to Begin?* p. 66.

10. Abram Tertz (pseud.), *On Socialist Realism* (New York, 1960), p. 43.

beyond the realm of the known; the unexplored territory of doubt, confusion, and unresolved contradiction is declared out of bounds. When these policies reached the West through the medium of the Communist Party, they were not significantly altered to meet conditions of artistic independence. The writer on the Left was to be set tasks by the Party and reprimanded when he failed to carry out his duties. W. H. Auden, for example, was encouraged by the Party to visit Spain during the Civil War. As Claud Cockburn recalls, "what we really wanted him for was to go to the front, write some pieces saying hurrah for the Republic, and then go away and write some poems, also saying hurrah for the Republic." [11] The easy cynicism of such statements conveys a good deal about the attitude of the Party toward Western writers: they were instruments, tools. One wonders what it was able to make of its commissioned product, Auden's ironic, sophisticated, difficult "Spain 1937"; or how it might have justified such policies to Marx himself, who once wrote: "The writer in no way regards his works as a *means*. They are *ends in themselves;* so little are they a means for him and others that, when necessary, he sacrifices *his* existence to *theirs,* and, like the preacher of religion, he takes as his first principle: 'Obey God more than men.' " [12]

Orwell's attitude toward the left-wing pressure to write propaganda was fundamentally hostile. He recognized the age as one which "conspires to turn the writer, and every other kind of artist as well, into a minor official, working on themes handed to him from above and never telling what seems to him the whole of the truth" (*CEJL* 4: 60). Yet the obvious hostility of these words should not be understood as a rejection of political involvement by a writer whose fundamental impulse was purely aesthetic. Unlike many of the fellow-travelers of the decade, he remained deeply interested in politics and political ideology throughout his life. Although he might not have written political books in a less political age, it is difficult to believe that he could have been as indifferent to social forces as he once claimed: "In a peaceful age I might have written ornate or merely descriptive books, and might

11. "A Conversation with Claud Cockburn," *The Review*, nos. 11–12, p. 51.

12. "Debaten ueber Pressfreiheit," reprinted in Karl Marx and Frederick Engels, *Literature and Art: Selections from Their Writings* (New York, 1947), p. 63.

have remained almost unaware of my political loyalties" (*CEJL* I: 4).

Orwell's career in fact reveals that he had a far greater tolerance for and involvement in politics than most of his literary contemporaries. Considering the pressures of his time, his political attitudes remained strikingly unapocalyptic. He had no faith in the possibility of a *total* transformation of society. Most of his fellow writers drifted into revolutionary politics partly through an impatience with the banality and slowness of democratic, evolutionary social change. It was almost as if they could not afford the time for anything likely to take longer than an instantaneous revolution, and their impatience is suggested in Auden's poem:

> Today the expending of powers
> On the flat ephemeral pamphlet and the boring meeting.
> ["Spain 1937"]

In contrast to such tedious preparations, the revolution itself was glorified—in Christopher Caudwell's sarcastic phrase—"as a kind of giant explosion which will blow up everything they feel to be hampering them." [13]

Orwell's conviction that real and lasting social changes come about slowly meant that he was less subject to such impatience. He knew that politics is the realm of expediency and compromise, of pressure and delay, of progress and reaction. Many of his fellow writers on the Left were essentially bored by politics and outraged by the triviality of the "solutions" it brought forth to the great human problems. This impatience gave them little staying power, and their associations with the revolutionary parties were predictably short-lived. Orwell, by contrast, remained an active socialist all his life, a fact which also helps to explain his attitude toward propaganda. A writer may devote his energies to writing "the flat ephemeral pamphlet" from Party dictation if he feels this is merely a short phase of his career, and if he is sure the Party understands the best way to bring the prerevolutionary movement to a revolutionary end. Orwell felt that both of these attitudes were thoroughly naïve. He assumed that a worldwide socialist

13. *Illusion and Reality: A Study of the Sources of Poetry* (New York, 1947), p. 283.

society might not be brought into being for decades, or even centuries, if indeed it were ever to come about. And he was too convinced of the failures of Marxism as a predictive system and the Communist Party as an agent of social change to believe that he would be helping the cause of socialism by accepting communist ideology without question.

In addition, Orwell was profoundly suspicious of ideology per se as a guide to literary creation. It was not merely Marxism he distrusted, but any theory of history that claimed to predict the future in detail with such dogmatic self-confidence. Every previous revolution had created as many problems as it had solved, most of which could hardly have been anticipated beforehand. The solutions to these problems were arrived at, if at all, only through the collaboration of many men. No ideology would have helped them as much as their own powers of observation. The writer was one of these observers. His sensitivity to the quality of life around him helped to identify and publicize the unresolved problems of his time. To surrender his initiative in choosing subjects and recording impressions meant to deny his own powers of vision, his ability to see and call attention to the new forms of frustration and conflict which life so unpredictably invents. In this process, the socialist revolution would be no different from the revolutions of the past. No mere doctrine could be relied upon to understand and assess the nature of the human stress that its triumphs and failures might bring about. The writer's most valuable social duty was to record that stress before it was generally acknowledged and understood, and certainly before it had been assigned a place in a political program. The hierarchical arrangement proposed by Lenin is reversed: it is the political party that must learn from the socially observant writer, not vice versa, because the party is more likely to develop a vested interest in its own policies and to ignore the suffering those policies might bring about.

If the idea of the writer's freedom means anything at all, Orwell writes in "The Prevention of Literature," it means "the freedom to criticise and oppose" (*CEJL* 1: 59). His work comes alive only when he is not ratifying what is already generally known. A truth for him must be subjective, his own discovery ratified by his own feelings. Orwell insists that this cannot be falsified, that a writer finds it psychologically impossible to "misrepresent the scenery of his own mind: he cannot say with any conviction that he likes what he dislikes, or believes what he disbelieves. If he is forced to do so, the only result is that his creative faculties dry up" (*CEJL* 4: 65). The policy of presenting writers with themes or attitudes that it is their task to "realize" in works of art ignores the essential nature of artistic creation and condemns the artist to impotence. He may put the words down on the page, but if they do not express a subjective truth for him, they simply will not live. A directed art is a contradiction in terms.

"To accept an orthodoxy," Orwell says in one of his late essays, "is always to inherit unresolved contradictions" (*CEJL* 4: 411). Yet the system of belief itself must deny the existence of such contradictions because they challenge the completeness and truth of its own dispensation. An ideology-dominated organization will regularly accuse its internal critics of heresy and attempt to exclude them from the ranks of the true disciples. For example, deviations from the orthodox Marxist position are dismissed simply by adding the suffix "ism": economism, opportunism, reformism, left-wing deviationism, Trotskyism, and so on. The effect is to suggest that the rebel group is creating a rival system and isolating itself from the original movement rather than working toward its reformation. The analogies to the medieval Church are obvious, and Orwell frequently draws attention to them (see, for example, *CEJL* 4: 61).

Orwell believed that any form of orthodox belief is incompatible with literary creation, but he felt that certain elements in communist and other totalitarian ideologies offered greater danger to the writer than any previous creed. The unprecedented thing about the Party line was that it was so unstable, that it changed from one day to the next. The doctrines of totalitarian states, unlike the more fixed beliefs of the older orthodoxies, "are always liable to be altered at a moment's notice" (*CEJL* 4: 66). Orwell gives the example of the sudden shifts of attitude demanded when Stalin's policy toward Hitler was reversed, first in 1939, at the time of the Nazi-Soviet Pact, and then again in

1941, when Russia joined the Allies. A more recent example might be the post-1956 vilification and subsequent partial rehabilitation of Stalin himself.

In both cases writers were expected to respond immediately to the shifts in policy. But, as Orwell says, such rapid shifts are psychologically impossible for the writer: "If he is to switch his allegiance at exactly the right moment, he must either tell lies about his subjective feelings, or else suppress them altogether. In either case he has destroyed his dynamo. Not only will ideas refuse to come to him, but the very words he uses will seem to stiffen under his touch" (*CEJL* 4: 66). Behind this idea is an assumption about the connection between sincerity and artistic vitality. It is worth noting that Orwell criticizes such procedures not because they are immoral (they may or may not be) but because as a policy for literature they are *impossible,* because they do not work even if the writer forces himself to try. By comparison, the Catholic orthodoxy of the Middle Ages at least permitted the writer to believe the same things all his life, and thus left his day-to-day responses relatively untouched.

Political propaganda demands not only ideological orthodoxy but impersonality in art. Orwell's inability to write propagandistically was the product not only of his naturally heretical cast of mind but of his insistence that the artist cannot refine himself out of his work. Even Orwell's most blatantly political works are highly personal, as his constant use of autobiographical material even in his documentaries demonstrates. Yet many of the critics on the Left insisted that the personality of the writer has no place in a work of political importance. As Karl Radek said in his speech to the first conference of Soviet writers in 1934, "We must turn the artist away from his 'inside,' turn his eyes to these great facts of reality which threaten to crash down upon our heads." [14] There was no leisure, especially by the late thirties, for a "personal" art. Everywhere, Marxist literary critics called for an end to spiritual autobiography. As Randall Swingler wrote in the influential English journal *Left Review*, the revolution is communal, not individual, and it requires of the writer "a giving away of

14. Zhdanov et al., *Problems of Soviet Literature*, p. 179.

the self . . . a death of the self." [15]

Orwell saw the point of these demands yet could not respond sympathetically. Critics who made them reduced the complex process of literary creation to its component parts and then pretended that the same work could be done with only a few of the fragments. His own sense of the mixed motives of writers and the psychological complexity of successful literary composition assured him that such demands could not be met. He recognizes that one of the essential components of his own work is political, that it is invariably when he lacks a political purpose that he is "betrayed into purple passages, sentences without meaning, decorative adjectives and humbug generally" (*CEJL* 1: 7). Yet it is equally true of his work that when it does not simultaneously fulfill a private need it becomes indistinguishable from the political ephemera his age turned out. The difficult task which faced him, and which he spent his life trying to solve, was to write about public issues in works of personal sincerity that would stand the test of rigorous aesthetic scrutiny. If he was seldom successful in this ambitious undertaking, it can at any rate be said of him that he did not try to make his task any simpler, and that in refusing to do so he was swimming against the current of his times.

ii

To call Orwell an internal critic of socialism, as I have done, suggests that he deserves to be considered seriously not only as a writer but as a socialist thinker. His contribution to the history of socialist thought was not, however, original in the way that the writings of Lenin, Trotsky, Eduard Bernstein, or Sidney Webb— to name only a few influential post-Marxian socialists—clearly were. Orwell's theoretical ideas were in fact derived from these and lesser writers. Yet his position in the history of socialist thought seems to me important. Orwell was not a theorist but a tester of theories, a skeptical observer attempting to assess the validity of certain accepted or controversial socialist ideas.

He wrote in an age that was ripe for such work. The three

15. *Left Review* 1 (1934): 78.

decades of his adult life—the 1920s, 1930s, and 1940s—were important for the socialist movement because for the first time its theories could be tested against reality. The movement had been transformed from the relatively weak opposition force of the previous century into one of the principal shaping powers of the modern world. Socialism, whether revolutionary or evolutionary, had become a mass movement that could make and unmake governments, seize power, and transform existing societies. In Germany, France, and England, parties calling themselves socialist were strong enough to control parliamentary bodies and to attract even the political careerists anxious to join a crescent movement. In the Soviet Union, such a party had seized control and was rapidly turning an ancient feudal country into a modern state attempting to put socialist ideas into practice.

These formidable successes seemed to demand a reassessment of socialist theory. As Orwell wrote, "the whole left-wing ideology, scientific and Utopian, was evolved by people who had no immediate prospect of attaining power. It was, therefore, an extremist ideology, utterly contemptuous of kings, governments, laws, prisons, police forces, armies, flags, frontiers, patriotism, religion, conventional morality, and, in fact, the whole existing scheme of things" (*CEJL* 4: 409–10). Orwell's words suggest that the wholesale rejection of the old order is characteristic of the adolescent stage of a great social movement, when its chief motive force is (often legitimate) outrage. Adult power, on the other hand, carries with it a whole new set of problems, essentially those of construction rather than of destruction.

Orwell was concerned with the maturity of the socialist movement, and particularly with the relationship between its youthful ideals and its adult responsibilities. He knew that this was a crucial stage in its growth, and one in which the temptations to forget or deny its original aspirations and act like any other government in power would be hard to resist. He was to concentrate particularly on the discrepancies between theory and practice, not always with a view to condemning the latter as a betrayal of the former. He wanted to know which part of the socialist program was in fact realizable, which was not, and why. As evidence he used the actual practice of nominally socialist leaders, parties, and governments, of which he was a close and clinically minded student. It is only in the sense that Marx can truly be called a *scientific* socialist that Orwell might be considered his disciple; but he was to turn the method against the master himself and expose what he took to be the utopian element in Marxist doctrine.

As a socialist, Orwell was neither the creator of a new system nor the unquestioning adherent of an established one. Although his fundamental loyalty was, broadly speaking, to the evolutionary rather than the revolutionary wing of the movement, he did not hesitate to use the ideas of each in the assessment of the other. In his most pessimistic moments, he felt that the revolutionist scorn for the methods of socialist reformers, and the reformist fears of revolutionary dictatorship, had both proven to be perfectly valid and had thus deprived the movement of a plausible theory of tactics. Yet in calling attention to such tragic failures, Orwell was not expressing his own disillusionment with the ideals of socialism but asking the committed to acknowledge the possibility that their ideals might never actually be put into practice. If he had been a profoundly original socialist thinker, he might have gone on to propose a set of tactics that took these failures into account and used them as the foundation for a new and more realistic policy. In this, he remained a critic rather than a creator. Yet the criticism of an accepted orthodoxy is an essential element in keeping it alive. By constantly raising embarrassing questions about socialist assumptions, Orwell was trying to force the movement to scrutinize itself in order to determine whether it was built on reality or fantasy. There is a certain ruthlessness in his demand that socialism stand naked before the mirror. But one must keep in mind that the movement was his movement, its exposure his own, its failures ones he would feel deeply. Unlike many of his fellow socialists, however, he was unwilling to live a life of sustaining illusion.

By this point in history, socialism has evolved into a movement with so many contradictory ideals, theories, and policies, and so many rival organizations, that one wonders whether one can still speak of it in the singular rather than the plural. Yet Orwell always treated it as a single, coherent movement, a tree with many branches. Despite the extraordinary infighting and continuing schisms that characterized the behavior of the various left-wing groups in the thirties and forties, he consistently treated "The Left" as a unifiable, if not unified, body. It is important to keep this assumption in mind while reading the following pages, since it accounts for Orwell's tendency to generalize on the grand scale. When assessing his critique of socialism specifically, it helps to understand how he used the word and what he took to be the essential aims of the movement. His ideas will, I hope, be clearer if we grasp the psychological roots of his faith before examining the specific ideas and political policies he came to endorse.

How and why socialists come to the movement often determines their choices within it; certainly this was true of Orwell. He was drawn to socialism neither because of its economic theories nor its links with pacifism nor its criticism of the chaotic and inefficient element in capitalism. The emotional source of Orwell's socialism was his hatred of hierarchy in any form. He simply could not tolerate the fact that the world is divided into masters and servants. As he says in *The Road to Wigan Pier*, at a certain point in his life he was suddenly overwhelmed by the imperative necessity of finding an escape "from every form of man's dominion over man" (*RWP*, p. 150). His first encounter with privilege, in the snobbish preparatory school he describes in "Such, Such Were the Joys," may have predisposed Orwell to search for such an escape; but the more immediate motivation was his sense of guilt in having associated himself for the first five years of his adult life with British imperialism in Burma. As a colonial policeman, he was there to protect the powerful from the weak, and he had not hesitated to use his own position in ways which later revolted him. He recalls the faces "of subordinates I had bullied and aged peasants I had snubbed, of servants and coolies I had hit with my fists in moments of rage" (*RWP*, p. 149).

As a way of expiating these human crimes, Orwell resigned from his post at the age of twenty-four and then began literally to put himself in the place of his victims, or of people like them. The attempt to deny his own middle-class status and sink down into the world of the poor is recorded in some of his early works, particularly in *Down and Out in Paris and London, A Clergyman's Daughter*, and *Keep the Aspidistra Flying*. Yet to turn himself into a derelict did not make life any more tolerable for his fellow victims; it had no social utility but merely assuaged his own conscience. When Orwell understood this, he began to search for a social system that promised to end the division between oppressors and oppressed in all of its manifestations, the subtle as well as the obvious ones. He came to despise the forms of hierarchy the world had invented, whether of birth, wealth, race, or even talent. The foundation of his socialist faith was an absolutely uncompromising international egalitarianism, even if that were to mean—in practice—shared misery. His motto could have been the William Morris quotation the workers in *Major Barbara* emblazon on the walls of their church: "NO MAN IS GOOD ENOUGH TO BE ANOTHER MAN'S MASTER." This does not, of course, mean that he did not recognize different levels of ability among men; merely that he felt such gifts entitled no one to a greater share of the world's wealth, power, or honor than their "inferiors." It is entirely characteristic that he insisted the *first* act of Britain's newly elected "socialist" government in 1945 should be "to abolish all titles, the House of Lords and the Public Schools" rather than to set up a National Health Service or a program of public housing.[16]

Orwell hated the master-servant relationship because it corrupted both parties and robbed them of their natural dignity. He recounts a painful incident during the Spanish Civil War which illustrates the psychological effects of that relationship. There had been some trivial thefts in his company. The officer in charge arbitrarily accused "a wild-looking boy from the back streets of Barcelona" of being the thief:

> The wretched boy allowed himself to be led off to the guardroom to be searched. What most struck me was that he barely attempted to protest his innocence. In the fatalism of his attitude you could see the desperate poverty in which he had been bred. The officer ordered him to take his clothes

16. T. R. Fyvel, "The Years at *Tribune*," in *The World of George Orwell*, ed. Miriam Gross (London, 1971), p. 115.

off. With a humility which was horrible to me he stripped
himself naked, and his clothes were searched. Of course
neither the cigars nor the money were there; in fact he had
not stolen them. What was most painful of all was that he
seemed no less ashamed after his innocence had been
established. That night I took him to the pictures and gave
him brandy and chocolate. But that too was horrible—I
mean the attempt to wipe out an injury with money. For a
few minutes I had half believed him to be a thief, and that
could not be wiped out. [*CEJL* 2: 254-55]

The born victim and the born ruler; each acts his part in an
almost predestined way. The victim's humility and shame become
reflex responses; the ruler shifts uneasily between arbitrary
assertion of power and the guilty gestures of charity. Orwell
suggests that no amount of good will on either side can make this
fundamental disparity of *power* tolerable. The task is to shatter the
molds from which such men are made.

Orwell's socialism, then, is a vision of an end to all forms of
privilege. As he says in *Homage to Catalonia*, "The thing that
attracts ordinary men to Socialism and makes them willing to risk
their skins for it, the 'mystique' of Socialism, is the idea of
equality; to the vast majority of people Socialism means a classless
society, or it means nothing at all" (*HC*, p. 112). There is a strong
Utopian element in this vision, and since the attack on pre-
scientific socialism by Marx and Engels such ideas have often
been treated as soft-headed and naïve. Yet Orwell was not
predicting that an egalitarian society would come into being; here
he differs markedly from the Oscar Wildes and William Morrises
of the movement. His own feelings about the future were far from
optimistic, as we shall see. But he insisted that the ideals of
Utopian socialism had in no way been discredited by the Marxist
insistence on the inevitability of class war and revolution or the
Leninist concern with tactics. The time had come to rehabilitate
the sound elements in the Utopian vision, if only to remind
socialists exactly what they were fighting for.

Orwell felt that Marxists in particular had refused to think
seriously about the exact nature of a socialist society on the

principle that the future cannot be predicted in detail. Lenin, for example, praised Marx's refusal to describe what is to come: "There is no trace of an attempt on Marx's part to conjure up a utopia, to make idle guesses about what cannot be known." [17] Too often, Marx's disciples assumed that the only obstacle to socialism was the existence of capitalism, and that after the destruction of the capitalist system socialism must inevitably follow. The idea betrays its Rousseauistic roots; capitalist man is alienated and unnatural; socialist man will be free; socialism as a system will evolve naturally and create itself. Orwell feared such laissez-faire attitudes because he could not believe that only unselfish impulses would fill the vacuum created by the destruction of capitalism. If socialism were to come at all, it would have to be defined, created, and defended. Otherwise the forces that had produced the forms of oppression peculiar to capitalism would invent a new set of "socialist" oppressions. Human freedom would not be served by a change of masters. Historically, the Utopian socialists' obsession with ends and indifference to means had been followed in the Marxist era by an obsession with means and an indifference to ends. A healthy movement demanded a clear sense both of ideals and of tactics, and its followers must not permit it to forget either. It was in this spirit that Orwell, who was very un-Utopian in temperament, nevertheless felt called upon to remind the socialist movement of its Utopian heritage.

Orwell's attitude toward Marx and his modern disciples has generally been misunderstood. Isaac Deutscher, for example, suggests that he rejected Marxism because "the dialectical-materialist philosophy had always been too abstruse for him." [18] Yet

17. *The State and Revolution* (chap. 5, pt. 1), in Lenin, *Selected Works in Three Volumes*, 2: 369. Marx's own early attempts to describe the final stage of communism are couched in imprecise but glowingly idealistic terms. For example: "*Communism* as the *positive* transcendence of *private property*, as *human self-estrangement*, and therefore as the real *appropriation of the human* essence by and for man; communism therefore as the complete return of man to himself as a *social* (i.e., human) being—a return become conscious, and accomplished within the entire wealth of previous development" (Karl Marx, "Private Property and Communism," in *Economic and Philosophic Manuscripts of 1844*, ed. Dirk J. Struik [New York, 1964], p. 135).

18. Isaac Deutscher, " '1984'—The Mysticism of Cruelty," in his *Heretics and Renegades and Other Essays* (London, 1955), p. 45.

Orwell's work indicates that he had read Marx with care and understanding. That he remained unconvinced and highly critical does not mean that he could not follow Marx's arguments; or rather, it could mean that only to a Marxist. Richard Rees recalls that at the socialist summer school run by *The Adelphi* in 1936, Orwell "astonished everybody, including the Marxist theoreticians, by his interventions in the discussions. . . . At one of the sessions I noticed a leading Marxist eyeing him with a mixture of admiration and uneasiness." [19] And Orwell's essays reveal not only a detailed familiarity with Marxist texts but also a fundamental admiration for his contribution to the socialist movement.[20]

His quarrel was not so much with Marx as with Marxism. It is worth recalling that Marx himself was the first man to make this distinction. The theory of dialectical materialism had been evolved in the mid-nineteenth century—at a particular stage of capitalism—and some of its predictions and generalizations had been proved false even in Marx's lifetime. Marx had seriously underestimated the adaptability of capitalism, the likelihood of political and economic reform, and the force of nationalism. Yet his disciples treated his theories as laws and his prophecies as facts. It was this dogmatic element in Marxism that Orwell found an intolerable obstacle to human progress. Long before, Engels had understood and fought against the tendency of the disciples to reduce Marx's thought to a set of unquestionable doctrines. He had written of the Social Democratic Federation, for example, that it had "ossified Marxism into a dogma" and "contrived to reduce the Marxist theory of development to a rigid orthodoxy." [21]

By contrast, one can see how aware Marx and Engels were of the tentative nature of their conclusions in the preface they wrote to the *Communist Manifesto* a quarter of a century after its first

19. *George Orwell: Fugitive from the Camp of Victory* (London, 1961), p. 147.

20. See, for example, his discussion of the *context* of the famous quotation, "Religion is the opium of the people," *CEJL* 2: 18; his reference to Marx's unfamiliar critique of *Timon of Athens*, *CEJL* 2: 128; and his insistence on Marx's seminal importance, *CEJL* 3: 98.

21. Karl Marx and Frederick Engels, *On Britain* (Moscow, 1962), pp. 574, 582.

publication. Here they felt obliged to note that "this programme
has in some details become antiquated." [22] Such revisionism is a
natural consequence of Engels's call for an end to "final solutions
and eternal truths." He insists that "one is always conscious of the
necessary limitation of all acquired knowledge, of the fact that it
is conditioned by the circumstances in which it was acquired." [23]
It was in this open and critical spirit, and in reaction against
Marxist scholasticism, that Orwell read Marx. He treated
Marxism as the dialectical system of thought it claimed to be, not
as a repository of final truths.

Orwell's critique of Marxism concentrated on what he took to
be its anachronisms and untenable assumptions: its theories of
class and revolution, its historicist tactics, its materialist basis and
consequent neglect of psychology, and its refusal to think seriously
about the nature of a socialist *state*. He used the history of the
century after Marx began to write as his basic data—a set of
events Marx had tried, but largely failed, to foresee. The
widening gulf between an affluent bourgeoisie and an impoverished proletariat which Marx had predicted, and on which he
had based his faith in revolution, had certainly failed to
materialize. The extraordinary general prosperity produced by
the technology of the industrial countries had been more widely
distributed than Marx had foreseen; as a consequence, the
workers of the world had more to lose than their chains. Their
attitudes had grown imperceptibly but steadily more conservative.
The clichés of Marxist propaganda simply did not meet the test of
observation.

Take, for example, the image of the bourgeois man of property.
In the Marxist propaganda of Orwell's day, the landlord
regularly appeared as a fat, greedy, and hardhearted capitalist in
a top hat. But as Orwell observed in *The Road to Wigan Pier*, the
worst slum landlord is as likely to be "a poor old woman who has
invested her life's savings in three slum houses, inhabits one of
them and tries to live on the rent of the other two—never, in
consequence, having any money for repairs" (*RWP*, p. 58). The

22. Marx and Engels, *Selected Works in Two Volumes*, 1: 22.
23. "Ludwig Feuerbach and the End of Classical German Philosophy," in
Marx and Engels, *Selected Works in Two Volumes*, 2: 388.

Marxist system did not make sufficient allowance for the existence
and importance of this buffer-class, which modern industrial
societies were producing in increasing numbers. "The class
in-between" Orwell called them—reduced gentlefolk, affluent
workers, minor officials. A proletarian revolution was very
unlikely to appeal to them, and they would do everything in their
power to make it impossible. No form of socialism that ignored
the increasing importance of this modern class could hope to
triumph.

That Engels, at any rate, was aware of this trend in modern
capitalism is suggested by an observation he made in a letter to
Marx: "The English proletariat is actually becoming more and
more bourgeois, so that this most bourgeois of all nations is
apparently aiming ultimately at the possession of a bourgeois
aristocracy and a bourgeois proletariat *as well as* a bourgeoisie." [24]
His tone indicates that he is outraged by the idea; yet in the last
century his prophecy has been fulfilled not only in England but in
most of the industrial countries of the world. This fact has vital
consequences for the socialist movement, which a less doctrinaire
Marxism would have understood and incorporated. Marx himself
had suggested that England might find its way to socialism
without going through a revolution;[25] yet the rhetoric of class
conflict, proletarian dictatorship, and the extermination of the
bourgeoisie remained the language of the official Marxist groups.

The Marxism of the Communist Party was fundamentally
insensitive to local conditions because it was dominated by Soviet
policy and the thought of its leaders. Orwell noted that its theories
did not grow out of the conditions existing in other countries but
were deduced from Marxist dogma or were dictated by Lenin and
Stalin. Because revolution had succeeded in Russia, it became
international communist policy. The first Soviet leaders, for
example, insisted that Marx's belief in the possibility of evolutionary socialism in England must be abandoned. Lenin preached
revolution for all countries: "Today, in 1917, in the epoch of the

24. Marx and Engels, *On Britain*, pp. 537–38.

25. See his speech to the Hague Congress (1872), Marx and Engels, *On Britain*,
p. 494; and Engels's preface to Marx's *Capital*, Marx and Engels, *Selected Works in
Two Volumes*, 1: 467.

first great imperialist war, this restriction made by Marx is no longer valid. . . . Today, in Britain and in America, too, 'the preliminary condition for every real people's revolution' is the *smashing*, the *destruction* of the 'ready-made state machinery.' " [26] And Trotsky insisted that only "outright revolutionary force" could compel the bourgeoisie to surrender its privileges: "History has not yet devised any other method. England will be no exception." [27] Neither Lenin nor Trotsky really knew England as well as Marx and Engels, yet this fact did not prevent them from issuing such pronouncements.

Orwell came to feel that a classic Marxist revolution was simply not a realistic possibility in a country like England, in which national solidarity had proven over the centuries to be a far more powerful force than class division. As he put it in *The English People*, "civil war is not *morally* possible in England. In any circumstances that we can foresee, the proletariat of Hammersmith will not arise and massacre the bourgeoisie of Kensington: they are not different enough" (*CEJL* 3: 15). It should be emphasized that Orwell was merely describing these conditions, not praising them. There were times in his life when, because of his impatience with the methods of reform, he really wished for a violent revolution in England. In 1940, for example, he wrote: "Only revolution can save England. . . . I dare say the London gutters will have to run with blood. All right, let them, if it is necessary" (*CEJL* 1: 539). Yet he did not permit his wishes to cloud his vision or his theories to contradict facts. And he reluctantly concluded that England must reach socialism through the route of reform or not at all.

A more serious objection to Marxism was that its conviction of the inevitable triumph of socialism legitimized any method of reaching it. This "historicist" [28] claim is the assumption behind the communist principle that the end justifies the means. Since a

26. *The State and Revolution* (chap. 3, pt. 1), in Lenin, *Selected Works in Three Volumes*, 2: 332.

27. Leon Trotsky, *Whither England?* (New York, 1925), p. 50.

28. I use Popper's term for the doctrine that the social sciences should "furnish us with long-term historical prophecies." K. R. Popper, *The Open Society and Its Enemies* (New York, 1963), 1: 3.

successful proletarian revolution is bound to create a socialist
society, all tactics that serve the revolution are taken to be
socialist in effect. This includes such policies as the formation of
elitist revolutionary conspiracies; the rejection of democracy,
personal liberty, and honesty; the liquidation of hostile groups;
forced industrialism and collectivization; and so on. In essence,
the present generation is sacrificed to the future. This may just
conceivably be tolerable if the future good is absolutely assured,
but if it is no better than a hope, the policy is quixotic as well as
suicidal.

Orwell describes such fanatical commitment to a cause with
sympathetic irony in *Nineteen Eighty-Four*, when Winston and Julia
dedicate themselves to serve Goldstein's mythical Brotherhood in
the following catechism:

> "You are prepared to give your lives?
> "Yes."
> "You are prepared to commit murder?"
> "Yes."
> "To commit acts of sabotage which may cause the death of
> hundreds of innocent people?"
> "Yes."
> "To betray your country to foreign powers?"
> "Yes."
> "You are prepared to cheat, to forge, to blackmail, to
> corrupt the minds of children, to distribute habit-forming
> drugs, to encourage prostitution, to disseminate venereal
> diseases—to do anything which is likely to cause demoraliza-
> tion and weaken the power of the Party?"
> "Yes."
> "If, for example, it would somehow serve our interests to
> throw sulphuric acid in a child's face—are you prepared to
> do that?"
> "Yes." [*NEF*, p. 177]

And so on. In this scene, the logic of end-justifies-means is
pushed to the brink of absurdity and beyond, particularly because
O'Brien, the questioner, is an agent of the Party merely posing as
a conspirator in order to force Winston and Julia into an

outrageous position. The scene parodies the initiation ritual of an extremist revolutionary group. That in this instance the group may not even exist, and certainly has little chance of success, adds to the irony of Orwell's picture of fanatical "idealistic dedication." Only an absolute hatred for the present and an obsession with the future can explain such behavior. Orwell felt that the teleological element in Marxism had much to answer for. It is worth recalling that a crucial difference between "revisionist" democratic socialism and revolutionary Marxism is that the former is present-oriented. As Eduard Bernstein explained in his *Evolutionary Socialism*: "I am not concerned with what will happen in the more distant future, but with what can and ought to happen in the present, for the present and the nearest future." [29]

Engels had written, "to make a science of socialism, it had first to be placed upon a real basis." [30] Orwell would have agreed with the general principle but rejected its Marxist application, for Marx and Engels had taken *real* to be a synonym for *materialist*. Orwell rejected economic determinism as an explanation of human behavior and world history, though his own attitudes were I think determinist in a different way. Marx's analysis of the history of presocialist society along materialist lines had certainly been a necessary corrective to the general wooliness of Utopian thought, but his conception of history had been turned into a simplistic and dangerous tool for predicting the future. Marxists took from the *Communist Manifesto* the slogan, "The theory of the Communists may be summed up in the single sentence: Abolition of private property," [31] and treated this revolutionary economic act as a guarantee of the triumph of socialism.

In this instance, Marx and Engels cannot so easily be distinguished from their disciples. They often treat the mere fact of capitalist expropriation as the equivalent of the abolition of all classes. As soon as the "old conditions of production" are swept away, they say in the *Manifesto*, the proletariat will "have swept

29. *Evolutionary Socialism: A Criticism and Affirmation*, trans. Edith C. Harvey (New York, 1961), p. 163.

30. "Socialism: Utopian and Scientific," in Marx and Engels, *Selected Works in Two Volumes*, 2: 128.

31. Marx and Engels, *Selected Works in Two Volumes*, 1: 47.

away the conditions for the existence of class antagonisms, and of classes generally, and will thereby have abolished its own supremacy as a class." [32] This optimistic picture of postrevolutionary society was to have the most serious consequences for the socialist movement. It led to the confusion of state ownership with socialism and discouraged Marxist thinkers from insisting on safeguards to protect and preserve the newly won freedom of the working class.

Orwell consistently attacked this element in Marxist thought— the idea that the abolition of private property necessarily brings with it an end to hierarchy and privilege. As he says in *The Lion and the Unicorn*:

> It has become clear in the last few years that "common ownership of the means of production" is not in itself a sufficient definition of Socialism. . . . Centralised ownership has very little meaning unless the mass of the people are living roughly upon an equal level, and have some kind of control over the government. "The State" may come to mean no more than a self-elected political party, and oligarchy and privilege can return, based on power rather than on money. [*CEJL* 2: 80]

This was, indeed, just what had happened in the Soviet Union after the Revolution, and Orwell uses that historical fact as the basis for his skeptical critique of economic determinism. If class divisions and the exploitation of man by man had survived a tremendous economic transformation like the Russian Revolution, such behavior might well have a noneconomic first cause.

This conclusion led Orwell to reexamine the "psychologism" that Marx and Engels had so contemptuously rejected as an explanation for human behavior. It seemed more and more likely that some actions could be better accounted for by a theory of psychological rather than economic motives. Engels had insisted that "the final causes of all social changes and political revolutions are to be sought, not in men's brains . . . but in changes in

32. Ibid., p. 54.

the modes of production and exchange." [33] But perhaps "men's brains" are less malleable than this implied and their motives not so easy to understand. "The main weakness of Marxism," Orwell wrote, is "its failure to interpret human motives. . . . As it is, a 'Marxist analysis' of any historical event tends to be a hurried snap-judgment based on the principle of *cui bono?* . . . Along these lines, it is impossible to have an intuitive understanding of men's motives, and therefore impossible to predict their actions." [34]

For this economic determinism Orwell eventually substituted a psychological one. Psychology was the new science of the twentieth century, as economics had been of the nineteenth. The obsession with the power-motive which came to dominate Orwell's thought in the 1940s and which is treated as the ultimate cause of totalitarianism in *Nineteen Eighty-Four*, was in its way as rigid and reductive an explanation of human behavior as the principle of cui bono. In its crudest form, it becomes indistinguishable from such ahistorical formulas as Acton's "Power tends to corrupt, and absolute power corrupts absolutely." [35] Deutscher has accused Orwell of adopting "the oldest, the most banal, the most abstract, the most metaphysical, and the most barren of all generalizations"—that "sadistic power-hunger" is the source of all political betrayals.[36] Yet Orwell's exaggerated dependence on the formula must be understood as a dialectical response to the complete rejection of all psychological explanations in Marxist theory. Neither Marx nor his disciples had been able to predict the triumph of a "socialist" totalitarianism, and no Marxist explanation for Stalinism—neither the "cult of personality" nor Trotsky's "stage of economic scarcity"—seemed to get to the heart of the matter.

This gap in Marxist theory was not merely an intellectual flaw. In a successful political program, a failure to foresee disaster

---

33. "Socialism: Utopian and Scientific," in Marx and Engels, *Selected Works in Two Volumes*, 2: 136.
34. George Orwell, "The English Civil War," *New Statesman and Nation*, 24 August 1940, p. 193.
35. Orwell quotes this familiar epigram in "In Pursuit of Lord Acton," *Tribune*, 29 March 1946, p. 19.
36. Deutscher, " '1984'—The Mysticism of Cruelty," p. 48.

increases the difficulty of preventing it. The psychological naïveté of Engels's prediction that the postrevolutionary state will simply wither away, for example, is indirectly responsible for the lack of democratic safeguards in such states when they come into being. His description of the process ignores the fact that the postrevolutionary world will be run by people who will make choices, possibly in their own interest rather than in that of society as a whole. As he describes it in a well-known passage, the whole transitional period unfolds passively, "naturally," without the agency of the human will: "State interference in social relations becomes, in one domain after another, superfluous, and then dies out of itself; the government of persons is replaced by the administration of things, and by the conduct of processes of production. The state is not 'abolished.' *It dies out.*" [37] Yet the Soviet state has not shown the slightest tendency to dissolve naturally. Shortly after the Revolution, Lenin was already predicting rather ominously that the "inevitable" withering away of the state might be "protracted" and was refusing to offer a time-table.[38] Over the next thirty years, Orwell was to see the process reversed; far from dying out, the Soviet state had consolidated its power, created a new bureaucracy, and perfected new forms of coercion.

This was the form of socialism that had been foreseen with remarkable prescience by the nineteenth-century anarchists. Even before Marxism had been formulated in a sytematic way, Proudhon had reminded his readers that the government of all must nevertheless be ruled by the few, and that all delegated authority was potentially tyrannical. No matter how many "agents of the people" were chosen, the danger was the same: "It is always the government of man, the rule of will and caprice. I ask what this pretended revolution has revolutionized?" [39] And forty years later, Kropotkin insisted that the phrase "revolution-

37. "Socialism: Utopian and Scientific," in Marx and Engels, *Selected Works in Two Volumes*, 2: 151.
38. *The State and Revolution* (chap. 5, pt. 4), in Lenin, *Selected Works in Three Volumes*, 2: 379.
39. P. J. Proudhon, *What Is Property: An Inquiry into the Principle of Right and of Government*, trans. Benj. R. Tucker (London, n.d.), 1: 56.

ary government" was as hopelessly contradictory as "white blackbird." [40] Orwell's terrifying picture of a triumphant "social- ist" state in *Nineteen Eighty-Four* has encouraged some of his readers to stress his sympathy with philosophical anarchism. Deutscher dismisses him as "at heart . . . a simple-minded anarchist"; George Woodcock thinks that Orwell's socialism "had far more affinity with Proudhon's variety than with Marx's"; and Ray- mond Williams stresses Orwell's relentless criticism of all forms of association.[41]

Orwell certainly had a fundamental respect for the anarchist criticism of Marx as well as a liking for individual anarchists as people. In Spain, he felt most sympathetic to the anarchist forces and wrote to a friend that he would have joined them if he had understood the internal conflicts of the Left better when he arrived (*CEJL* 1: 289). "Though their principles were rather vague," he later wrote, "their hatred of privilege and injustice was perfectly genuine" (*HC*, p. 64). Yet it is a mistake to think of Orwell's socialism as based on philosophical anarchism. He was as critical of the unrealistic element in its theory as that in Marxist ideology. Even before he went to Spain, Orwell treated his own anarchist sympathies as childish wish-fulfillment. After his early years in Burma, he says, he "worked out an anarchistic theory that all government is evil, that the punishment always does more harm than the crime and that people can be trusted to behave decently if only you will let them alone. This of course was sentimental nonsense. I see now as I did not see then, that it is always necessary to protect peaceful people from violence" (*RWP*, p. 148). He also recognized that a 'modern industrial society demands complex forms of organization, "with all the repressive apparatus that that implies" (*CEJL* 4: 49).

Marxism and anarchism, despite their century-old quarrel, shared a basic faith in "liberated" human nature that Orwell felt

40. P. Kropotkin, "Revolutionary Government," *Kropotkin's Revolutionary Pam- phlets*, ed. Roger N. Baldwin (New York, 1927), p. 238.

41. Deutscher, " '1984'—The Mysticism of Cruelty," p. 47; George Woodcock, *The Crystal Spirit: A Study of George Orwell* (Boston, 1966), p. 28; Raymond Williams, *Culture and Society 1780-1950* (London, 1958), pp. 290-91. Woodcock, however, also understands some of Orwell's reservations about anarchism (ibid, pp. 26-30).

to be misguided and dangerous. Both the belief that the socialist state would wither away, and that it was not necessary in the first place, seemed to him naïve. He saw that modern society was not evolving in that direction, that it was moving toward greater and greater centralization and state power. Despite his own nostalgia for a simpler and more primitive world, he knew this process to be irreversible. In an important letter written shortly before Orwell began work on *Nineteen Eighty-Four*, he wrote, "Whether we like it or not, the trend is towards centralism and planning and it is more useful to try to humanise the collectivist society that is certainly coming than to pretend . . . that we could revert to a past phase" (*CEJL* 4: 103). Anarchism was useful because it had been the first movement to alert people to the potential dangers of a centralized state. Orwell was anxious to use this insight not in order to endorse Proudhon's revolutionary formula—"NO GOVERNMENT" [42]—but in order to make sure that the powerful government which seemed inevitable was democratically elected, restrained by law, and subject to recall.

Perhaps Orwell's most powerful doubt about the socialist movement was a result of its sectarianism. Too many of the major philosophical or tactical disagreements in its history had resulted in a permanent split and the creation of still another hostile group—Utopian socialists, revolutionary Marxists, anarchists, Social-Democrats. It seemed impossible for the disciples of these opposing ideologies to acknowledge the validity of the criticisms they made of each other's ideas and methods. The practice of each group was to discredit and then to exclude its own critics, thus protecting its own ideological purity. Yet history had shown that each of these rival systems was intellectually and pragmatically vulnerable, and that none had succeeded in creating a real socialist society, despite considerable opportunity to do so. In part, this failure could be explained by the refusal of each group to learn from its critics, by the nearly universal hostility and defensiveness of the movement as a whole. If the ideals of socialism were not to be written off by history as simply

---

42. P. J. Proudhon, *General Idea of the Revolution in the Nineteenth Century*, trans. John Beverley Robinson (London, 1923), p. 126.

unrealizable, and if the movement was ever to evolve a coherent
and plausible set of tactics, the various sects that had tried to
bring socialism into being would have to agree on what had gone
wrong and why.

It was on this principle that Orwell's critique of *English*
socialism—which had remained largely anti-Marxist, antianar-
chist and antiutopian, and to which he was basically sympathetic
—became as searching as his analysis of the Continental movements. Orwell has often been treated as an essentially English
socialist, "in the tradition of Owen and William Morris." [43] This
does not mean, however, that he found it easy to ally himself with
the policies of any of the various English socialist organizations.
Here too, he was looking at a set of "socialist" assumptions
critically, with a sort of clinical detachment, just as he had done
with the ideas of Marx and the anarchists. His grudging support
for the Labour Party, for example, was constantly undermined by
his sense that it had betrayed part of the essential content of socialism: internationalism, absolute egalitarianism, and democracy.

The various English groups that had preached the doctrine in
the nineteenth and twentieth centuries had regularly forgotten at
least one of these ideals. That Britain was still, in Orwell's day, a
powerful imperial nation, made it difficult for any English
socialist movement to stress the issue of international equality.
Indeed, when H. M. Hyndman, the leader of the Marxist-
oriented Social Democratic Federation, first summarized Marx's
theories for an English audience in the 1880s, his imperial pride
produced a curious amalgam of socialism and the white man's
burden: he hoped that the English would "knit together the great
democracies near and far *under our flag,* and *deal out to our
dependencies* a full measure of that justice which alone can secure
for us and for ours *the leadership* in the social reorganization which
will be our greatest claim to respect and remembrance from
countless generations of the human race." [44]

Although probably no British socialist of the 1930s and 1940s
would have used such language, the essential betrayal of the

43. John Atkins, *George Orwell, a Literary Study* (London, 1954), p. 13.
44. *The Text-Book of Democracy: England for All* (London, 1881), p. 6. Italics added.

internationalism of the movement had not really changed. In 1935, the chief spokesman for the Labour Party could write that poverty would soon be a thing of the past "for those who live in countries where the resources of science are available," though "all the millions in Asia and Africa who live in primitive conditions" would of course have to wait until their own economies could produce the necessities of life.[45] Ten years later, when that same writer had become the first Labour prime minister with real parliamentary power, Orwell could still point to the anomaly of a "socialist" party which could not tell the truth about British imperialism: Britain "lives partly by exploiting the coloured peoples. To continue exploiting them is incompatible with the spirit of Socialism, while to stop doing so would entail a difficult reconstruction period during which our own standard of living might fall catastrophically. In one form and another this problem comes up again and again, and, except for the minority who have travelled outside Europe, I have never met an English Socialist who would face it" (*CEJL* 3: 396). "Socialism in one country" could have been the slogan of more than one local movement.

It was only in 1918, nearly a generation after its foundation, that the Labour Party committed itself to a specifically socialist program. At that time, it vowed "to secure for the producers by hand or by brain the full fruits of their industry, and the most equitable distribution thereof that may be possible, upon the basis of the common ownership of the means of production and the best obtainable system of popular administration and control of each industry and service." [46] Yet the Party's left-wing critics—Orwell among them—would say that time has proven these bold words merely a paper commitment. The Labour Party could not be counted upon to put its official faith into practice, even when it had the opportunity to do so. Its practical policies had never been radical enough to please its own militant socialist wing: "we know what the history of the Labour Party has been" (*CEJL* 1: 337–38),

45. Clement R. Attlee, *The Will and the Way to Socialism* (London, 1935), p. 13.
46. Quoted in G. D. H. Cole, *A History of the Labour Party from 1914* (London, 1948), p. 56.

Orwell wrote laconically, in explaining why he was leaving it to join the disaffiliated Independent Labour Party.[47]

Despite his temporary departure from the Labour Party, however, Orwell never felt entirely alienated from it. Many of his attitudes were shared by such critical Labour M.P.'s as Aneurin Bevan and Michael Foot, with whom he was associated while literary editor of *Tribune*. Bevan had been the rebel within the Labour camp, always at the center of controversy but on the inner rim of the world to which he felt loyal. He took his task to be the Party's reconstruction along socialist lines, and he became its most uncompromising internal critic. Also like Orwell, he was constantly accused of disloyalty by various left-wing groups. But he was faithful to what he took to be the essential elements of the Party, the program, and the cause, not to their momentary manifestations, which often struck him as hopelessly compromised. What Bevan was to the Labour Party, Orwell tried to be to the Socialist movement as a whole.[48]

Orwell's criticism of the Labour Party was, however, tempered by his awareness that its unreliable socialism was not so much a betrayal as an accurate reflection of the real attitudes of the British working class. Continental socialists had long been astonished by its indifference to theory. Kropotkin comments on "the lack of general ideas" and the unradical program of the British working class compared to its Continental counterparts.[49] And Engels notes with dismay that the English bourgeois intelligentsia "understand things better and take them up more passionately than the workers." [50] The British working class could be radical in its tactics, as its history of industrial conflict clearly shows; but its demands were of the sort that socialists usually dismiss as "palliatives"—the higher wages and social insurance of the affluent society and the welfare state. Such policies were

47. See Orwell's critical appraisal of the postwar Labour government, "Britain's Struggle for Survival," *Commentary* 6 (1948): 343–49.

48. See Michael Foot, *Aneurin Bevan: A Biography*, 2 vols. (London, 1962 and 1973), and Bevan's own *In Place of Fear* (London, 1952).

49. P. Kropotkin, *Memoirs of a Revolutionist* (London, 1899), 2: 313–14.

50. Karl Marx and Frederick Engels, *Selected Correspondence 1864–1895*, trans. Dona Torr (New York, 1942), p. 419.

fundamentally liberal rather than socialist, since they did not involve the reconstruction of society or the abolition of classes. That the ruling class could and did accommodate such demands may well have kept it in power.

Orwell understood that the workers by and large supported the Labour Party not because of its paper socialism, since "most of them don't know what Socialism means," but because they relied upon it to provide "full employment, free milk for school-children, old-age pensions of thirty shillings a week, and, in general, a fair deal for the working man." [51] His attitude toward this state of affairs was highly ambiguous. He certainly wanted the working class to be more radical in its demands, to be unsatisfied with anything but an international egalitarian society. Yet he was unwilling to teach the workers what they *ought* to want. Behind this lies his own middle-class guilt and dislike of hierarchy: to make the workers into a revolutionary proletariat was in practice a form of intellectual coercion. English socialism had been from the start dominated and controlled by the middle class along paternalistic lines. Robert Owen insisted that he did not manage but rather "governed" the factory at New Lanark because he saw the need "to introduce principles in the conduct of the people." [52] Shaw's advice to the public benefactor in "Socialism for Millionaires" was "Never give the people anything they want: give them something they ought to want and dont." [53]

Orwell hated this *de haut en bas* strain in English socialism. He had no objection to middle-class support for the movement, only to middle-class direction and control. Yet the pioneers and early leaders of socialism in Britain had almost all come from the bourgeoisie—William Morris, H. M. Hyndman, Engels, Beatrice Webb. In the thirties, their places were taken by a new generation of middle-class intellectuals fresh from the universities. Orwell thought of himself as a rather marginal member of the same class, which might explain his hostility toward it. In any case, he would certainly have agreed with Morris's final rejection of bourgeois

51. George Orwell, "The British General Election," *Commentary* 1 (1945): 68.
52. *The Life of Robert Owen by Himself* (London, 1920), p. 78.
53. Bernard Shaw, *Essays in Fabian Socialism* (London, 1932), p. 119.

socialism: it is, Morris said, "impossible that the change can be made from above to below." [54]

Finally, Orwell disliked the curiously administrative form of socialism which the Fabian-trained leaders of the Labour Party had evolved. The planned society was too often taken as the equivalent of the classless one. The mentality was fundamentally bureaucratic, the root emotion being not so much hatred of privilege as dislike of inefficiency and chaos. H. G. Wells had complained that Marx's form of socialism was "unattractive to people who had any real knowledge of administration," and he congratulated the Fabian Society for correcting this unfortunate situation by finding a way "to convert Revolutionary Socialism into Administrative Socialism." [55] His own version of the socialist future is obsessed with planning and grows out of a hatred of anarchic mess: "In place of disorderly individual effort, each man doing what he pleases, the Socialist wants organized effort and a plan. . . . That and no other is the essential Socialist idea." [56]

Although they might have expressed themselves more cautiously, the Webbs were in essential agreement with the spirit of this statement. Their faith in administrative experts amounts to the creation of a new heroic type. The "disinterested professional expert who invents, discovers, inspects, audits, costs, tests or measures," they assure their readers, "will find expression, and his freedom will be exercised without limitation, in the process of discovery and measurement, and in the fearless representation of whatever he finds, without regard either to the *amour propre* of the management or to the rebellious instincts of any grade of employees." [57] The Webbs' sharp sense of class division in this plan for their "Socialist" Commonwealth is worth noting. Its logical culmination was the Labour Party program for state socialism. In the words of Clement Attlee, "The managers of great

54. William Morris, "Monopoly: or, How Labour is Robbed," *Collected Works* (London, 1915), 23: 251.

55. *New Worlds for Old: A Plain Account of Modern Socialism* (London, 1912), p. 261.

56. Ibid., p. 26. One is reminded of Pound's violent dismissal of the Fabians as "crying for . . . a new dung-flow cut in lozenges" (canto 15).

57. Sidney and Beatrice Webb, *A Constitution for the Socialist Commonwealth of Great Britain* (London, 1920), p. 198.

businesses are bound to look after the narrow interests of their shareholders. When these great aggregations of capital are transformed into State enterprises, *the managers will be able to carry on their work* with the substitution of the motive of service for that of profit." [58] Such a plan led inevitably to the Managerial Society and the New Class.

Orwell was convinced that this fixation on the administration and economic structure of a socialist society was a fundamental perversion of the original aims of the movement. Although common ownership and centralized control might well be necessary first steps in the creation of an international socialism, they must not be confused with the goal itself. Furthermore, the cult of the expert could lead to a new form of hierarchy, more stable precisely because it was so necessary to society. It is important to remember, Orwell says, that "Socialism, if it means only centralised ownership and planned production, is not of its nature either democratic or equalitarian." [59] These fears for the principle of equality in a bureaucratized socialist society are sharply expressed in the class divisions of *Nineteen Eighty-Four*: "The new aristocracy was made up for the most part of bureaucrats, scientists, technicians, trade-union organizers, publicity experts, sociologists, teachers, journalists and professional politicians. These people, whose origins lay in the salaried middle class and the upper grades of the working class, had been shaped and brought together by the barren world of monopoly industry and centralized government" (*NEF*, pp. 210–11).

All of these misgivings about the English socialist movement only underline Orwell's extreme eclecticism. He was unwilling to be an uncritical disciple of any existing sect and really preached a kind of socialist ecumenicalism. That is why he says "when the real English Socialist movement appears . . . it will cut across the existing party divisions. It will be both revolutionary and democratic. It will aim at the most fundamental changes and be perfectly willing to use violence if necessary. But also it will recognize that not all cultures are the same, that national

58. Attlee, *The Will and the Way to Socialism*, p. 38. Italics added.

59. George Orwell, "Revolt in the Urban Desert," *Observer*, 10 October 1943, p. 3.

sentiments and traditions have to be respected if revolutions are not to fail." [60] He was far from certain that such a form of socialism would ever materialize, but he devoted most of his life to trying to bring it about.

In working for that end, Orwell had raised far more questions than he had been able to answer, and eventually he brought himself to the edge of despair. It is worth reiterating that he did not do so to embarrass the socialist movement, either in his own country or anywhere else. He concentrated on the problematic aspects of socialism, not because he felt he had solved them, but because he knew that if no sympathetic critic of the movement aired them in the first place they would only provide ammunition for the real enemies of socialism. He thought of himself as contributing to a century-old movement, of whose continuing development his own work might one day be treated as an essential stage; and he knew that he was working in conjunction with other writers and thinkers in this reassessment of the history of socialism.

Perhaps, finally, Orwell's originality lies less in his ideas than in his insistence that these problems would have to be presented honestly to, and solved by, the *whole* of society, not just by its intellectuals. His decision to reveal the conflicts of his own mind and faith in literary works that were to prove highly popular and influential, seemed to many of his peers a public betrayal. In this he differed markedly from most of the left-wing writers of his time, for his trust in the basic decency and intelligence of ordinary people made him anxious to expose rather than to hide the flaws he saw in the socialist movement. That the conflict of ideas and the disagreements about social policies must be argued out in the public forum rather than among the intelligentsia was his most passionately held democratic belief, one which was to bring him into conflict repeatedly with the left-wing publishers, parties, and intellectuals of his time.

60. George Orwell, "Fascism and Democracy," in *The Betrayal of the Left*, ed. Victor Gollancz (London, 1941), p. 214.

2

The Quarrel with the Intelligentsia

The dispute we have been tracing concerning socialist ideals and tactics has a long history, and the various positions Orwell took will be recognizable to anyone acquainted with it. Far less familiar, largely because it is the product of Orwell's character and personal experience, is his lifelong family quarrel with the personnel of British left-wing movements, both with the Communist Party regulars and with the fellow travelers who turned to the Left in the thirties. This quarrel is worth tracing in detail, not only because it suggests something of the complexity of the period—its civil wars—but because its history reveals the growing depth and seriousness of Orwell's mind. Certainly no antipathy could have begun as more of an instinctive, mindless revulsion. His contempt for the London, middle-class, left-wing intellectual was founded on envy, spite, ignorance, and a kind of puritanism.

Orwell had been to the fashionable school he describes in his autobiographical essay "Such, Such Were the Joys," and he had won a scholarship to Eton. The normal next stop for someone with his abilities and interests would clearly have been Oxford or Cambridge; yet he did not go on to a university but spent the next five years as a British policeman in Burma.[1] This choice was to set him apart from the group who might otherwise have been his peers. It was not just that compared to people like Auden, Isherwood, MacNeice, C. Day Lewis, and Spender he had come

1. Orwell makes it clear that after cramming to win the scholarship to Eton, he was determined to "'slack off' and cram no longer" (*CEJL* 4: 363). This decision meant, in effect, that he would not be able to go to a university, since his family was not wealthy enough to send him without a scholarship. See Sonia Orwell, "A Reply to Mary McCarthy," *Nova* (June–July 1969), p. 20, and the letter from A. S. F. Gow, Orwell's classical tutor at Eton, quoted in Jeffrey Meyers, "Review Article: George Orwell, the Honorary Proletarian," *Philological Quarterly* 48 (1969): 531.

from a less firmly upper-middle class family. His ambiguous status never receded into the past for him, as it did for many other scholarship boys who allowed themselves to join the establishment. It seems likely that Orwell's painful exclusion from the London literary set was in some perverse, idealistic way sought by him rather than forced upon him; it became a symbol of his purity and his seriousness.

It was not a clean break, however, for Orwell's snide references to the "parlour Bolshie" hardly suggest he had chosen his isolation without regret. His attacks on the socialist bourgeoisie are suspect by their very excess. Here, for example, is a description of them in a letter written in 1936: "And then so many of them are the sort of eunuch type with a vegetarian smell who go about spreading sweetness and light and have at the back of their minds a vision of the working class all TT [tuberculin-tested, or pasteurized], well washed behind the ears, readers of Edward Carpenter or some other pious sodomite and talking with BBC accents" (*CEJL* 1: 216). The tone is characteristic of Orwell's attacks on the intelligentsia during the 1930s. In *The Road to Wigan Pier* (1937) he writes: "One sometimes gets the impression that the mere words 'Socialism' and 'Communism' draw towards them with magnetic force every fruit-juice drinker, nudist, sandal-wearer, sex-maniac, Quaker, 'Nature Cure' quack, pacifist and feminist in England" (*RWP*, pp. 173–74). This outraged dismissal, so obsessed with surfaces and so narrow in its sympathies, ignores the obvious fact that even the most legitimate and serious revolutionary movements will be supported by a very motley collection of rebels. But there is more to it than that, for such passages also suggest Orwell's strained attempt to associate himself with working-class values, earthy and commonsensical, vulgar but "straight" and brutally honest.

Orwell's violent rejection of the unconventional element in social protest is almost certainly the product of inner stress. This is nowhere more apparent than in his review of Cyril Connolly's novel, *The Rock Pool*, in which he argues that "even to want to write about so-called artists who spend on sodomy what they have gained by sponging betrays a kind of spiritual inadequacy. For it is clear that Mr Connolly rather admires the disgusting beasts he

depicts. . . . The fact to which we have got to cling, as to a
life-belt, is that it *is* possible to be a normal decent person and yet
to be fully alive" (*CEJL* 1: 226). If this had really been a "fact"
for Orwell, rather than a desperate wish, he would hardly have
chosen to compare it to a life-belt. It does not require much
psychological insight to sense the uncertainty behind such violent
rejections. They recall the ambiguous class hatred of Orwell's
hero in *Keep the Aspidistra Flying*, an almost clinical study of
obsession.

It is difficult to see how a penetrating and persuasive analysis of
the world of political action could grow out of such private wars,
but eventually it did. Orwell's reflex hostility to middle-class
socialists made him preternaturally sensitive to their flaws of mind
and of motive. His criticism of the left-wing intelligentsia becomes
steadily more analytic and insightful in his mature years. It is
possible that the turning point between the early intemperate and
highly personal attacks and the later ones came with actual
exposure. In the early thirties, Orwell was looking at the London
literary world from the outside. By the late thirties he had more or
less arrived: at any rate his name was beginning to be known.
Around 1936, Cyril Connolly acted as a kind of go-between; he
says that he tried to overcome Orwell's "prejudice against the
Left-wing university group of the 'thirties which I so admired,"
and that his letters "show a gradual thawing from the defensive
attitude he adopted to the London literary scene." [2] A letter
Orwell wrote to Stephen Spender in 1938 certainly bears him out:

> You ask how it is I attacked you not having met you, & on
> the other hand changed my mind after meeting you. I don't
> know that I had exactly attacked you, but I had certainly in
> passing made offensive remarks abt "parlour Bolsheviks such
> as Auden & Spender" or words to that effect. I was willing to
> use you as a symbol of the parlour Bolshie because *a.* your
> verse, what I had read of it, did not mean very much to me,
> *b.* I looked upon you as a sort of fashionable successful
> person, also a Communist or Communist sympathiser, & I
> have been very hostile to the CP since about 1935, &

2. "Some Letters of George Orwell," *Encounter* 18 (1962): 56.

c. because not having met you I could regard you as a type & also an abstraction. Even if when I met you I had not happened to like you, I should still have been bound to change my attitude, because when you meet anyone in the flesh you realise immediately that he is a human being & not a sort of caricature embodying certain ideas. It is partly for this reason that I don't mix much in literary circles, because I know from experience that once I have met & spoken to anyone I shall never again be able to show any intellectual brutality towards him, even when I feel that I ought to. [*CEJL* 1: 313]

The letter leads us directly to one of Orwell's fundamental objections to the left-wing intelligentsia—indeed to any intelligentsia—that it is basically a closed world (or at best an incorporative one), addicted to coterie loyalty and exclusion, and constantly tempting its members to blunt honest criticism in the name of civility. England had a tradition of coterie socialists in the influential Fabian Society, which had frequently been attacked for its refusal to be absorbed by the proletarian movement. Engels had scornfully dismissed them as "an ambitious group here in London who have understanding enough to realise the inevitability of the social revolution, but who could not possibly entrust this gigantic task to the rough proletariat alone and are therefore kind enough to set themselves at the head." [3] And one of its own members, H. G. Wells, had complained that the Society was as difficult to join as a London club.

The sense of class identity and hierarchy was such a powerful force in English life that even the devotees of the idea of the classless society could not escape it. Orwell felt that most middle-class socialists were seriously ambivalent about their own class privileges, that they could discard them in theory but not in practice. He analyzed this attitude in a wartime essay:

In the last twenty years western civilisation has given the intellectual security without responsibility, and in England,

3. Karl Marx and Frederick Engels, *Selected Correspondence 1846–1895*, trans. Dona Torr (New York, 1942), p. 505.

in particular, it has educated him in scepticism while anchoring him almost immovably in the privileged class. He has been in the position of a young man living on an allowance from a father whom he hates. The result is a deep feeling of guilt and resentment, not combined with any genuine desire to escape. [*CEJL* 2: 314]

In *The Road to Wigan Pier*, Orwell observes that the middle-class socialist, or even communist, "is vastly more at home with a member of his own class, who thinks him a dangerous Bolshie, than with a member of the working class who supposedly agrees with him" (*RWP*, p. 137). His classic picture of this type is Ravelston, the rich and well-meaning socialist editor in *Keep the Aspidistra Flying*. Orwell's portrait is not ungenerous. Ravelston has a conscience, and his support of the oppressed is sincere enough. But between his ideas and his feelings there is a thick, protective layer of money and privilege—an elegant flat, a stylish mistress, intimate dinners at his favorite restaurant. And so the sharp words of his journal—with its theatrical title, *Antichrist*—are paper crusades:

> In a way, of course, he knew—it was precisely this that *Antichrist* existed to point out—that life under a decaying capitalism is deathly and meaningless. But this knowledge was only theoretical. You can't really *feel* that kind of thing when your income is eight hundred a year. Most of the time, when he wasn't thinking of coal-miners, Chinese junk-coolies and the unemployed in Middlesbrough, he felt that life was pretty good fun. [*KAF*, p. 105]

And later, in the restaurant, Ravelston thinks, "In Middlesbrough the unemployed huddle in frowzy beds, bread and marg and milkless tea in their bellies. He settled down to his steak with all the shameful joy of a dog with a stolen leg of mutton" (*KAF*, p. 123).

Not all the guilty pleasures of the middle-class socialist were material, however. Orwell grew more and more interested in the subtle forms of privilege, particularly as they found expression in taste, in coterie culture. It was obvious that the great literary revolution of the 1920s had produced a high culture much less available to the common reader than Victorian or Edwardian literature had been. Orwell's literary criticism is almost exclusively about the earlier, more popular literature. There are essays on Dickens, on Wells, on Kipling; and Orwell sees these writers as part of a loose tradition of writing that appealed to a really wide audience. Some of his other important literary essays deal with that tradition, with Swift, Shakespeare, Tolstoy, and comparable writers. Most of the rest examine the subliterature of popular culture—the detective story, boys' weeklies, the comic postcards of Donald McGill.

Orwell's literary criticism scarcely deserves that name. It is, rather, sociological analysis that concentrates on the question of the writer's audience, and the consistent standard of judgment is wide appeal. In the essay on Dickens, for example, he is fascinated by the inexplicable way in which his work has filtered down to a nonintellectual audience: "A music-hall comedian can (or at any rate could quite recently) go on the stage and impersonate Micawber or Mrs Gamp with a fair certainty of being understood, although not one in twenty of the audience had ever read a book of Dickens's right through. Even people who affect to despise him quote him unconsciously" (*CEJL* 1: 450). It is clear that this was the only kind of literary immortality Orwell felt was worth having—to become part of the *consciousness* of one's society.

By contrast, most of the great literature of the twentieth century, particularly recent poetry, was a closed world. The poet and the ordinary reader were no longer on speaking terms, and the recognition of this breach only tended to widen it, for "the concept of poetry as . . . something intelligible only to a minority, encourages obscurity and 'cleverness' " (*CEJL* 2: 331), as Orwell says in "Poetry and the Microphone." The charge is of course very familiar; in fact the attack on literary obscurity (seen as a symbol of the decadence of Western capitalism) was repeated ad nauseam by Marxist literary critics of the 1930s.

Orwell's attitude is unusual, however, because his disapproval of the coterie writing of the twenties is based on an honest acknowledgment that this obscurity coexists with unquestioned artistic distinction. Unlike the orthodox Marxist critics, he is not ready simply to dismiss the literature of the twenties, because he knows only too well how good it is; his aesthetic sensitivity is at war with his cultural ideals. The modern writers he admired most and never tired of reading were Joyce, Eliot, and Lawrence (*CEJL* 2: 24). His complex response to their work is most clearly spelled out in "Inside the Whale." Also significant is the essay on Yeats, since Yeats's idealization of aristocratic values must have been deeply offensive to Orwell. Yet it is clear from the piece that he knows Yeats's work in detail; he quotes both familiar and highly unfamiliar passages from memory and is constantly qualifying his disapproval by acknowledging the power and brilliance of the poems. He concludes, ruefully, "By and large the best writers of our time have been reactionary in tendency" (*CEJL* 2: 276).

The real problem, however, was not merely literary but social and human. A narrowly based high culture creates and then steadily reinforces a particularly intransigent kind of class identity, much more difficult to dissolve than the class distinctions of money and property. Money and property are portable and can be expropriated in a socialist society. But the sense of a proletariat of intellect is internal and can be reinforced in a thousand humiliating ways which no mere transfer of property can affect. Orwell's profound dislike of coterie culture grew out of his sense that it encouraged the "fit audience, though few" to think of itself as made of a finer clay. In the essay on Kipling, he insists that this is largely a fiction, that it ignores "the emotional overlap between the intellectual and the ordinary man" (*CEJL* 2: 195).

Orwell had a deep commitment to the idea of the potential democracy of intellect. He distrusted not only the literary coterie but any group that thought of itself as chosen and of the rest of the world as benighted. As Lionel Trilling has put it, Orwell liberates us "from the belief that the mind can work only in a technical, professional way and that it must work competitively. He has the effect of making us believe that we may become full members of the society of thinking men." [4] This distrust of the expert—the

4. *The Opposing Self* (New York, 1959), p. 158.

prophet with access to secret lore—is even more apparent in Orwell's dislike of the Marxist ideologue, whether or not he is a member of the Communist Party. From the beginning Marxism had been a profoundly theoretical—even scholarly—movement; it grew out of a philosophical schism and was taken up largely by an ideologically oriented intelligentsia. The nineteenth-century Russian intellectuals, the grandfathers and fathers of the Revolution, were highly educated men alienated from their society and involved in a lifelong obsession with theory. As Martin Malia has argued, despite their generational distinctions, they were all "men of ruthlessly logical ideology, and this bond was far stronger than the social and philosophical differences between them." [5]

Such men tend to think of socialism as a maze of conflicting theories and programs, most of which could be identified as heretical. The analogy Orwell often uses is to the Catholic Church, with its emphasis on dogma and its domination by a priest caste that interposes itself between the ordinary man and truth. Orwell was, in effect, a Protestant socialist, insisting that every man have access to the Word, that he be considered competent to understand the world around him without the benefit of a socialist priesthood. In its more ideologically trained disciples, the socialist movement had degenerated into a pointless heresy-hunt. As Orwell says in his essay "The Prevention of Literature," "The Catholic and the Communist are alike in assuming that an opponent cannot be both honest and intelligent. Each of them tacitly claims that 'the truth' has already been revealed, and that the heretic, if he is not simply a fool, is secretly aware of 'the truth' and merely resists it out of selfish motives" (*CEJL* 4: 61).

The vocabulary of the orthodox Marxists consisted largely of literal translations from German or Russian. The characteristic of the "international" Marxist style, Orwell writes in one of his *Tribune* essays, is its appropriation, without adjustment to its new audience, of phrases and metaphors "from the defunct *Inprecor* and similar sources." For example, the communist "vocabulary of

5. "What Is the Intelligentsia?" in *The Russian Intelligentsia*, ed. Richard Pipes (New York, 1961), pp. 12–13.

abuse . . . includes such terms as hyena, corpse, lackey, pirate, hangman, bloodsucker, mad dog, criminal, assassin. Whether at first, second or third hand, these are all translations, and by no means the kind of word that an English person naturally uses to express disapproval" (*CEJL* 3: 110). This is part of Orwell's quarrel with international Marxism as a movement—that it neither grows out of nor is adapted to local conditions, that it generalizes illegitimately because it is out of touch with ordinary people. The same thing was true of almost all theoretically inclined socialists, whether they were communists or not. As Orwell says in *The Road to Wigan Pier*, socialist literature, "even when it is not openly written *de haut en bas*, is always completely removed from the working class in idiom and manner of thought" (*RWP*, p. 175). Finally, it is the tendency of all elites, no matter what their official motives, to impose their vision of the world on the rest of society, whether by consent or by force. For many people who call themselves socialists, Orwell goes on to say, "revolution does not mean a movement of the masses with which they hope to associate themselves; it means a set of reforms which 'we', the clever ones, are going to impose upon 'them', the Lower Orders" (*RWP*, p. 179).

In essence, Orwell felt that too many members of the left-wing intelligentsia were really using the idealistic content of socialism as a way of releasing and legitimizing their own interest in power. This was particularly ironic for people who professed to believe in the end of class hierarchy, for despite the purity of their professed aims, there was an underlying wish to dominate and control the movement. The persecution of heretics was symptomatic. Any kind of crusade is, after all, a holy war; and in a holy war, there are no rules. One is not obliged to treat the devil as a fellow human being. The violent emotions released in left-wing antifascism were frightening in their suggestion of a naked lust for power, in their revelation of a suppressed brutality. Orwell's hero in *Coming Up for Air* uses a Left Book Club lecturer's speech as an example:

I saw the vision that he was seeing. And it wasn't at all the kind of vision that can be talked about. What he's *saying* is

merely that Hitler's after us and we must all get together and
have a good hate. . . . But what he's *seeing* is something quite
different. It's a picture of himself smashing people's faces in
with a spanner. Fascist faces, of course. . . . That's what's in
his mind, waking and sleeping, and the more he thinks of it
the more he likes it. And it's all O.K. because the smashed
faces belong to Fascists. [*CUA*, pp. 151–52]

These are serious charges, yet Orwell keeps coming back to
them in the last decade of his life, though usually in a less extreme
form. He was led to make them in the first place, I think, by the
apparently anomalous discovery of a similarity in *style* between
the intelligentsia of the Left and the Right. It is important to
remember that in the middle and late thirties fascism and
communism were treated as polar opposites. There was hardly
anyone who argued that their similarities might finally be more
significant than their differences. The term *totalitarianism* had not
yet come into vogue, and toward the end of the decade, Orwell
struggled to find a word that would point to their common
elements.

The essential quality he was trying to isolate was an emotional
identification with authoritarian autocracy. In a letter written in
1939 to Herbert Read, he predicted that England would move
toward "a fascising process leading to an authoritarian régime,
i.e. some kind of austro-fascism. So long as the objective, real or
pretended, is war against Germany, the greater part of the Left
will associate themselves with the fascising process, which will
ultimately mean associating themselves with wage-reductions,
suppression of free speech, brutalities in the colonies etc. Therefore the revolt against these things will have to be against the Left
as well as the Right" (*CEJL* 1: 386).

Orwell's vision of a totalitarian Britain was certainly one of his
more clouded prophecies, to which he was particularly prone in
the late thirties. He says that "the sin of nearly all left-wingers
from 1933 onwards is that they have wanted to be anti-Fascist
without being anti-totalitarian" (*CEJL* 3: 236). The emotional
addiction to totalitarian methods was, however, the exclusive
property of neither the Left nor the Right. Rather, it seemed to be

a disease peculiar to intellectuals. How else could one explain the apologists among both the fascist and the communist intelligentsia for the worst excesses of the regimes with which they associated themselves—the official ignorance of or refusal to acknowledge such outrages to common decency as the concentration camps, the secret police, the show trials? One of the unholy marriages of the twentieth century was that between "progressive impulses" and the "admiration for power and cruelty," Orwell writes in his essay on James Burnham. "It would be grossly unfair," he goes on, "to suggest that power-worship is the only motive for russophile feeling, but it is one motive, and among intellectuals it is probably the strongest one" (*CEJL* 4: 174).

Here, as elsewhere, the standard by which Orwell measures the intelligentsia is the common people. The worship of power, he claims, is simply incomprehensible to the ordinary Englishman. As he put it in his quasi-sociological study, *The English People*:

> From Carlyle onwards, but especially in the last generation, the British intelligentsia have tended to take their ideas from Europe and have been infected by habits of thought that derive ultimately from Machiavelli. All the cults that have been fashionable in the last dozen years, Communism, Fascism, and pacifism, are in the last analysis forms of power worship. It is significant that in this country, unlike most others, the Marxist version of Socialism has found its warmest adherents in the middle class. . . . One must conclude that in this matter the English common people have lagged behind their century. They have failed to catch up with power politics, "realism", *sacro egoismo* and the doctrine that the end justifies the means. [*CEJL* 3: 7–9]

It is significant that O'Brien, the sadistic villain of *Nineteen Eighty-Four*, should also be its most intelligent character. The greatest temptation for the intellectual lay precisely in the power of his mind. The sense of his own superiority led logically enough to the feeling of the inferiority of others. With the merest touch of noble fire, this condescension or contempt could be turned into an excuse for domination. The benighted did not understand; they obviously needed to be led. Orwell's friend Richard Rees recalls that "when Socialists told him that under Socialism there would be no such feeling of being at the mercy of unpredictable and irresponsible powers, Orwell commented: 'I notice people always say "*under* Socialism". They look forward to being on top—with all the others underneath, being told what is good for them.' " [6] The only kind of socialism most left-wing intellectuals could take seriously assumed that all classes were equal, but some classes were more equal than others. They had cast themselves in the role of the philosopher-kings of the Left.

This was the secret wish of the Russophile English intelligentsia, as Orwell says in his essay on Burnham: "the wish to destroy the old, equalitarian version of Socialism and usher in a hierarchical society where the intellectual can at last get his hands on the whip" (*CEJL* 4: 179). The naked, uncompromising quality of such statements makes one wonder if Orwell is not simply returning to the mindless hostility and private obsession of some of his earliest attacks on the bourgeois intellectuals. Have such statements been tested by skepticism, by objective observation? Do they have any basis in fact? Or are they merely the violent expression of Orwell's profound personal dislike? It seems to me absurd to think of Orwell as a dispassionate, scientific observer willing to assume the innocence of the intellectuals until they had been proven guilty. His role was not really that of judge but of prosecuting attorney. And in preparing his brief, he had come upon a particularly damaging piece of evidence—the attitude of the left-wing intelligentsia toward the Soviet Union. It was on this foundation that he built his case.

Orwell is not condemning all left-wing intellectuals but only those who consistently acted as apologists for Stalin and Soviet policy during the 1930s. Unlike most English leftists, he never approved of what was happening in the Soviet Union. This meant that he never went through the sudden crisis of conscience that events like the Moscow Trials or the Hitler-Stalin Pact forced on so many socialists. There was no disenchantment because there had never been an infatuation. In dissociating himself from the

6. Richard Rees, *George Orwell: Fugitive from the Camp of Victory* (London, 1961), p. 153.

standard pattern of left-wing attitudes toward Russia, Orwell wrote in 1946: "I could never be disappointed by the STALIN regime, because I never expected any good to come of it. . . . I do not believe in the possibility of benevolent dictatorship, nor, in the last analysis, in the honesty of those who defend dictatorship. Of course, one develops and modifies one's views, but I have never fundamentally altered my attitude towards the Soviet regime since I first began to pay attention to it some time in the nineteen-twenties." [7]

Insofar as Orwell developed and modified his views, they progressed from doubt to certainty, from vague distrust to positive rejection. The trouble at first was simply lack of information. Too many of the reports coming from Russia were contradictory or incomplete; or else they were clearly the work of biased observers, determined to find utopia in everything they were permitted to see. The late 1920s and early 1930s were the age of a new kind of Grand Tour—the Western socialist's ecstatic trip to the Soviet Union, from which he brought back news of wonders. The culmination of this movement was the Webbs' two-volume scholarly love-letter, *Soviet Communism: A New Civilisation?* (1935). The answer to the rhetorical question of their title was a decided yes; in later editions the question mark was removed.

By this time, however, a very different kind of report had begun to appear, from people who had expected to find a paradise and discovered instead a terror-ridden state: books like Gide's influential (and bitterly attacked) *Retour de l'U.R.S.S.* (1936) and Eugene Lyons's *Assignment in Utopia* (1938). Although the Purge Trials and Orwell's observation of the methods of the Communist Party in Spain had convinced him that his doubts about the Soviet Union were well-founded, he was not yet completely certain he was right. In his review of the Lyons book, he could still say: "Meanwhile the truth about Stalin's régime, if we could only get hold of it, is of the first importance. Is it Socialism, or is it a peculiarly vicious form of state-capitalism? All the political

7. George Orwell, annotations to Randall Swingler's "The Right to Free Expression," *Polemic*, no. 5 (September–October 1946), p. 53. For a detailed study of the attitudes of other intellectuals on the Left, see Neal Wood, *Communism and British Intellectuals* (New York, 1959).

controversies that have made life hideous for two years past really circle round this question" (*CEJL* 1: 333). By 1940, no doubt remained. Russian policy since 1928 had simply been an instrument "tending to keep the ruling clique in power"; and both Russia and Nazi Germany were "rapidly evolving towards the same system—a form of oligarchical collectivism" (*CEJL* 2: 26, 25).

The growing distrust of the Soviet Union during the late thirties came to a climax in 1939 with the Hitler-Stalin Pact. Russia's sudden and completely unexpected betrayal of the anti-Fascist policy of a decade opened the eyes of many intellectuals on the Left and made them reexamine their attitudes. Nevertheless, the effect was shortlived, since within two years of the Pact, Russia was again an ally in the fight against Germany. The painful truths of the previous decade were too readily forgotten, the British Communist Party greatly expanded its membership, and even the *New Statesman* could assure its readers, when Russia began to set up its puppet regimes in Eastern Europe, that "a parallel drawn between the Soviet encroachments and those of Nazi Germany before the war . . . is stupid, misleading and extremely dangerous. For the first object of Soviet policy is to preserve the peace." [8] This curious ability to forget or ignore the facts about Soviet totalitarianism finally convinced Orwell that the left-wing intelligentsia's worship of Russia had nothing to do with lack of information but rather satisfied some deep need. In 1946 he could write that the new orthodoxy of the Left consisted simply in never criticizing Stalin: "the bulk of the English literary intelligentsia has looked on at torture, massacre and aggression without expressing disapproval and perhaps in the long run without feeling it." [9]

Possibly even more important than this secret identification with power was the intellectual dishonesty that accompanied it. The left-wing intellectual's attitude toward Russia could be dangerous for him, since more than any other opinion he held it was a test of his orthodoxy, the key to how he was judged by his

8. "Russia and the West," *New Statesman and Nation* 30 (1945): 223.
9. Orwell, annotations to Swingler, "Right to Free Expression," p. 53.

peers. For this reason, it was a kind of litmus test for integrity of mind. In order to find anything wrong with the Soviet Union, he would have to stop running with the pack. So Orwell could write in 1944, in a letter to Middleton Murry, that "for people like ourselves, who suspect that something has gone very wrong with the Soviet Union, I consider that willingness to criticize Russia and Stalin is *the* test of intellectual honesty. It is the only thing that from a literary intellectual's point of view is really dangerous. . . . The thing that needs courage is to attack Russia, the only thing that the greater part of the British intelligentsia now believe in" (*CEJL* 3: 203–04).

In the same year Orwell was painfully exposed to the orthodox habit of mind in left-wing circles when he tried to get *Animal Farm*, which he had just finished, into print. The book was effectively suppressed for so long that Orwell wrote to his agent that he was ready to publish it at his own expense (*CEJL* 3: 187). The fear of criticizing Stalinist Russia was a local condition, and one that would pass. But the principle behind it—intellectual honesty— would always be in danger no matter what the reigning orthodoxy. It was possible, Orwell realized with great prescience in 1946, that by the 1950s it might be "as dangerous to praise STALIN as it was to attack him two years ago. But I should not regard this as an advance. Nothing is gained by teaching a parrot a new word. What is needed is the right to print what one believes to be true, without having to fear bullying or blackmail from *any* side." [10]

The fear of criticizing Soviet Russia was merely symptomatic. It grew out of a hierarchy of values in which efficacy is more important than honesty, and out of an assumption that the only way to fight an ignoble opponent is to adopt his methods. The suppression of truth in left-wing circles had the complicity of those who saw it as truth. The most frightening propagandistic achievement of the twentieth century, as Orwell saw it, was the disappearance of objective history and the willingness of intellectuals to work toward its elimination. The constant restructuring of the past to make it conform to the present—one of the familiar

10. Ibid.

methods of Soviet history—seemed to him both new and especially sinister. No matter how intolerable the present is, the sense of alternative possibilities that objective history inevitably presents can still liberate the imagination and perhaps lead to significant change. But once the past is perpetually "rectified" to conform to the present, this escape is no longer possible. When Winston Smith attempts to escape the society of 1984, he creates a little world out of the pathetic fragments of the past—trivial objects, anecdotes, memories. They are the apparently forgotten interstices in that society where sanity still seems possible.

The whole subject of the disappearance of an objective past came to haunt Orwell in the 1940s. It first appears in his work in *Homage to Catalonia*, when it suddenly occurs to him that no unbiased account of the Barcelona uprising will ever be possible, since "future historians will have nothing to go upon except a mass of accusations and party propaganda" (*HC*, p. 160). This insight is generalized by 1942 in the essay "Looking Back on the Spanish War," where Orwell voices his fear that "the very concept of objective truth is fading out of the world" (*CEJL* 2: 258). In *Animal Farm*, the threat posed by the animals' memory of the heroic days of the revolution is solved by the systematic recasting of what actually happened, a process that culminates in the secret rewriting of the Seven Commandments on the barn door. By *Nineteen Eighty-Four* this rewriting of history has become a major government industry, in which the hero is engaged: " 'Who controls the past,' ran the Party slogan, 'controls the future: who controls the present controls the past' " (*NEF*, p. 38).

Very few intellectuals would have been able to tolerate such methods without a high-minded excuse. There were several available for them to choose from: that "we can only combat Communism, Fascism or what not if we develop an equal fanaticism," as Orwell puts it (*CEJL* 4: 478); that internal criticism of a movement "objectively" helps the other side, since it can be used as propaganda by them; that most people are not capable of facing an ambiguous reality and need to have the issues purified to preserve their commitment. All of these excuses for the suppression of damaging truth turn on a schizophrenic distinction between what one knows and what one claims to be

true—an occupational disease of propagandists that is called
"reality control" or "doublethink" in the language of *Nineteen
Eighty-Four:*

> To know and not to know, to be conscious of complete
> truthfulness while telling carefully constructed lies, to hold
> simultaneously two opinions which cancelled out, knowing
> them to be contradictory and believing in both of them; to
> use logic against logic, to repudiate morality while laying
> claim to it, to believe that democracy was impossible and
> that the Party was the guardian of democracy; to forget
> whatever it was necessary to forget, then to draw it back into
> memory again at the moment when it was needed, and then
> promptly to forget it again: and above all, to apply the same
> process to the process itself. That was the ultimate subtlety:
> consciously to induce unconsciousness, and then, once again,
> to become unconscious of the act of hypnosis you had just
> performed. Even to understand the word "doublethink"
> involved the use of doublethink. [*NEF*, pp. 38–39]

The passage suggests that the whole technique of "reality
control" was invented by a benevolent power to protect the sanity
and the innocence of the propagandist, to make the consciousness
of lying tolerable by disarming the conscience. The brain's
potential waywardness is kept in check by transforming it into an
efficient machine controlled by the will. All of Winston Smith's
difficulties in *Nineteen Eighty-Four* arise from his imperfect mastery
of the technique. His violent and total repudiation of a regime he
has been serving without compunction for years is the product of
the long, frustrated attempt to eliminate the part of his mind that
remembers dangerous truths *despite* the efforts of his will. Orwell
is, I think, suggesting that Winston's sudden and disastrous
apostasy is the logical pattern for intellectuals who attempt to
suppress their doubts in the first place. His awakening is a kind of
allegorical version of the breakdown of the many communist
intellectuals who—at an arbitrary moment—can no longer
successfully deny the unpalatable truths they have been refusing
to acknowledge for years: suddenly they surge toward the surface.
The result is a mental cataclysm, in which the sense of revulsion

with oneself, one's former associates, and even the ideology for which one has been fighting, combine to produce a complete breakdown. This experience has often been described by its survivors, not only by former communists in such books as *The God That Failed*, but by other faithful servants of a creed, for example, by John Stuart Mill in the section of the *Autobiography* he calls "A Crisis in My Mental History." The whole process was finally dangerous to the cause of socialism itself, for, as Orwell says in an essay in *Tribune*, pro-Soviet propaganda may induce "a sudden revulsion" in which the formerly faithful "may reject the whole idea of Socialism" (*CEJL* 4: 36), not merely the more unsavory aspects of its local manifestation.

Orwell is characteristically attacking propaganda not only because it is immoral but because it doesn't work. This conviction turns on a distinction between its short- and long-term results. If "unpleasant truths" were made public in the first place rather than being suppressed they would certainly have a momentarily damaging effect, and they might very well strengthen the other side. But this effect would be short-lived compared to what happens when the facts are not related honestly in the first place. The trouble with the suppression of facts is that they never *stay* suppressed. Sooner or later, inevitably, they are brought to light; and when people feel that essential information has been withheld from them, their anger is likely to be much more extreme, their rejection much more violent, than it would have been if they had been told the truth in the first place. So Orwell writes to a friend in 1938, "my position has always been that this kind of controversy could die a natural death and cause comparatively little harm if people would refrain from telling lies in the beginning" (*CEJL* 1: 364).

The crucial point here is psychological: it concerns people's ability to do without myths or sustaining illusions, to accept reality in its naturally ambiguous state. In "Why I Write," Orwell suggests that he first thought of writing as a vocation when he realized that he had "a facility with words and a power of facing unpleasant facts" (*CEJL* 1: 1). In that context, he treats this power as a special gift rather than as a common human characteristic. Yet his whole insistence on the efficacy of honesty in political writing is, I think, based on the assumption that the "power of facing unpleasant facts" is widespread, perhaps nearly universal. He would hardly have agreed with Eliot that "human kind cannot bear very much reality." His whole argument for honesty is founded on a fundamental trust in human nature, on the conviction that people are capable of tolerating ambiguity and can do without the cant and the fraudulent purification of tarnished ideals which have always been thought necessary to inspire political action.

Orwell sees this as the final, and the most insulting, condescension of the Left toward the people: the feeling that they cannot be told the whole truth, that embarrassing facts must be kept from them, as they are from children. Socialism had a large collection of unpalatable truths it was keeping well hidden. Orwell regularly pointed out two important ones which the English Left suppressed: that British prosperity depended ultimately on the exploitation of the colored races, and that mere "state Socialism" was perfectly compatible with a brutally repressive totalitarian regime. To admit these facts meant to question the millennial element in socialism, the idea that with its establishment utopia will have arrived. Orwell's demand for an end to political myths attacks the theory that to make people work for any ideal wholeheartedly, you must nurture their chimerical conception of it. He clearly believed that for most people complete realism and passionate dedication are compatible, that lies are not the necessary aliment of enthusiasm.

His quarrel is really with the theory of social change proposed by writers like Georges Sorel. *Reflections on Violence*, a book Orwell had read, crystallizes the central ideas against which he fought. Sorel insists that all great political and religious movements owe their effectiveness not to realism but to myths. The adherents of such movements are inspired by an inner certainty that their cause is absolutely just and must triumph. Their myths are "anticipations of the future . . . which recur to the mind with the insistence of instincts in all the circumstances of life," and which take the form of utopian visions. In order to dedicate himself wholeheartedly to a cause and to suppress his own weakness, laziness, and willingness to compromise, a man "must have in himself some source of conviction which must dominate his whole consciousness, and act before the calculations of reflection have time to enter his mind." As soon as such myths are abandoned by the more skeptical among the adherents of any sect, the movement loses its fundamental vitality and begins to decay. Sorel suggests that the beginning of the end for the Catholic Church, for example, came when such myths as the Church militant and the struggle with Satan were discredited by the spread of the "sophisticated" habit of mind among educated Catholics.[11] In order to bring a socialist society into being, Sorel felt, the movement must inspire a faith comparable to the ideal visions of the great religions.

It was precisely this position that Orwell was attacking. He insisted that socialism as a theory had reached its maturity and must now resolutely strip itself of its childish illusions. It was time for a realistic vision of the socialist future. As he writes in a *Tribune* piece that specifically mentions Sorel:

> The real answer is to dissociate Socialism from Utopianism. . . . Socialists are accused of believing that society can be—and indeed, after the establishment of Socialism, will be—completely perfect; also that progress is *inevitable*. Debunking such beliefs is money for jam, of course.
>
> The answer, which ought to be uttered more loudly than it usually is, is that Socialism is not perfectionist, perhaps not even hedonistic. Socialists don't claim to be able to make the world perfect: they claim to be able to make it better. . . . It is all summed up in Marx's saying that after Socialism has arrived, human history can begin. [*CEJL* 3: 64]

It is, however, a mistake to think of millennial socialism only as a fraud consciously perpetrated by the intelligentsia upon the common people in order to make them more dedicated, even if this was how some "realist" intellectuals in politics defended it. Orwell insisted that the true reason socialism had been turned into a religion was that intellectuals *needed* religions: it was the

11. Georges Sorel, *Reflections on Violence*, trans. T. E. Hulme and J. Roth (New York, 1967), pp. 125, 207, 42–43.

price they had to pay for their liberation from patriotism and traditional piety. Yet this liberation from King and Country on the one hand, and God and the Church on the other, had no effect whatever on the emotional need to identify with some kind of external authority. The religious feeling had not been transcended; it had merely been transferred. And the elements of irrationality, illusion, and intolerance were at least as evident in the new guise as in the old. Orwell analyzes this condition among English Communists in "Inside the Whale":

> But I do not think one need look farther than this for the reason why the young writers of the 'thirties flocked into or towards the Communist Party. It was simply something to believe in. Here was a church, an army, an orthodoxy, a discipline. Here was a Fatherland and—at any rate since 1935 or thereabouts—a Fuehrer. All the loyalties and superstitions that the intellect had seemingly banished could come rushing back under the thinnest of disguises. [*CEJL* 1: 515]

Orwell's most sustained analysis of this element in the British intelligentsia is the essay "Notes on Nationalism," where he catalogs the various kinds of substitute faiths to which intellectuals had become addicted. The term *nationalism* is misleading, as Orwell realizes; he chooses it only because no other word has been coined for the condition of mind he describes. Its most salient characteristics are obsession, instability, and indifference to objective truth; one might add intolerance, a lust for power, and utopianism. "Nationalists" believe absolutely in the *exclusive* truth of their cause. It explains the world to them and has no apparent internal contradictions. Such faiths have the logical consistency and absolute coherence of madness, since they do not bother to take the contradictory aspects of reality into account. One might say that "national" beliefs are the easiest to hold because they can incorporate and absorb any experience, no matter how apparently alien or superficially threatening, without calling the bases of the belief into question.

Orwell treats this mental condition not as a mass but as a class neurosis. His analysis of it occasionally reminds one of Freud's *The*

Future of an Illusion, in which religious belief is placed under the same kind of detached scrutiny. Freud's cautiously optimistic conclusion is that the need for religious consolation—indeed for the whole concept of a benevolent supernatural force that will eventually rectify the abuses of nature—is part of the childhood of man; and that someday humanity will be able to do without such sustaining illusions: "surely infantilism is destined to be surmounted. Men cannot remain children for ever; they must in the end go out into 'hostile life'. We may call this *'education to reality'*." [12]

It was precisely this hostile reality that the English political intelligentsia—of whatever persuasion—could not accept. Orwell felt that their whole identification with a cause was an all-or-nothing affair, and this made it necessary for them to adopt all the intellectual abuses he exposed: the intolerance of internal criticism, the blindness to any evidence damaging to their cause, and the abandonment of moral scruple in the methods used to defend it. We are dealing here with a passionate will-to-faith, so powerful that it sweeps all opposition from its path—in short, fanaticism. Every such sect has at least one "unpleasant fact" that it finds intolerable and therefore inadmissible. For example, Orwell says, it is emotionally impossible for the communist to admit that "If she had not been aided by Britain and America, Russia would have been defeated by Germany"; or for the pacifist to acknowledge that "Those who 'abjure' violence can only do so because others are committing violence on their behalf" (*CEJL* 3: 378). The denial of such intolerable facts and the construction of ingenious theories to explain them away is an activity that provides work for the intelligentsia: the manufacture and dissemination of sustaining illusions. What Orwell is calling for, on the other hand, is an unfanatical, a nonutopian, an illusion-*free* socialism. Helping to create such a movement is the underlying aim of most of his mature work.

Yet in pursuing this goal, he could not help inventing a myth of his own. He felt he had a set of natural allies, not among the

12. Sigmund Freud, *The Future of an Illusion*, trans. W. D. Robson-Scott, ed. James Strachey (Garden City, N.Y., 1964), p. 81.

intelligentsia, but in the English common people. Orwell saw them as having no need for substitute faiths, partially because they had never really given up their traditional ones: they still loved their country and they had never abandoned the ethical content of Christianity. They were not deracinated; they were not apostates. And so they were likely to treat politics with a pragmatism and realism (as well as a moral scrupulousness) rare in their ideologically committed intellectual superiors. It was his hope that their essential soundness and decency might one day be prized by the English intelligentsia, when they came to realize they had as much to learn from the common people as to teach them. He sought to heal the rift between the disillusioned realists who had given up politics as a hopelessly sullied world and the passionately self-deceived who could see no wrong in their cause. This breach had produced a tragic divorce between energy and sense; the two parties must be reconciled.

The emphasis on reformation and reconciliation is one of the marks of Orwell's mature work. One sometimes has the feeling, in reading his early books, that his dislike of the intellectuals led him to imagine a future society in which they would be, in some mysterious way, completely eliminated. By the end of his career, he writes about them in a very different spirit. Here, for example, is part of the conclusion of "Notes on Nationalism":

> As for the nationalistic loves and hatreds that I have spoken of, they are part of the make-up of most of us, whether we like it or not. Whether it is possible to get rid of them I do not know, but I do believe it is possible to struggle against them, and that this is essentially a *moral* effort. It is a question first of all of discovering what one really is, what one's own feelings really are, and then of making allowance for the inevitable bias. . . . The emotional urges which are inescapable, and are perhaps even necessary for political action, should be able to exist side by side with an acceptance of reality. [*CEJL* 3: 380]

The passage speaks of "us" rather than "them." It does not simply reject one segment of society as hopelessly alien and dangerous. Here Orwell clearly identifies himself with the intellectuals and their peculiar difficulties, and he treats their painful internal struggle against their own irrational needs with full sympathy. "Men cannot remain children for ever," as Freud said. The struggle to abandon their childlike, millennial faith and substitute for it a hard, realistic dedication would certainly not be easy. Yet Orwell too was cautiously optimistic: "The emotional urges which are inescapable, and are perhaps even necessary for political action, should be able to exist side by side with an acceptance of reality." Certainly they did in him, and he was too much of an instinctive egalitarian to treat this as a special gift. The one "unpleasant fact" Orwell himself could not face was that fanaticism has always been, and will always be, the only fuel on which radical movements can run. But to say this is to assume that it *is* a fact, which he would certainly have denied.

3

The Making of a Socialist

"I have seen wonderful things & at last really believe in Socialism, which I never did before" (*CEJL* 1: 269), Orwell wrote to Cyril Connolly from Spain. And ten years later he recalls, "The Spanish war and other events in 1936–37 turned the scale and thereafter I knew where I stood" (*CEJL* 1: 5). Both quotations suggest that Orwell's commitment to socialism was the product of external events, the crises of the 1930s that moved so many writers of his generation to the Left. His socialism was unusual, however, not only because it outlasted the events that helped to create it, but because at every stage it combined an extraordinary reluctance with an extraordinary persistence. Orwell's socialism was not a phase but a lifelong commitment; yet throughout his career it had to contend with the most powerful doubts and reservations. In some fundamental way, Orwell was an *unwilling* socialist. Like other writers of his time, he moved toward political awareness slowly and with many misgivings. But Orwell's reluctant socialism was not merely the product of a basically apolitical nature forced into political awareness by the age. The conflict was both deeper and narrower, for socialism is an optimistic faith and Orwell was a temperamental pessimist. He was to write in 1940, at the end of a decade of ideology, that "the only 'ism' that has justified itself is pessimism" (*CEJL* 1: 533). Yet he knew that "Socialism is in the last analysis an optimistic creed" and the socialist, "a person who believes 'the earthly paradise' to be possible." [1]

Although he carefully tried to detach the millennial element from socialism and insisted that no transformation of society could eliminate many of the forms human unhappiness takes, Orwell as

George Orwell, "What Is Socialism?" *Manchester Evening News*, 31 January 1946, 2.

a socialist would have accepted certain fundamentally optimistic assumptions: that many of the major human problems can be solved by a reconstruction of society; that the competitive drive in human beings which supports a system of inequality need not be stronger than the sense of communal loyalty; that the means used to transform society (whether revolutionary or reformist) do not necessarily compromise the hope of creating a world without privilege.

In calling himself a socialist, Orwell was in effect affirming his belief in these ideas. Yet compared to most of the visionaries on his side of the fence, he spoke of the coming triumph of socialism with much less faith and assurance. He was inhibited by a kind of reflex despondency that finds expression in almost all his works and eventually comes to dominate his vision. The fear that human hopes will come to nothing, that all projects for the improvement of society are doomed, has its roots in Orwell's earliest sense of himself. His social pessimism grows out of an original conviction of *personal* failure, as the memories of his schooldays in "Such, Such Were the Joys" make clear. A line of verse, he tells us, crystallized his feelings of frustration at that time: "The armies of unalterable law." [2] The line came to stand for all of his own apparently insuperable shortcomings: "according to that law I was damned. I had no money, I was weak, I was ugly, I was unpopular, I had a chronic cough, I was cowardly, I smelt. . . . The conviction that it was *not possible* for me to be a success went deep enough to influence my actions till far into adult life. Until I was about thirty I always planned my life on the assumption . . . that any major undertaking was bound to fail" (*CEJL* 4: 360–61).

This pessimism finds clear expression in Orwell's early, presocialist fiction. *Burmese Days* (1934), *A Clergyman's Daughter* (1935), and *Keep the Aspidistra Flying* (1936) all move inexorably toward defeat. Each begins with an intolerable situation, flirts with the possibility of release from it, and ends either in despair or resignation. The element of social criticism in the three books is

2. Actually, "the army of unalterable law" in Meredith's "Lucifer in Starlight." Orwell's memory of the line suggests an even greater sense of helplessness.

very strong; the misery Orwell describes is at least in part the product of anonymous social forces. His targets are often institutional: British colonialism, the Anglican church, private schools, the advertising industry, the wage structure, the system of casual labor, and so on. The major character in each of these novels is appalled by the conditions of his life as they are determined by such institutions. Yet the attempt to escape is illustory: the forces of the society are stronger than the potential rebel. He can only choose between suicide and surrender, although he may keep his scrap of dignity even in defeat. His adjustment to the society becomes a life sentence.

All of these novels were written before Orwell's "conversion" to socialism and each seems imaginatively trapped in the system it describes. *Burmese Days*,for example, is shrewdly diagnostic about the evils of imperialism but suggests no way out of the morass. Not a single character in the novel is liberated enough from the world Orwell describes to have any real perspective on it. The disease is known; the cure is not.[3] This absence of political understanding is even more evident in *A Clergyman's Daughter*, partly because of the miscellaneousness of its satirical targets. If there is a single root to most of the evils described in that book it is money; Dorothy slowly comes to understand its "mysterious power" in the course of the novel (*CD*, p. 214). Yet this insight is treated as a terminal fact, not as the first step in a political education. Orwell's obsession with money both here and in his next novel is fetishistic; he takes the symbol for the real power. His social protest does not as yet rest on a theoretical foundation.

Keep the Aspidistra Flying comes closer to having a coherent political vision, and yet it too is finally balked by its obsession with money. The book seems to have all the building blocks for a commitment to socialism yet emphatically refuses to create such a structure. Gordon Comstock's diatribes against the bourgeoisie and his keen awareness of the omnipotence of money are basic

3. Orwell's picture of Burma in the 1920s virtually ignores the political movement for independence that began to grow powerful in those years. See the interesting account of this decade by Maung Htin Aung, "George Orwell and Burma," in *The World of George Orwell*, ed. Miriam Gross (London, 1971), pp. 20–30.

socialist components. Here are two quotations: "What he realised, and more clearly as time went on, was that money-worship has been elevated into a religion. Perhaps it is the only real religion—the only really *felt* religion—that is left to us. Money is what God used to be" (*KAF*, p. 56). "Then came money, that universal commodity for which all others could be exchanged. But when men invented money they little suspected that they were creating a new social power, the one universal power to which the whole of society must bow." The first passage comes from *Keep the Aspidistra Flying*, the second from Engels's *The Origin of the Family, Private Property and the State*.[4]

Yet though Orwell's hero is ripe for conversion to socialism, he scornfully rejects the faith. Socialism, in the novel, is an enthusiasm of the young or a comfortable creed for the guilty rich. Gordon's sarcastic dismissal of it is so violent as to be suspicious. Socialism to him means "Four hours a day in a model factory, tightening up bolt number 6003. Rations served out in grease-proof paper at the communal kitchen. Community-hikes from Marx Hostel to Lenin Hostel and back. Free abortion-clinics on all the corners." And when his socialist friend encourages him to study Marx, he replies that he would sooner read Mrs. Humphry Ward (*KAF*, pp. 109-10). Rather than become a socialist, Gordon finally surrenders unconditionally to the money god. He becomes a part of the army of wage-slaves with a kind of passionate despair that comes close to triumph, if only because the choice he makes confirms the rightness of his own political despondency: there is no way out.

What turned such an instinctive pessimist into a socialist? And how were these antithetical impulses—the faith in a socialist future and the gloomy fear that society was incapable of improvement—combined in Orwell's life and work? These questions can only be answered by tracing his political ideas and commitments in time, through the two decades of his career. Although he says he went through a phase of youthful Lenin-worship at school, and although a couple of the articles he published

4. Karl Marx and Frederick Engels, *Selected Works in Two Volumes* (Moscow, 1962), 2: 267-68.

in French journals in his twenties occasionally strike an anticapitalist note, Orwell's early published writings in England are rooted in the tradition of reformist liberalism. His outrage at exploitation, inequality, and destitution are fundamentally moral, and his proposed solutions to these problems combine a faith in the possibility of a change of heart in the middle class with a trust in the power of government regulation and reform.

One of his earliest published pieces, the *New Statesman* essay "Common Lodging Houses" (1932), describes the conditions in London dormitory accommodations for the poor and insists that significant improvements could be made in such places by passing and enforcing sensible Council regulations providing, for example, cubicles and more comfortable beds (*CEJL* 1: 99–100). At no point in the essay does Orwell raise the question of why society forces human beings to live under such conditions. He seems to accept the situation as inevitable: for the poor always ye have with you. The appalling school described in *A Clergyman's Daughter* could, Orwell implies, be improved by regular government inspection: "Only the tiny minority of 'recognised' schools—less than one in ten—are officially tested to decide whether they keep up a reasonable educational standard. As for the others, they are free to teach or not to teach exactly as they choose. No one controls or inspects them except the children's parents—the blind leading the blind" (*CD*, p. 261). But the fundamental question of why such schools should be run as profit-making enterprises at all, which is at the heart of the problem, is barely raised.

Again and again in these early works, we have the sense of a writer who neither understands why things are as they are in his society nor can imagine the possibility of a really different world. For example, in the hop-picking section of *A Clergyman's Daughter*, he insists that the exploitation of the hop-pickers is inevitable. The farmers were not to blame: "the low price of hops was the root of the trouble" (*CD*, p. 132). Such passages suggest Orwell's inability to think outside the socioeconomic framework of his society, his acceptance of its basic structure as inevitable.

This is particularly apparent in Orwell's most direct analysis of poverty, the nonfictional *Down and Out in Paris and London*, published in 1933 but written and revised between 1930 and

1932. Orwell's first priority in that book is to describe the lives of the poor in vivid detail, primarily because he knows that this exotic landscape is almost entirely unfamiliar to the middle-class audience he is trying to reach. His rare proposals for ways of alleviating the deprivation and suffering he describes are all cautiously meliorist. For example, he suggests that the life of tramps in the casual wards could be improved if "each workhouse could run a small farm, or at least a kitchen garden, and every able-bodied tramp who presented himself could be made to do a sound day's work" (*DOPL*, p. 206). In the context of the book, this is roughly comparable to a scheme for improving hell by planting trees in its streets. Orwell's concluding paragraph, in which he proposes some new attitudes and actions for himself and his middle-class reader, is equally unruffled:

> Still I can point to one or two things I have definitely learned by being hard up. I shall never again think that all tramps are drunken scoundrels, nor expect a beggar to be grateful when I give him a penny, nor be surprised if men out of work lack energy, nor subscribe to the Salvation Army, nor pawn my clothes, nor refuse a handbill, nor enjoy a meal at a smart restaurant. That is a beginning. [*DOPL*, p. 213]

"Well just," one feels after reading this conclusion to Orwell's harrowing exposé of poverty and destitution. Certainly none of these resolutions would have much effect on the tramps and beggars he describes. *Down and Out* is a classic instance of unradical thinking, despite its very fresh observation. The social misery the book depicts seems to demand more forceful and coherent counsel. The cautious program of changed middle-class attitudes and institutional tinkering that Orwell proposes is painfully inconsequential and futile in comparison to the magnitude of the problems his book raises. It is perhaps Orwell's understanding of this disparity that makes his suggestions for improvement so rare and unobtrusive in his narrative. At this point in his career, it can fairly be said that he knows what he hates but has little idea why it exists, and knows even less what to do about it. A socialist would have to be able to answer all three questions.

Given his own unformed political attitudes in the early 1930s, Orwell's best work of the period tends to be detached and analytic. He is still very far from being a prophet, but he is from the first a keen and accurate reporter. The fine documentary essay, "A Hanging," is among his earliest works, and his first novel, *Burmese Days*, contains vivid sketches of British colonial types and their characteristic attitudes. It is the sense of sharply observed detail in these works, and in *Down and Out*, that makes them permanently valuable, rather than the persuasiveness of their vision. But to find a solution one must first feel the urgency of the problem. This the experiences recorded in Orwell's earliest works gave him, and he hoped his writings would pass that awareness on to his readers.

To understand the transition from this unformed political consciousness to Orwell's socialist faith, one has to have some further sense of the forces in the early thirties that were moving liberal intellectuals to the Left. The radicalization of the Left in England began with a sense of the failures of piecemeal reform and the tactics of gradualism. Two Labour governments in the twenties and early thirties had not been able to avert an economic crisis that resulted in industrial failure and mass unemployment. And the growing strength of fascist regimes in Germany and Italy only reinforced the idea that things were getting not gradually better but rapidly worse. The sense of urgency these events created translated itself into an impatience with gradual solutions to social problems and a demand for more radical thought and action.

We can see this disillusionment with the principle of the inevitability of gradual reform even in the chief spokesmen for that theory. Both Shaw and the Webbs, the major architects of the Fabian Society, began to think seriously about revolutionary alternatives to the Fabian program of institutional permeation. To read through Beatrice Webb's diary of the period is to become aware of her growing disillusionment and her search for an alternative program of social transformation—an uneasiness that finally led her and Sidney to idealize the Soviet Union. She writes in one of the entries for 1931:

> What I am beginning to doubt is the "inevitability of gradualness", or even the practicability of gradualness, in the

transition from a capitalist to an equalitarian civilisation. Anyway, *no leader*, in our country, has thought out *how to make the transition*, without upsetting the applecart. Sidney says "it will make itself", without an acknowledged plan accepted by one party in the state and denounced by the other. We shall *slip into the equalitarian state* as we did into political democracy —by each party, whether nominally Socialist or anti-Socialist, taking steps in the direction of curtailing the tribute of rent and interest and increasing the amount and security of reward of labour. But this cannot be done without transferring the *control* of the savings of the country; and I don't see how that is to be done gradually or without a terrific struggle on clearly thought-out lines. . . . Sidney says, "All I know is that I don't know how to do it." [5]

Shaw too attacked the triviality and futility of gradual reform from within capitalism, particularly in the extraordinary report on his trip to the Soviet Union, *The Rationalization of Russia* (written 1932). He insisted that "the corruption of a predatory society cannot be cured by reforms within that form of society: it is fundamental." [6] And his attack on the existing system includes a denunciation of its petty concessions to the oppressed:

We cannot smash Capitalism without smashing its institutions; and its institutions include not only its predatory and oppressive organs but the defensive, humanitarian, palliative and popular brakes and checks and safeguards and franchises and "liberties" which it has consented to partly in fear of rebellion and partly in a natural recoil from its own worst villainy in pursuit of profits. [7]

In such extreme statements, the bourgeois prophets of parliamentary reform seemed to be ratifying the revolutionary vision of Marx and Engels rather than the more measured assumptions of traditional English socialism.

5. *Beatrice Webb's Diaries 1924–1932*, ed. Margaret Cole (London, 1956), pp. 265–66.

6. Bernard Shaw, *The Rationalization of Russia*, ed. Harry M. Geduld (Bloomington, Ind., 1964), p. 38.

7. Ibid., p. 40.

The search for radical alternatives to present reformist policies did not push all English leftists to theoretical Marxism and the cult of Russia, however. It often expressed itself in an impatience with the Labour Party as an institution, or with the compromises of its leaders. The Party was constantly accused by its more radical members of betraying the principles of socialism, and in 1932 the left-wing Independent Labour Party—which Orwell was later to join—finally disaffiliated from the larger organization. In a manifesto justifying the action, its chairman insisted that the working class "must break with the policies of reformism; then they must unite on a policy of revolutionary Socialism." [8]

The pressures that turned Fabian gradualists into apologists for revolution and alienated the Labour Party's left wing changed Orwell from a humanitarian liberal into a socialist. Middle-class reformers characteristically reject capitalist society and its palliatives only when they become convinced that it is on the verge of breakdown. Orwell recorded this sense of crisis in *The Road to Wigan Pier*: "It hardly needs pointing out that at this moment we are in a very serious mess, so serious that even the dullest-witted people find it difficult to remain unaware of it. We are living in a world in which nobody is free, in which hardly anybody is secure, in which it is almost impossible to be honest and to remain alive" (*RWP*, p. 170). The crucial question for someone hesitating between liberal reform and socialism was whether the system was bankrupt. As Orwell says, "before you can be sure whether you are genuinely in favour of Socialism, you have got to decide whether things at present are tolerable or not tolerable" (*RWP*, p. 123). By 1936 he, along with many of the writers of his generation, had become convinced of the need for a complete social transformation.

Between 1935 and 1938, Orwell's socialist sympathies gradually developed into a firm political commitment. In 1936, he attended the Adelphi Centre summer school in Essex, an institution which its sponsors conceived as "a centre of non-sectarian Socialism,"

8. A. Fenner Brockway, *Socialism at the Crossroads: Why the I.L.P. Left the Labour Party* (London, 1932), p. 7. For a history of the I.L.P.'s troubled relations with the Labour Party, see Robert E. Dowse, *Left in the Centre: The Independent Labour Party 1893–1940* (London, 1966).

based "on the conviction of the desirability of a classless society." [9] Although Orwell was sharply ironic about the attempt by such institutions to turn proletarians and "repentant bourgeois" into "brothers for ever" (*RWP*, p. 163), his participation in the program makes clear that he was reading and thinking about socialism in a serious way. He also began to move from observation to participation in British socialist politics. His allegiance throughout this period was to the Independent Labour Party (I.L.P.), the splinter group that thought of itself as the socialist conscience-in-exile of the Labour Party. When he went to Spain at the end of 1936, he traveled with I.L.P. credentials, which accounted for his joining the affiliated P.O.U.M. (Partido Obrero de Unificación Marxista) militia when he arrived rather than the communist-dominated International Brigades.

By 1938, he had officially joined the I.L.P. because, as he explains in the Party's journal, the political situation of the late thirties forced one "to be actively a Socialist, not merely sympathetic to Socialism." He chose the I.L.P. rather than another socialist party because it represented a "body of people who can be depended on, even in the face of persecution, not to compromise their Socialist principles" (*CEJL* 1: 337–38). Although Orwell broke with the Party because of its pacifist stand during World War II, his political sympathies during the rest of his life were always with the left wing of Labour supporters. Immediately after his break with the I.L.P., he began to contribute to the left-wing Labour weekly, *Tribune*, and eventually became its literary editor.

Before committing himself to socialism, however, there was another barrier Orwell had to surmount—his attitude toward the working class. He makes clear in *The Road to Wigan Pier* that his middle-class indoctrination had taught him to think of the working class with mingled fear and revulsion. This was the unacknowledged impediment that prevented the romantic revolutionism of his youth from becoming a genuine socialism. He describes himself as being, at the age of seventeen or eighteen, "both a snob and a revolutionary," a "Socialist" who agonized

9. John Middleton Murry, "The Adelphi Centre," *Adelphi* 11 (1936): 199.

over the sufferings of the working class yet "hated them and despised them when I came anywhere near them" (*RWP*, pp. 141–42). When Orwell returned from Burma, he embarked on a systematic attempt to purge himself of these unwilled but potent reactions. Yet his plans for self-cure were still essentially romantic, as *Down and Out in Paris and London* makes clear. He sought out the extremes of poverty and destitution—the dishwashers, the beggars, the tramps; but in temporarily joining the world of the outcast he was still ignoring the working class, of which such people were not at all typical. His determination to touch bottom on the social ladder allowed him to skip several important rungs in his descent. As one Marxist critic has pointed out, this romantic search for absolute destitution is a characteristically liberal rather than socialist attitude: "The miscellaneous tramp group strike a very resonant chord in the liberal mind, for they more than anyone else correspond with classical liberal free men." With the class-conscious proletariat, on the other hand, Orwell seemed "to have had virtually no contact"; nor did he sympathize with them "except in so far as he could envisage them in their liberal character of poor men who deserved a better chance." [10]

To some extent, these charges are legitimate socialist objections to Orwell's politics throughout his career; yet they seem distinctly more applicable to the period before 1936. His months with the Wigan miners were Orwell's first extended contact with the working class, and a good deal of *The Road to Wigan Pier* attempts to record exactly how that class works and lives. The choice of Wigan was deliberate, he explains, because he wanted to see "the most typical section of the English working class at close quarters"; and he understands that the exposure was personally indispensable in making him a socialist (*RWP*, p. 123). Such attempts to overcome crucial impediments by first recognizing their exact nature and then deliberately trying to surmount them are characteristic of Orwell throughout his life.

Living with the Wigan miners, far more than his excursions into the world of the down and out, finally released him from the

10. Peter Thirlby, "Orwell as a Liberal," *Marxist Quarterly* 3 (1956): 241–42.

childhood fear of the working class and removed one of the last barriers to his socialism. He wrote to Cyril Connolly from Wigan, with naïve surprise, that the miners "are very nice people, very warm-hearted & willing to take me for granted" (*CEJL* 1: 163). The reaction recalls his description of the "baptism" of being welcomed by the tramps on his first excursion to a doss-house many years before: "my fears vanished. Nobody questioned me, nobody showed offensive curiosity; everybody was polite and gentle and took me utterly for granted" (*RWP*, p. 153). Both these passages suggest that the greatest impediment to Orwell's socialist commitment was his middle-class fear that the "lower orders" could not be trusted to respond simply as human beings, that they were mysteriously alien creatures.

When Orwell finally overcame this prejudice, he could at last declare himself a socialist. *The Road to Wigan Pier* and all his subsequent works make it clear that his new attitude toward the working class largely determined the particular form his socialism took. The phrase "solidarity with the working class" suggests some of the worst left-wing cant of the thirties, but for Orwell the idea had a precise meaning. Unlike many theoretical socialists, he did not try to transform the working class by making it more radical and self-conscious. He consistently supported its point of view even when he was disappointed by its lack of militancy or political awareness. This meant that Orwell deliberately inhibited some of his criticisms of the working class. Several significant critical passages in the diary he kept during his months in Wigan did not find their way into the final draft of the book. For example, he complains of working-class apathy at a protest meeting: "I suppose these people represented a fair cross-section of the more revolutionary element in Wigan. If so, God help us. Exactly the same sheeplike crowd—gaping girls and shapeless middle-aged women dozing over their knitting—that you see everywhere else" (*CEJL* 1: 181). This passage does not appear in the completed *Road to Wigan Pier*. Yet the book is full of quite savage attacks on the pretensions of middle-class socialists—Orwell's own world, which he felt he had a right to criticize.

In questioning the attitudes of the reformers among the middle class, Orwell is putting his own previous meliorism under critical scrutiny. Although *The Road to Wigan Pier* struck many of its first readers as insufficiently revolutionary, it was certainly much closer to preaching radical solutions than anything Orwell had written previously. His attacks on "bishops, politicians, philanthropists and what not" who "enjoy talking piously about 'slum clearance' " could apply almost as well to himself at an earlier stage. As with other moves to the Left in the period, Orwell's impatience with such traditional liberal methods grows out of an awareness that they have not worked: "all this talk has led to surprisingly small results. So far as one can discover, the congestion [in the slums] is no better, perhaps slightly worse, than it was a dozen years ago" (*RWP*, p. 66).

Yet though Orwell was ready to call himself a socialist in 1936, he was still confused about two important questions. One was tactical: exactly how was socialism to be brought into being? The other concerned the relationship between socialism and industrialism. Orwell's impatience with the theory of evolutionary change did not immediately turn him into a supporter of revolution. He insists that insurrection "in a strongly governed country like England, could only lead to futile massacres and a régime of savage repression" (*RWP*, p. 91). This distrust of revolution really leaves him without a theory of tactics. He is impatient with the slow and unreliable process of reform and yet afraid of revolution. The passages in *The Road to Wigan Pier* that deal with *how* society is to be transformed are marked by extreme vagueness: "It seemed to me then—it sometimes seems to me now, for that matter—that economic injustice will stop the moment we want it to stop, and no sooner, and if we genuinely want it to stop the method adopted hardly matters" (*RWP*, pp. 150–51). Despite the obtuseness of much of Victor Gollancz's foreword to the original edition of *The Road to Wigan Pier*, he was clearly right in insisting that Orwell had paid no attention to "*the means* of transition to a Socialist society." [11] We will see that Orwell never really solved this problem, although he thought about it constantly in later years. At this point, his refusal to think about the tactics of establishing socialism suggests a kind of complacency

11. Left Book Club Edition (London, 1937), p. xxiii.

and intellectual laziness. Later on, as he gives the question more serious thought, his confusion becomes more poignant. He might have said, with Sidney Webb, "All I know is that I don't know how to do it."

Orwell's doubts about the socialism he professed went beyond the question of tactics. *The Road to Wigan Pier* also demonstrates his reluctance to accept the apparently inevitable link between socialism and industrialism, a link reinforced by the Soviet Union's program of rapid industrialization. Although Orwell accepted the inevitability of the vast expansion of industry, he could not pretend to welcome it: "The sensitive person's hostility to the machine is in one sense unrealistic, because of the obvious fact that the machine has come to stay. But as an attitude of mind there is a great deal to be said for it. The machine has got to be accepted, but it is probably better to accept it rather as one accepts a drug—that is, grudgingly and suspiciously. Like a drug, the machine is useful, dangerous and habit-forming" (*RWP*, p. 202).

What offends Orwell is the assumption that industrialism has anything at all to do with the egalitarian *ideals* of socialism, which could presumably be put into practice equally well in either an agricultural or an industrial economy. He is repelled by the nexus of thought "Socialism——progress——machinery——Russia——tractor——hygiene——machinery——progress" (*RWP*, p. 207) and insists that the association is merely fortuitous. His greatest fear is that the collectivism to which the advance of machine-technique will inevitably lead "need not necessarily be equalitarian." And he goes on to imagine, in a vision that anticipates *Nineteen Eighty-Four*, "a world-society, economically collectivist—that is, with the profit principle eliminated—but with all political, educational and military power in the hands of a small caste of rulers and their bravos" (*RWP*, p. 214).

Orwell could not fully accept socialism as a faith until he had managed to separate it entirely from industrialism. In an advanced country like England, and particularly in a mining town like Wigan, this was impossible. Only when he went to Spain at the end of 1936 did he find proof that the ideals of socialism could be realized in a setting that had nothing to do with industrial organization. As he says in *Homage to Catalonia* of the front where he fought, "there was no one there except the peasants and ourselves, and no one owned anyone else as his master" (*HC*, p. 111). Despite the futility of the fighting in which he was involved, Orwell confesses that his months at the front "formed a kind of interregnum in my life, quite different from anything that had gone before and perhaps from anything that is to come, and they taught me things that I could not have learned in any other way" (*HC*, p. 110). His passionate belief in socialism after his Spanish experience is entirely different in tone from the grudging socialist allegiance that the events of the previous years had finally wrung out of him: he had seen the future and it worked.

/ Perhaps Orwell's most powerful doubt about socialism was the product of his natural pessimism: he had never been convinced that human beings could really live in a state of equality.)Class distinctions and class identity had so pervaded all of his previous experiences, whether at school, in Burma, or in England upon his return, that it was difficult for him to believe in the possibility of their annihilation. Orwell's training had made him intensely aware of the universal nature of power and privilege, exploitation and snobbishness. Could such a way of life really be swept away; and if so, at what cost?

The Road to Wigan Pier still shows Orwell very much concerned about these questions and far from confident that they can be answered reassuringly. On the one hand, he insists that he wanted "to escape not merely from imperialism but from every form of man's dominion over man" (*RWP*, p. 150). On the other hand, he worries that "to abolish class-distinctions means abolishing a part of yourself. . . . For to get outside the class-racket I have got to suppress not merely my private snobbishness, but most of my other tastes and prejudices as well. I have got to alter myself so completely that at the end I should hardly be recognisable as the same person" (*RWP*, p. 162). This fear for the survival of one's identity, though it was seldom confessed so honestly, made many a middle-class socialist fundamentally uncertain in his commitment. Orwell's class fear still inhibited his socialism, and so he hesitantly concludes in *The Road to Wigan Pier* that "the only sensible procedure is to go slow and not force the pace" (*RWP*, p. 169).

Spain changed his mind. Here was a postrevolutionary society, one in which the pace *had* been forced, in which "land had been seized by the peasants, industries collectivised, big capitalists killed or driven out, the Church practically abolished" (*CEJL* 1: 287). Yet all of this had occurred without the destruction of anything Orwell thought worth preserving. On the contrary, Barcelona, and the Aragon front where he was stationed, gave him the sense of achieved human brotherhood. His descriptions of this moment in Spain's history are lyrical in their intensity and involvement:

> Up here in Aragon one was among tens of thousands of people, mainly though not entirely of working-class origin, all living at the same level and mingling on terms of equality. . . . Many of the normal motives of civilized life—snobbishness, money-grubbing, fear of the boss, etc.—had simply ceased to exist. The ordinary class-division of society had disappeared to an extent that is almost unthinkable in the money-tainted air of England. . . . One had been in a community where hope was more normal than apathy or cynicism, where the word 'comrade' stood for comradeship and not, as in most countries, for humbug. One had breathed the air of equality. [*HC*, p. III]

Furthermore, Spain proved to him that a classless society could work, despite the gloomy predictions of those who insisted that without a privileged class all societies break down. Barcelona was a large, complex modern city which, despite its abolition of class privilege, was obviously still functioning. But the real test was the militia, the volunteer fighting force that had abolished all forms of inequality between officers and men. Could such an army—in which "everyone from general to private drew the same pay, ate the same food, wore the same clothes, and mingled on terms of complete equality" (*HC*, p. 26)—work? To Orwell's amazement, he found that it could. Although he acknowledged that the P.O.U.M. militia, which he had joined and in which he eventually became an acting lieutenant, had some problems, he was certain that its policy of equality had proven to be a powerful cohesive force.[12]

Such experiences were presumably what Orwell had in mind when he wrote to Connolly, "I have seen wonderful things & at last really believe in Socialism." Before Spain, the ideal of a classless society, of an end to the whole pattern of servility and mastery, had been *only* an ideal for him, connected with no concrete reality and perhaps no more than a hopeless vision. His new conviction that such a world could actually be brought into being reinforced his dedication to socialism decisively, since he could finally feel that he was fighting for a distinct human possibility. Furthermore, he had lived in this society of the future for half a year without a single regret for his lost middle-class identity, about which he had still been concerned in *The Road to Wigan Pier*.

It should be clear that the confirmation of Orwell's socialist commitment is at every stage a conquest of one of his fears—his fear of poverty, of the "alien" working class, and finally of the loss of his middle-class tastes and values. In each case, the concern had proven to be artificial and insignificant, a barrier erected by his own class training that could be removed without regret. This conquest of his own misgivings finally reinforced the hesitant hope with which he ends *The Road to Wigan Pier*—the hope that the middle class "may sink without further struggles into the working class"—and convinced Orwell that "when we get there it will not be so dreadful as we feared" (*RWP*, p. 230).

Orwell's experience in Spain made his socialism a living faith; paradoxically, however, it also planted the seeds of his strongest doubts. For though he had seen a classless society established, he had also watched it die. To return to Barcelona after several months at the front early in 1937 was to be aware of how quickly

12. Later historians of the Spanish Civil War do not share Orwell's faith in the militia. Burnett Bolloten, for example, concludes that the defects of the militia system "were indubitably among the principal reasons for General Franco's swift advance up the Tagus valley towards the Spanish capital" (*The Grand Camouflage* [London, 1961], p. 208). Orwell's attraction to the militia as a realization of his ideal of community clearly blinded him to its defects as a combat force in modern warfare.

the city had reverted to its prerevolutionary class distinctions. The streets were once again full of "fat prosperous men, elegant women, and sleek cars. . . . The normal division of society into rich and poor, upper class and lower class, was reasserting itself" (*HC*, pp. 117–18). Although there were desperate shortages of food and tobacco, anything could be purchased for money. The smart restaurants had reopened; the trains again had first-class coaches and dining cars. In the armed forces, a similar pattern was evident. The hierarchically organized Popular Army was being built up by official propaganda at the expense of the democratically run militias. Everywhere a classless society seemed to be reverting to its bourgeois origins.

Even more disturbing was the conflict among the parties supporting the Government. The unity that had characterized the early days of the war was breaking down; fierce internal struggles for power and sway were destroying the vital accord of the Left. Orwell became directly involved in this civil war *within* the civil war when the party to whose militia he had been assigned—the P.O.U.M.—was officially suppressed by the Government. Earlier he had been a witness and participant in the Barcelona street fighting, in which anarchists and communists, workers and civil guards were shooting at each other behind hastily erected barricades while the "real" war went on in the rest of the country. The uneasy alliance of the Popular Front was visibly breaking down into its hostile component parts at the same time as an ostensibly socialist commonwealth was reestablishing the old class demarcations.

It would be difficult to exaggerate the despair with which Orwell watched all this happen. He says of the Barcelona fighting, for example, that "it was one of the most unbearable periods of my whole life. I think few experiences could be more sickening, more disillusioning or, finally, more nerve-racking than those evil days of street warfare" (*HC*, p. 139). Orwell began to fear that fascism would triumph because the Left could not unite to fight it. Far from using the external danger to cement their own unity, the socialist parties seemed to be diverting most of their energies to the wars within their own camp. Accusations and counteraccusations, lies and rumors, power plays and open fighting—these had established a pattern for conflict among socialist factions. But if such groups could not even unite among themselves when their cause and their lives were clearly in danger, what hope did they have of ever creating an undivided society?

To put the question in this way is to cast it in terms that are more general and more tragic than Orwell would have used at the time. The odd thing about *Homage to Catalonia* is that it ends optimistically, despite everything Orwell saw that could so easily have pushed him the other way. He was perfectly aware of the apparent failure of logic here, and yet he says: "When you have had a glimpse of such a disaster as this—and however it ends the Spanish war will turn out to have been an appalling disaster, quite apart from the slaughter and physical suffering—the result is not necessarily disillusionment and cynicism. Curiously enough the whole experience has left me with not less but more belief in the decency of human beings" (*HC*, p. 247).

Does this conclusion merely represent a failure of nerve, and has Orwell's "power of facing unpleasant facts" deserted him? A more plausible explanation, I think, is to be found in the way his mind worked. He was, first of all, a close observer of facts and only much later an interpreter of them. His fundamental distrust of ideology did not give him a reliable basis for understanding new phenomena. He knew *what* had happened in Spain, but he did not know *why*. Orwell saw this need for time and distance from events as a characteristic of his nature. When the P.O.U.M. was suppressed, he says, "I did not make any of the correct political reflections. I never do when things are happening. . . . Afterwards I can see the significance of events, but while they are happening I merely want to be out of them" (*HC*, p. 228).

This unwillingness—or inability—to supply instant interpretations of experiences as they occur is related to a kind of brooding quality in Orwell's mind that keeps making him go back to certain incidents again and again in a struggle to find their deeper meaning. Some of the titles of his essays suggest this habit of mind: "Looking Back on the Spanish War," "Second Thoughts on James Burnham." It is also related to the nostalgic passages in books like *Coming Up for Air* and *Nineteen Eighty-Four*, and to the vivid re-creation of distant memories in "Such, Such Were the Joys."

Orwell's attempt to understand the significance of the abortive revolution he saw in Spain involved the same kind of brooding reflection over a long period of time. His first attempts to explain what had happened, in *Homage to Catalonia* and in several pieces of journalism written at about the same time, temporarily resolved the question by exposing the villain—the Communist Party. In a book review published shortly after his return from Spain, he says that "Communism is now a counter-revolutionary force; that Communists everywhere are in alliance with bourgeois reformism and using the whole of their powerful machinery to crush or discredit any party that shows signs of revolutionary tendencies" (*CEJL* 1: 270). And in *Homage to Catalonia* he insists that the Communists were working "not to postpone the Spanish revolution till a more suitable time, but to make sure that it never happened" (*HC*, p. 70).

Although he never abandoned his conviction that the Communist Party had suppressed the socialist revolution in Spain, in the subsequent decade Orwell came to see that this explanation merely begged the crucial questions. Why would a party officially dedicated to socialist ideals be willing to work against the classless society just when it showed signs of materializing? How had the old privileges managed to reassert themselves, and why had the working class permitted it to happen? Is there perhaps something in the nature of revolutions that dooms them to failure? Such questions go deeper into human nature and society than any mere assignment of blame. Orwell's attempt to answer them in the years following the publication of *Homage to Catalonia* would involve him in the most fundamental doubts and threaten his newly won faith in the socialist cause. The optimistic conclusion of his book about Spain was to be tested by continual exposure to events and ideas that seemed to demand a very different response, and that provided his natural pessimism with abundant fuel.

4

Socialism vs. Pessimism

In *Homage to Catalonia*, Orwell treats the Spanish war as a unique event. He writes as a participant and journalist rather than as a historian or detached observer. Time brought perspective but no consolation: the betrayal of the revolution Orwell had witnessed in Spain was to obsess him for the rest of his life. As he continued to brood about it, the unique event began to seem more and more typical, the doubts and fears it raised, to be confirmed and extended by everything he saw happening in the world. The Spanish war was the pebble thrown into the pond; its ripples would fan out until every placid corner of Orwell's mind had felt the disturbance. Finally, it would threaten the very basis of his faith, not only in socialism, but in human decency.

As Europe moved inexorably toward war, traditional ideas were shaken, political faiths abandoned, policies discredited and reversed almost from day to day. The ideological and tactical confusion of the Left in this period could hardly be exaggerated. Disillusioned communists abandoned the Party as impatient social reformers turned toward revolution; pacifists demanded rearmament or preventive war; a former Labour minister became the leader of the British fascist movement; a whole generation of "international" socialists discovered they were willing to die for their country. Such extraordinary shifts of allegiance now seem like the last desperate gestures of people who for the moment could see only the bankruptcy of the faction or policy they had been supporting. Auden's "September 1, 1939" captures the mood:

> I sit in one of the dives
> On Fifty-second Street
> Uncertain and afraid
> As the clever hopes expire
> Of a low dishonest decade.

Orwell's new socialist faith was equally threatened by the events of the late 1930s. Too many of the received ideas of the Left did not seem to be confirmed by what was actually happening. In 1940, Orwell was to describe the previous decade as "an age in which every *positive* attitude has turned out a failure. Creeds, parties, programmes of every description have simply flopped, one after another" (*CEJL* 1: 533). The Left had declared its belief in an absolute opposition between socialism and fascism. To such people, the Hitler-Stalin pact must have been not merely a nightmare but absolutely incomprehensible. To understand it involved abandoning some of their fundamental political assumptions. In the eyes of most Western socialists of the thirties, Hitler was a tool of German capitalism and Nazism was not a revolutionary movement. Orwell saw the desperation with which socialists ignored the more and more apparent similarities between the Soviet and Nazi regimes. "National Socialism," he insists, "*is* a form of Socialism, *is* emphatically revolutionary, *does* crush the property owner just as surely as it crushes the worker" (*CEJL* 2: 25).

What had happened in Spain was merely the prelude to the worldwide triumph of tyranny. This idea, which took possession of Orwell as World War II broke out, brought him close to despair, a despair he records in his important essay, "Inside the Whale":

> What is quite obviously happening, war or no war, is the break-up of *laissez-faire* capitalism and of the liberal-Christian culture. Until recently the full implications of this were not foreseen, because it was generally imagined that Socialism could preserve and even enlarge the atmosphere of liberalism. It is now beginning to be realised how false this idea was. Almost certainly we are moving into an age of totalitarian dictatorships—an age in which freedom of thought will be at first a deadly sin and later on a meaningless abstraction. The autonomous individual is going to be stamped out of existence. [*CEJL* 1: 525]

Far from standing against this trend, socialism—or rather one form of socialism—seemed to be one of its chief moving forces. Somehow the fundamental socialist ideals had been perverted in the process of institutionalizing collectivist economic theory. Behind this betrayal lay the false but widely accepted assumption that "if you make the necessary technical advance the moral advance will follow of itself," as Orwell put it in a letter to a friend. But Hitler had shown the absurdity of the belief that "Socialism *in itself* need work any real improvement" in the fundamental quality of human life (*CEJL* 1: 532).

The war also brought into question the Marxist belief that nationalism was a dying movement and that "the proletariat has no country." During the thirties, many of Orwell's attacks had been directed against the parochialism and complacency of the loyal British subject. His own outlook was, at least in theory, strongly internationalist. The war made him discover the depth and intensity of his own patriotism, an untapped and quite unsuspected reserve of feeling that suddenly asserted itself when he understood England's danger. It is clear from what Orwell wrote in the early years of the war that his loyalties were profoundly dislocated. Less than a year before, he had been saying that England would certainly go fascist in the event of a European war and that he did not believe such a war "can do the slightest good or even that it makes much difference who wins." [1] Such cynicism evaporated completely in the event. By 1940 Orwell was writing with self-lacerating irony, "It is all very well to be 'advanced' and 'enlightened', to snigger at Colonel Blimp and proclaim your emancipation from all traditional loyalties, but a time comes when the sand of the desert is sodden red and what have I done for thee, England, my England?" (*CEJL* 1: 535).

Such feelings were neither perverse nor uncommon, although they did conflict with the ideals of international socialism. The ideologue, when confronted with such conflicts, must see his experience as in some way already accounted for by the ideology he accepts. Orwell's distrust of theory made him respond quite differently. If socialism said that fascism and communism had nothing in common, that an economic advance was inevitably a

1. Letter to Lady Rees, 23 February 1939, "Some Letters of George Orwell," *Encounter* 18 (1962): 61. See also the letter to Herbert Read, 4 January 1939 (*CEJL* 1: 377–78).

moral advance, that the working class had no country, then something was wrong with the theory, which would have to be altered. Orwell's socialist assumptions were constantly under scrutiny. He was a revisionist as a matter of course and would have scorned any ideology that uses the word *revisionism* as a term of contempt.

Orwell's socialism was shaped, not only by world events and by his own experience, but also by a wave of important analyses of the Soviet and Nazi states that appeared in the West in the late thirties and forties. He lists a group of books written by what he calls "The Pessimists": Voigt's *Unto Caesar*, Russell's *Power*, Hayek's *Road to Serfdom*, Burnham's *Managerial Revolution*, and a number of others. Such studies "deny that a planned society can lead either to happiness or to true progress." Although Orwell's attitude toward these writers is critical, he concludes "that they and other writers of kindred tendency have uttered much useful criticism of the folly and wickedness of the Totalitarian age." [2]

The Voigt and Russell books were published in 1938, and Orwell reviewed the latter in the *Adelphi*. These two early analyses of totalitarianism treated Communist Russia and Nazi Germany as variants of the same state—millennial, revolutionary, collectivist, tyrannical, and hierarchically organized and controlled. Voigt concludes that the secular messianism of both movements is responsible for the abandonment of moral scruple in the states they have created. Soviet "socialism," for example, "is by no means incompatible with inhuman oppression or, for that matter, with extreme economic inequality." The attempt to establish the Kingdom of Heaven on Earth "is always the Procrustean Bed which can be made to fit mankind only by war, terrorism, the prison, the concentration camp, the firing squad, and the hangman's rope." [3] Russell stresses the inevitable abandonment of decency in societies ruled by ideological fanatics: "being fanatics, they will be severe; being severe, they will be opposed; being opposed, they will become more severe. Their power-impulses will wear, even to themselves, the cloak of religious zeal, and will

2. George Orwell, "The Intellectual Revolt (1)," *Manchester Evening News*, 24 January 1946, p. 2.

3. F. A. Voigt, *Unto Caesar* (London, 1938), pp. 4, 251.

therefore be subject to no restraint. Hence the rack and the stake, the Gestapo and the Cheka." [4]

By far the most important and influential exposé of the totalitarian state, however, was Trotsky's *The Revolution Betrayed*, published in England in 1937. It is clear that Orwell read the book with care, since much of Emmanuel Goldstein's "Theory and Practice of Oligarchical Collectivism," in *Nineteen Eighty-Four*, is based on it and even mimics Trotsky's style. Orwell has often been called a Trotskyite, and not only in the days when such an accusation was the standard form of abuse employed by the radical Left. Yet he was very far from being a disciple. He wrote in 1939, for example: "Trotsky, in exile, denounces the Russian dictatorship, but he is probably as much responsible for it as any man now living, and there is no certainty that as a dictator he would be preferable to Stalin, though undoubtedly he has a much more interesting mind" (*CEJL* 1: 381). Nevertheless, Orwell learned a great deal from *The Revolution Betrayed*, in part because it was an analysis of the Soviet state written by someone who knew it from the inside. It was thus far more detailed and factually reliable than the reports by Western observers that Orwell had previously used. Trotsky himself dismisses such books as "dilettante journalism," the products of "an international school which might be described as *Bolshevism for the Cultured Bourgeoisie*, or more concisely, *Socialism for Radical Tourists*." [5]

Even more important, *The Revolution Betrayed* helped Orwell to connect his experience in Spain with what was happening in the Soviet Union and Germany. For although Trotsky does not deal with the Spanish Civil War in this book (it was written in 1936), he discusses the fate of successful revolutions at length, and much of what he says must have reinforced Orwell's impressions of Spain.[6] Trotsky analyzes the revival of bourgeois habits and privileges in postrevolutionary Russia in passages that could well

4. Bertrand Russell, *Power: A New Social Analysis* (London, 1938), pp. 196–97.

5. Leon Trotsky, *The Revolution Betrayed: What Is the Soviet Union and Where Is It Going?* trans. Max Eastman (London, 1937), p. 10.

6. Trotsky's later pamphlet, *The Lesson of Spain: The Last Warning* (London [1938]), would have confirmed Orwell's sense of a betrayed socialist revolution in that country as well as supported his defense of the P.O.U.M.

have reminded Orwell of his return to Barcelona after fighting at the front: "Limousines for the 'activists', fine perfumes for 'our women', margarine for the workers, stores 'de luxe' for the gentry, a look at delicacies through the store windows for the plebs—such socialism cannot but seem to the masses a new re-facing of capitalism, and they are not far wrong."[7] In 1935, the officers' corps of the democratically run Red Army was restored by decree "in all its bourgeois magnificence," a military hierarchy "beginning with lieutenant and ending with marshal."[8] Yet these important changes were taking place without transforming the property relations of Soviet society. The new aristocracy of Party functionaries, Trotsky points out, owns nothing:

> From the point of view of property in the means of production, the differences between a marshal and a servant girl, the head of a trust and a day labourer, the son of a people's commissar and a homeless child, seem not to exist at all. Nevertheless, the former occupy lordly apartments, enjoy several summer homes in various parts of the country, have the best motor cars at their disposal, and have long ago forgotten how to shine their own shoes. The latter live in wooden barracks, often without partitions, lead a half-hungry existence, and do not shine their own shoes only because they go barefoot.[9]

This betrayal of all the revolution had promised, this cynical abandonment of the ideal of equality and a classless society, raised the most profound theoretical problems for the socialist. Was there then no relation between property and privilege? Were all societies doomed to repeat the pattern of exploitation and internal division? In trying to answer such fundamental questions, Orwell and Trotsky eventually parted company, for despite its

7. Trotsky, *The Revolution Betrayed*, p. 117.
8. Ibid., pp. 210–11. Orwell understood the significance of such gestures. He notes in his "War-time Diary," "This morning's *News Chronicle* announces that saluting of superior ranks has been reinstituted in the Red army. A revolutionary army would *start* by abolishing saluting, and this tiny point is symptomatic of the whole situation" (*CEJL* 2: 355).
9. Trotsky, *The Revolution Betrayed*, p. 226.

black picture of Stalinist Russia, *The Revolution Betrayed* is basically an optimistic book. Trotsky explains the appalling events he describes in historical rather than psychological or philosophical terms: the revolution in Russia was inevitably betrayed because it took place in an economically backward country. Since, in addition, the expected international socialist revolution did not materialize, the Soviet regime has had to function as an economy of scarcity, surrounded by a hostile world rather than the sympathetic proletariat of other countries. The injustice, poverty, forced industrialization, and tyranny of Soviet society were thus historically inevitable, Trotsky says: "If the State does not die away, but grows more and more despotic, if the plenipotentiaries of the working class become bureaucratized, and the bureaucracy rises above the new society, this is not for some secondary reasons like the psychological relics of the past, etc., but is a result of the iron necessity to give birth to and support a privileged minority *so long as it is impossible to guarantee genuine equality.*" [10]

Such a theory makes the achievement of the original goals of the revolution only a matter of time. When privilege is no longer a historical necessity, when an economy of abundance has been achieved, a second (and final) socialist revolution will come, as Trotsky predicts: "All indications agree that the further course of development must inevitably lead to a clash between the culturally developed forces of the people and bureaucratic oligarchy. There is no peaceful outcome for this crisis. No devil ever yet voluntarily cut off its own claws. The Soviet bureaucracy will not give up its positions without a fight. The development leads obviously to the road of revolution." And once it is begun, such a revolution "will not this time stop half-way." [11] The idea that the revolution could be permanently prevented from fulfilling its goals would have struck Trotsky as nonsensical.

Much of Trotsky's book expounds a theory of the inevitable *stages* of revolution, a subject that haunted Orwell's imagination and was finally to produce *Animal Farm*. Trotsky constantly compares the Russian and French revolutions, and finds many

10. Ibid., p. 59. Italics added.
11. Ibid., pp. 271, 219.

similarities in their development. Nor is he averse to generalization: "It is sufficiently well known that every revolution up to this time has been followed by a reaction, or even a counter-revolution. This, to be sure, has never thrown the nation all the way back to its starting-point, but it has always taken from the people the lion's share of their conquests. The victims of the first reactionary wave have been, as a general rule, those pioneers, initiators, and instigators who stood at the head of the masses in the period of the revolutionary offensive." [12] A pessimistic observer might modify Marx's theory that revolutions are the engines of history by commenting that some of the trains seemed to shuttle back and forth between two fixed points. But Trotsky insists that even in the inevitable counter-revolution, the nation is never brought *all* the way back to its starting point.

In Orwell's speculations about revolution as a method for achieving socialist goals, this was one of the major points at issue. He became far less confident than Trotsky that real progress was achieved through revolution, and his own view at times approaches Lord Acton's gloomy conviction that every revolution "makes a wise and just reform impossible." [13] As early as 1938, the central idea of *Animal Farm* was running through Orwell's mind: "It would seem that what you get over and over again is a movement of the proletariat which is promptly canalised and betrayed by astute people at the top, and then the growth of a new governing class. The one thing that never arrives is equality. The mass of the people never get the chance to bring their innate decency into the control of affairs, so that one is almost driven to the cynical thought that men are only decent when they are powerless" (*CEJL* 1: 336). Clearly Orwell still hesitates to accept this idea: he says he is "almost driven" to it. It remained an unresolved issue in his mind for years, and one can see why. His socialist faith made him need to deny it; his temperamental pessimism must have found it congenial. He could neither resolve the question nor forget it—perhaps the ideal condition for the creation of a vital literary work.

12. Ibid., pp. 88–89.
13. Quoted in Orwell's "In Pursuit of Lord Acton," *Tribune*, 29 March 1946, p. 19.

Orwell's uncertainty about revolution eventually produced *Animal Farm* and was responsible for the considerable ambiguity of the book. An ironic allegory is bound to mystify many of its readers, no matter how easy it is to identify the historical parallels on which it is based. We know that Orwell had a great deal of difficulty getting *Animal Farm* into print, and it is generally assumed that publishers rejected it because they did not want to publish an anti-Soviet satire in the middle of the war. Yet T. S. Eliot's letter of rejection from Faber makes it clear this was not the only problem the book raised. Eliot complains that "the effect is simply one of negation. It ought to excite some sympathy with what the author wants, as well as sympathy with his objections to something: and the positive point of view, which I take to be generally Trotskyite, is not convincing." [14] He goes on to suggest that Orwell "splits his vote" by refusing to confirm any of the standard Western attitudes toward the Soviet Union.

Eliot's argument suggests a thoroughly confused sense of Orwell's purpose. If *Animal Farm* can be said to have a "positive point of view" at all, it is certainly not Trotskyite: Snowball is hardly its tragic hero. The difficulties of understanding *Animal Farm* largely stem from its interpretation as an exclusive attack on the Soviet Union. Orwell's purpose, however, is more general: he is interested in tracing the inevitable stages of any revolution, and he shapes his fable accordingly. This is not to deny that the literal level of the story is almost exclusively based on Soviet history. But although Russia is his immediate target, Orwell says the book "is intended as a satire on dictatorship in general." [15] He was faithful to the details of Soviet history, yet he did not hesitate to transform some of its most important elements.

The most striking of these is the omission of Lenin from the drama. Major (the idealist visionary who dies before the revolution takes place) is clearly meant to represent Marx, while Napoleon and Snowball act out the conflict in the postrevolutionary state between Stalin and Trotsky. Lenin is left out, it

14. Quoted in Anthony Lewis, "T. S. Eliot and 'Animal Farm,' " *New York Times Book Review*, 26 January 1969, p. 16.

15. MS letter to Leonard Moore, 17 December 1947, Berg Collection, New York Public Library.

seems to me, because Orwell wants to emphasize the enormous disparity between the ideals of the revolution and the reality of the society it actually achieves. Lenin was the missing link in this process, both visionary and architect of the new state, but from Orwell's longer historical perspective, his brief period of power must have seemed like an irrelevant interlude in the stark drama that was unfolding. The heirs of Lenin had in fact begun to transform him into a myth even before he was dead; they legitimized their power by worshipping at his shrine. In order to demythify the Russian Revolution and present the Bolshevik leaders as they really were, Orwell must have felt compelled to eliminate the mythical hero altogether.

Such radical departures from history are of course Orwell's prerogative in constructing a story intended to have more general significance. He says in a preface to *Animal Farm* that "although the various episodes are taken from the actual history of the Russian Revolution, they are dealt with schematically and their chronological order is changed; this was necessary for the symmetry of the story" (*CEJL* 3: 406). One might add that it was also necessary in order to achieve Orwell's purpose in writing it. This raises the question of how the topical and generic levels of satire in the book are related, and one might clarify the issue by citing the case of Swift, who was in some sense Orwell's model.

When *Gulliver's Travels* was first published, many read the book as an essentially partisan political document, a propaganda piece for the opposition party.[16] Yet Swift himself wrote to his French translator that, if *Gulliver's Travels* could only be understood in England, it was a failure, for "the same vices and the same follies reign everywhere . . . and the author who writes only for a city, a province, a kingdom, or even an age, deserves so little to be translated, that he does not even deserve to be read." [17] In the same way, *Animal Farm* is concerned both with the Russian Revolution and, by extension, with the general pattern of

16. See Bertrand A. Goldgar, "*Gulliver's Travels* and the Opposition to Walpole," in *The Augustan Milieu: Essays Presented to Louis A. Landa*, ed. Henry Knight Miller, Eric Rothstein, and G. S. Rousseau (Oxford, 1970), pp. 155–73.

17. *The Correspondence of Jonathan Swift*, ed. Harold Williams (Oxford, 1963), 3: 226.

revolution itself. As the Stalinist period recedes into the distant past, Orwell's book (if it survives as a literary work) will more and more be appreciated as generic rather than topical satire, just as *Gulliver's Travels* has come to be.

Orwell chose to write his book in the form of a fable partly to give the pattern of historical events permanent mythic life, to emphasize that he was dealing with typical, not fortuitous, events. He is interested in constructing a paradigmatic social revolution, and the pattern that emerges is meant to apply to the Spanish Civil War and to the French Revolution (the main character, after all, is named Napoleon) as well as to the Russian one. Orwell's story suggests that revolutions inevitably go through several predictable stages. They begin with great idealistic fervor and popular support, energized by millennial expectations of justice and equality. The period immediately following a successful revolution is the Eden stage. There is a sense of triumphant achievement; idealistic vision is translated into immediate reality; the spirit of community and equality are everywhere apparent. Old law and institutions are broken and replaced by an inner, yet reliable, concern for the common good. The state has, for the moment, withered away.

Slowly the feeling of freedom gives way to the sense of necessity and bondage, "we" becomes "I-they," spirit turns into law, improvised organization is replaced by rigid institutions, equality modulates to privilege. The next stage is the creation of a new elite which, because of its superior skill and its lust for power, assumes command and re-creates the class structure. Its power is first universally granted but gradually must be upheld against opposition by terror and threat. As time goes on, the past is forgotten or expunged; the new elite takes on all the characteristics of the old, prerevolutionary leadership, while the rest of the society returns to the condition of servitude. The transition is too gradual to be dramatic, although it has its dramatic moments, and it is constantly presented in the guise of historical inevitability or as a necessary response to conspiracy or external danger. A scapegoat is found to explain the disparity between ideal and actual. The exploited class remains exploited basically because of its doggedness and stupidity but also because, having no taste for power, it is inevitably victimized by the power-hungry. In every new society—even if it consists exclusively of those without previous experience of power—some will rise above their fellows and assume the available positions of authority. When their power and privileges are consolidated, they will fight to keep them. The only surviving vestiges of revolution will be its rhetoric and its (conveniently altered) history. The reality of "equality" and "justice" will have withered away, to be replaced by the state.

"The effect," Eliot had said, "is simply one of negation." His objection raises the question of whether *Animal Farm* should be considered in moral terms at all. At this point in his career Orwell's mind had begun to work in an increasingly analytic way. He was interested in understanding the structure of revolution rather than in proposing a better way to achieve social goals. Eliot complains that the book fails to "excite some sympathy with what the author wants." Yet great satire has often been written out of the despairing sense that "what the author wants" may be unattainable. Orwell's socialism is not an act of faith. If he has a "positive point of view" at all in writing *Animal Farm*, it is the hope that socialists will be able to face the hard truths he presents rather than continue to accept the various consoling illusions their movement has generated to account for its disappointments.

And yet realism is not his only goal; he is also finally a moralist. In the essay on Dickens, Orwell makes an important distinction between the moralist and the revolutionary, which I take to be crucial for an understanding of his purpose in *Animal Farm.* Dickens, he says, is a moralist: "It is hopeless to try and pin him down to any definite remedy, still more to any political doctrine. . . . Useless to change institutions without a 'change of heart'— that, essentially, is what he is always saying." Orwell realized that the need for a "change of heart" has been used as "*the* alibi of people who do not wish to endanger the *status quo*," but he insists that this does not make Dickens a reactionary apologist. The paradox can only be explained by understanding the writer's relation to the moment in which he writes:

> I said earlier that Dickens is not *in the accepted sense* a revolutionary writer. But it is not at all certain that a merely

moral criticism of society may not be just as "revolutionary"
—and revolution, after all, means turning things upside
down—as the politico-economic criticism which is fashionable at this moment. Blake was not a politician, but there is
more understanding of the nature of capitalist society in a
poem like "I wander through each charter'd street" than in
three-quarters of Socialist literature. Progress is not an
illusion, it happens, but it is slow and invariably disappoint-
ing. There is always a new tyrant waiting to take over from
the old—generally not quite so bad, but still a tyrant.
Consequently two viewpoints are always tenable. The one,
how can you improve human nature until you have changed
the system? The other, what is the use of changing the system
before you have improved human nature? They appeal to
different individuals, and they probably show a tendency to
alternate in point of time. [*CEJL* 1: 427-28]

The passage is remarkable for the sense it gives of Orwell's long
historical perspective and his ability to see a particular artistic
choice (Dickens's and, at this point, his own) as being in perpetual
conflict with its equally legitimate opposite. The attitude could be
described as dialectical, except that Orwell does not stress the
synthesis which grows out of each clash. Rather, he sees the
conflict as eternal: the point of view is far from the ultimate
optimism of Hegel and Marx. At a particular moment in time,
then, the moralist who voices his outrage at what is accepted, even
though he has no idea how things might be changed, is more of a
revolutionary than the "revolutionary" writer who endorses the
most advanced form of social engineering. Most revolutionaries,
as Orwell also points out in the Dickens essay, "are potential
Tories, because they imagine that everything can be put right by
altering the *shape* of society; once that change is effected, as it
sometimes is, they see no need for any other" [*CEJL* 1: 458].

It is at this moment—when a given revolution has more to
preserve than to transform—that it is ripe for the moralist's
exposé. Orwell felt that Soviet society had reached this stage,
although most of the socialist camp still saw in it only its earlier,
triumphant achievement. In performing this task, he hoped he

might also make his audience aware that the illusion they cherished was only a particular example of a temptation they would meet again—the habit of substituting wish for reality. It is, finally, impossible to talk about the political or moral purpose of *Animal Farm* without considering its tone. If the book is an exposé, it is certainly a remarkably unindignant one. Critics have praised its detachment, economy, and tight formal control; yet in a work with a serious political purpose, these qualities may not be as desirable as they are in purely aesthetic terms. There is truth in Mark Schorer's objection that *Animal Farm* "undid its potential gravity and the very real gravity of its subject, through its comic devices." [18] From the first page, Orwell's fable is marked by a sense of acceptance and composure. The satire is benevolent, the ridicule affectionate, the ingenuity and sophistication very far from impassioned preaching. It is as though the story of *The Revolution Betrayed* were retold a century later by a specialist in the ironies of history. Far more than *Nineteen Eighty-Four*, *Animal Farm* is written for posterity. The surprising thing is that it should have been the earlier book.

To describe the tone of *Animal Farm* in a few phrases is to suggest that it is consistent. Yet there are important moments in the book when Orwell's comic perspective is quite clearly abandoned. For example: "Napoleon stood sternly surveying his audience; then he uttered a high-pitched whimper. Immediately the dogs bounded forward, seized four of the pigs by the ear and dragged them, squealing with pain and terror, to Napoleon's feet. The pigs' ears were bleeding, the dogs had tasted blood, and for a few moments they appeared to go quite mad" (*AF*, p. 65). The passage stands at the beginning of the scene meant to parallel the Stalinist purge trials, and it is typical of the tone of gravity Orwell employs to describe the reign of terror that now begins at Animal Farm. The purge trials are the first events in Soviet history that Orwell considers tragically. Although terror was not, of course, invented by Stalin, there is something about the Moscow Trials which Orwell cannot treat as a predictable part of his paradig-

18. "An Indignant and Prophetic Novel," *New York Times Book Review*, 12 June 1949, p. 1.

matic revolution, something new in human history. It is, perhaps, the triumph of the big lie in Napoleon's justification for this slaughter of the innocents, the false confessions and abandonment of objective truth it involves. Here was something Orwell could not treat with composure and ironic detachment.

Orwell's tone in both *Animal Farm* and *Nineteen Eighty-Four* is determined by his sense of the uniqueness or typicality of the events he records. As long as he describes what he considers an inevitable stage of revolution, he can allow himself the long, detached historical perspective and the ironic tone that is its aesthetic correlative. When, on the other hand, he senses that some new, unexpected, and therefore perhaps avoidable form of tyranny has appeared, his response is very different: he permits himself the indignation of first discovery. *Nineteen Eighty-Four*, we will see, is different in tone from *Animal Farm* primarily because it is a reaction to certain terrifying events in modern history that could not have been foreseen in the first years of the century in which they occurred.

In order to understand Orwell's growing pessimism in the 1940s, it is worth recalling the fundamentally optimistic elements that still formed a part of his commitment to socialism at the beginning of the decade. His very guarded faith in the future rested on three assumptions: first, that although every revolution is betrayed and falls far short of its original goals, in the long view "progress is not an illusion"; second, that every oppressive regime is eventually destroyed by the people it oppresses; and third, that human greed and lust for power are probably not permanent impulses of human nature but are historically determined by the condition of scarcity and the competitive ethic it spawns.

The events of the late thirties and forties seemed to provide evidence that not even these vaguely hopeful beliefs could survive objective scrutiny. What observer of the methods of totalitarian rule in Russia and Germany could continue to believe in the slow but inevitable march of progress? As Orwell put it in his essay on H. G. Wells, "Creatures out of the Dark Ages have come marching into the present" (*CEJL* 2: 144). Only those who had lived under a totalitarian regime seemed able to grasp the extraordinary atavism of modern tyranny. The Russian writer

Yevgeny Zamyatin, whose novel of the future, *We*, greatly influenced Orwell in the conception of *Nineteen Eighty-Four*, had taken account of "the diabolism & the tendency to return to an earlier form of civilisation which seem to be part of totalitarianism" (*CEJL* 4: 485–86). Zamyatin's book, Orwell says, gives the regime of the future "the colour of the sinister slave civilisations of the ancient world" and shows an "intuitive grasp of the irrational side of totalitarianism—human sacrifice, cruelty as an end in itself, the worship of a Leader who is credited with divine attributes" (*CEJL* 4: 74–75).

More frightening even than this reversal of progress was the idea that such regimes might prove invulnerable to revolution. Orwell first mentions this possibility in 1939, in a review of a book about the Soviet Union that preached the inevitability of a new Russian revolution. In disputing this theory, Orwell is also calling into question the optimistic conclusion of *The Revolution Betrayed*:

> The terrifying thing about the modern dictatorships is that they are something entirely unprecedented. Their end cannot be foreseen. In the past every tyranny was sooner or later overthrown, or at least resisted, because of "human nature", which as a matter of course desired liberty. But we cannot be at all certain that "human nature" is constant. It may be just as possible to produce a breed of men who do not wish for liberty as to produce a breed of hornless cows. [*CEJL* 1: 380–81]

The growth of a movement resisting an oppressive state depends on certain conditions that a totalitarian regime might well succeed in stamping out. Its control of every aspect of human life narrowed the areas of independence its subjects could enjoy. Modern communication systems vastly increased the possibility of surveillance and thought-control. Previous autocratic societies had been full of interstices the state did not enter, small pockets of privacy in which a man or a small group of men could work out rebellious ideas and plans in some safety. Furthermore, the modern centralized apparatus of dictatorship—its control of the press, of publishing houses, of the schools, and all other organizations—gave it an unprecedented opportunity to indoctrinate its subjects. The fear that under such conditions rebellion is not a serious possibility lies at the heart of *Nineteen Eighty-Four*. Orwell originally thought of calling the book *The Last Man in Europe* (*CEJL* 4: 448), which would have presented Winston Smith's rebellious gesture as civilization's final, doomed attempt to fight against a repressive regime. By the end of the book, even Winston loves Big Brother; he has joined the "breed of men who do not wish for liberty."

It was entirely possible, then, that the totalitarian regimes of the twentieth century would be permanent rather than subject to the historical process. Marx had said that after the socialist revolution, history could begin. It seemed to Orwell more likely that after a revolution leading to the creation of a totalitarian state, history might end. The invention of atomic weapons made this more likely, since they served to make powerful states invulnerable to external attack. Hitler was finally overthrown only by losing a world war. Might the Nazi state still exist if German scientists had perfected the atomic bomb before or at the same time as their enemies? Although the three superstates in *Nineteen Eighty-Four* wage a limited kind of war incessantly, it is "warfare of limited aims between combatants who are unable to destroy one another, have no material cause for fighting and are not divided by any genuine ideological difference" (*NEF*, pp. 190–91). What hope is there for oppressed people in such countries?

Furthermore, one of the most "progressive" aspects of totalitarian regimes made their tyranny potentially more stable than the "reactionary" systems they had replaced—the fact that power and privilege were not hereditary. Hereditary institutions, Orwell suggests, "have the virtue of being unstable. They must be so, because power is constantly devolving on people who are either incapable of holding it, or use it for purposes not intended by their forefathers. It is impossible to imagine any hereditary body lasting so long, and with so little change, as an adoptive organisation like the Catholic Church. And it is at least thinkable that another adoptive and authoritarian organisation, the Russian Communist Party, will have a similar history" (*CEJL* 4: 456).

Such a state is less likely to become decadent than its

predecessors, first because it can secure the most able recruits from
all sectors of society, thus simultaneously making it an aristocracy
of talent and depriving the powerless of potential leaders, and
second because it can eliminate from its ranks all decadent,
untrustworthy, or incompetent members. The Inner Party in
Nineteen Eighty-Four is clearly selected by these principles: "The
child of Inner Party parents is in theory not born into the Inner
Party. Admission to either branch of the Party is by examination,
taken at the age of sixteen. . . . Between the two branches of the
Party there is a certain amount of interchange, but only so much
as will ensure that weaklings are excluded from the Inner Party
and that ambitious members of the Outer Party are made
harmless by allowing them to rise" (*NEF*, pp. 214–15). The
totalitarian state thus shrewdly deprives the potential rebel of two
of his strongest arguments—that the society is closed and that its
leaders are incompetent.

The adoptive rather than hereditary autocracy of totalitarianism created another, even more serious threat to human happiness: it encouraged and rewarded the power-mad. As Bertrand
Russell had argued in *Power*, "Where no social institution, such as
aristocracy or hereditary monarchy, exists to limit the number of
men to whom power is possible, those who most desire power are,
broadly speaking, those most likely to acquire it. It follows that, in
a social system in which power is open to all, the posts which
confer power will, as a rule, be occupied by men who differ from
the average in being exceptionally power-loving." [19] Of course
this might equally be said of a democracy in which elective office
is open to all, but at least in such governments there are some
safeguards against the worst abuses of power, safeguards a
totalitarian state does not have. This fear that the world would be
taken over by the power-mad became the most serious and
persistent obsession of Orwell's last years. As long as the existence
of privilege could be explained along economic lines, as a
necessary condition when there was not enough to go around, the
future offered some hope for a solution. But to Orwell it began to
seem more and more likely that money was merely a distraction

19. Russell, *Power*, p. 12.

on the road to power, and that the desire for power was an appetite which could of necessity never be satisfied universally. The displacement of greed by sadistic power-hunger seemed to Orwell a modern phenomenon that could only flourish once a certain level of universal comfort was attainable. Perhaps it could be understood as a postcapitalist phase: "Just as at the end of the feudal age there appeared a new figure, the man of money, so at the end of the capitalist age there appears another new figure, the man of power, the Nazi gauleiter or Bolshevik commissar. Such men may be individually corrupt, but as a type they are neither mercenary nor hedonistic. They don't want ease and luxury, they merely want the pleasure of tyrannising over other people." [20] If this theory was true, the socialist might well despair of his faith. He was taught to interpret oppression as an economic rather than a psychological fact. Yet at the very moment in human history when economic oppression is no longer a necessity for the survival of the few, equality seems more unattainable than ever. The demand for absolute power over others, Orwell writes in 1946, "has reached new levels of lunacy in our own age." This leads him to a question he could never answer: "What is the special quality in modern life that makes a major human motive out of the impulse to bully others?" (CEJL 4: 249).

The apparently irresistible cult of power brought Orwell to a deeper despair than any of his previous observations. Although he cannot explain its etiology, he records its triumphs in essay after essay written in the 1940s, and finally, of course, in Nineteen Eighty-Four. Orwell was particularly shaken by the realization that the worship of power was not merely limited to those anxious to exercise it. The totalitarian state satisfied many of the led as well as the leaders because the relationship seemed to fulfill a deep psychological need. The "cult of personality" spoke to some primitive instinct both in Germany and in the Soviet Union, despite the rebellious disaffection of the few. The true modern myth, Orwell says in "Raffles and Miss Blandish," "should be renamed Jack the Dwarf-killer" (CEJL 3: 222–23). The two-min-

20. George Orwell, "Will Freedom Die with Capitalism?" Left News (April 1941), p. 1684.

ute hate sessions in *Nineteen Eighty-Four*, the love for and identification with Big Brother, even Winston's fantasies while being
tortured, are all based on this insight. Winston and O'Brien forge
a symbiotic bond. As he awakes after a scene of terrible torture,
Winston is amazed to find that he feels no hatred: "The pain was
already half-forgotten. He opened his eyes and looked up
gratefully at O'Brien. At sight of the heavy, lined face, so ugly
and so intelligent, his heart seemed to turn over. If he could have
moved he would have stretched out a hand and laid it on
O'Brien's arm. He had never loved him so deeply as at this
moment" (*NEF*, p. 258).

What hope was there for the ideals of socialism, "equality" and
"the classless society," when such powerful psychological forces
were released and then systematically exploited? Orwell's growing
despair clearly arose from thwarted optimism. His socialist faith
began with a need to find a system that would provide an end to
"every form of man's dominion over man." But if the victim is
also in some crucial sense an accomplice, the whole theory of the
need to support the oppressed against the oppressor takes on the
character of an elaborate delusion: it is like interfering in a lovers'
quarrel.

Somewhere near the end of the nineteenth century, Beatrice
Webb had written in her diary, *"I have staked all on the essential
goodness of human nature."* Looking back many years later, she
recorded her disillusionment: "I realise how permanent are the
evil impulses and instincts in man—how little you can count on
changing some of these—for instance the greed of wealth and
power—by any change in machinery." [21] Orwell's career moved
toward a similar disenchantment, though he would probably have
rejected such ahistorical generalizations as being too vague and
temperamentally conservative. Yet he too had "staked all on the
essential goodness of human nature" as part of his socialist faith,
and it was precisely this belief which the present age called into
question.

It is easy enough to find historical explanations for Orwell's
growing pessimism, but part of the explanation must also come

21. *Beatrice Webb's Diaries 1924–1932*, ed. Margaret Cole (London, 1956), p. 79.

from his own psychological exigencies. His hatred of hierarchy and domination almost certainly began as a form of self-hatred, clearly rooted in his actions in Burma. But the very intensity of passages like that of Winston's awakening suggests that the whole pattern of sadistic action and masochistic response remained a living reality in Orwell's psyche long after his Burmese days were over. He seemed to understand the minds of the master and of the victim instinctively, and this natural sympathy suggests the strength of the sado-masochistic component in his own makeup. His political program was an attempt to find an ideal that would release him from this sense of himself while simultaneously releasing society from the condition of mastery and servitude. But the persistence of that wish in his fantasy, and its obvious latent power, might well have forced him to think again about whether such impulses were in fact controllable.

In the mid- and late 1940s, Orwell's thought at its most pessimistic finds a parallel in the ideas of James Burnham, the ex-Trotskyist author of *The Managerial Revolution*. Orwell reviewed several of Burnham's books, mentions him in a number of his journalistic pieces, and discusses him at length in a major essay called (in different editions) "Second Thoughts on James Burnham" or "James Burnham and the Managerial Revolution" (1946). Burnham's ideas are essentially variants of Trotsky's in *The Revolution Betrayed*, but the selection from Trotsky's thought and the attempt to bring him up to date are determined by Burnham's own absolute political despair. He was convinced not only that the Russian Revolution had been permanently betrayed but that the pattern of modern dictatorships would be repeated everywhere, whether in nominally capitalist or socialist countries. The managerial society whose universal triumph he predicts is characterized by permanent class stratification, autocratic rule, state ownership of the means of production, and "domination and exploitation by a ruling class of an extremity and absoluteness never before known." [22] The world would be divided into a few superstates, perpetually at war with each other; its ideals would

22. James Burnham, *The Managerial Revolution, or What Is Happening in the World Now* (London, 1942), p. 116.

be collectivist: "In place of the 'individual,' the stress turns to the 'state,' the people, the folk, the race. In place of gold, labour and work. In place of private enterprise, 'socialism' or 'collectivism.' In place of 'freedom' and 'free initiative,' planning. Less talk about 'rights' and 'natural rights'; more about 'duties' and 'order' and 'discipline.' " [23]

Burnham's book is a kind of terminal socialist document; it might be called *The Impossible Revolution*, a natural sequel to *The Revolution Betrayed*. A similar distinction can be made between *Animal Farm* and *Nineteen Eighty-Four*. Yet Orwell's attitude toward Burnham is, as with Trotsky, far from discipleship, although it seems to me that he appropriates much more from him than he is willing to acknowledge. Orwell nevertheless feels a strong need to dissociate himself from Burnham's gloom: he persistently rejects Burnham's conclusions and denies the plausibility of his predictions. These reactions are interesting because they point to a conflict in Orwell himself which I think he never resolved and which is evident in *Nineteen Eighty-Four*. His primary target is the political quietism that Burnham's sense of inevitability encourages. "Where Burnham and his fellow-thinkers are wrong," he writes, "is in trying to spread the idea that totalitarianism is *unavoidable*, and that we must therefore do nothing to oppose it." [24] In the long essay on Burnham, Orwell confidently predicts that the Russian regime will eventually become democratic or destroy itself, and that the slave societies Burnham envisions cannot last (*CEJL* 4: 180).

The strangest aspect of Orwell's relation to Burnham is how many of his criticisms could also be leveled against his own vision in *Nineteen Eighty-Four*. He says, for example, that "in all his talk about the struggle for power, Burnham never stops to ask *why* people want power. He seems to assume that power hunger, although only dominant in comparatively few people, is a natural instinct that does not have to be explained, like the desire for food" (*CEJL* 4: 177). But the question is precisely the same one which stops Winston Smith in *Nineteen Eighty-Four*, and which the

---

23. Ibid., p. 180.
24. George Orwell, "As I Please," *Tribune*, 14 January 1944, p. 11.

book does not really answer: "He understood *how;* he did not understand *why" (NEF,* p. 223). The closest thing to an answer is O'Brien's long speech about power, which is treated as the crucial revelation in the book. Yet nowhere in that speech does O'Brien explain *why* some people want power and, more particularly, why this hunger for power should have asserted itself so triumphantly in the twentieth century.

The subtitle of Isaac Deutscher's important essay on *Nineteen Eighty-Four,* "The Mysticism of Cruelty," underlines this irrational element in Orwell's belief.[25] O'Brien's answer to the question of the Party's motives has all the quality of an incantation and offers as few concessions to the rational mind: "Now I will tell you the answer to my question. It is this. The Party seeks power entirely for its own sake. We are not interested in the good of others; we are interested solely in power. Not wealth or luxury or long life or happiness: only power, pure power. . . . The object of persecution is persecution. The object of torture is torture. The object of power is power" *(NEF,* p. 269). Yet a few years before writing this, Orwell was categorically rejecting Burnham's conclusion that "Society is inevitably ruled by oligarchies who hold their position by means of force and fraud, and whose sole objective is power and still more power for themselves." [26]

One way to explain this disparity is to stress the changes in Orwell's attitudes in the last few years of his life, and particularly in his final illness, during which much of *Nineteen Eighty-Four* was written. There is, indeed, some truth in this explanation, although I think it has been exaggerated. I have tried to show that the conflict between optimism and pessimism is evident throughout Orwell's career, and that his fundamentally pessimistic cast of mind was constantly at war with his socialism. However, he could not easily acknowledge this fact about himself precisely because it conflicted with his basic political commitment and with his whole lifework. As a result, there is a curious lack of conviction in his more positive statements of the final years, as though he knew he was engaged in a hopeless task.

25. Isaac Deutscher, " '1984'—The Mysticism of Cruelty," in his *Heretics and Renegades and Other Essays* (London, 1955), pp. 35–50.
26. George Orwell, "Why Machiavellis of To-Day Fall Down," *Manchester Evening News,* 20 January 1944, p. 2.

The closest Orwell ever comes to acknowledging the effect of this despair on his political convictions is in one of the *Tribune* essays written in 1946: "When one considers how things have gone since 1930 or thereabouts, it is not easy to believe in the survival of civilisation. I do not argue from this that the only thing to do is to abjure practical politics, retire to some remote place and concentrate either on individual salvation or on building up self-supporting communities against the day when the atom bombs have done their work. *I think one must continue the political struggle, just as a doctor must try to save the life of a patient who is probably going to die"* (*CEJL* 4: 248–49; italics added). Political quietism was Orwell's greatest temptation. In "Inside the Whale," he writes of the desire to wash one's hands of politics with sympathy and perception, even though it is a wish against which he continues to fight in his own life and work.

This deeply divided internal state, this irresolvable conflict between political hope and despair, finds expression in *Nineteen Eighty-Four*. The controversy that has surrounded Orwell's book since it was first published centers on the question of his pessimism. So Deutscher writes: "Of course, Orwell intended *1984* as a warning. But the warning defeats itself because of its underlying boundless despair"; while George Woodcock interprets Orwell's book as a "statement of faith in humanity." [27] Such disagreements seem to me to arise from a confusion about Orwell's purpose. He once defined a writer's political aim as his "desire to push the world in a certain direction, to alter other people's idea of the kind of society that they should strive after" (*CEJL* 1: 4). In these terms, *Nineteen Eighty-Four* might be said to have a predominantly negative goal, since it is much more concerned to fight *against* a possible future society than *for* one. Its tactics are primarily defensive. Winston Smith is much less concerned with the future than with the past—which is of course the reader's present. He wants to recapture the modest individual liberty of Orwell's England. By comparison, his millennialism remains very unformed.

27. Deutscher, " '1984'—The Mysticism of Cruelty," p. 49; George Woodcock, *The Crystal Spirit: A Study of George Orwell* (Boston, 1966), p. 220.

The difficulty of interpreting *Nineteen Eighty-Four* grows out of Orwell's simultaneous interest in two quite distinct political questions: How can democratic states prevent the triumph of totalitarian methods in their own societies? How can totalitarianism be destroyed in states where it has established itself? Although Orwell's plot focuses on the latter, he knows he is writing primarily for an audience concerned with the former. Of course the two questions are related: demonstrating that an achieved totalitarian state is invulnerable should make readers outside the totalitarian camp fear its first incursions far more than they otherwise might. Yet the two questions must be kept distinct if one is to determine just how pessimistic Orwell became. It is possible, after all, that he was sanguine about prevention but hopeless about cure.

Actually, the matter is not so simple. His feelings about the future of the democratic regimes shifted constantly in the last decade of his life. As early as 1939, he wrote of the possibility "that we are descending into an age in which two and two will make five when the Leader says so" (*CEJL* 1: 376). Yet at other times he stressed the possibility that the inevitable planned societies of the future might be "humanised" (*CEJL* 4: 103). Orwell's theory of revolution in *Animal Farm* suggests that autocratic power is at first willingly conceded to the revolutionary leaders by the people. His last book can be interpreted as a warning intended to prevent such fatal concessions being made in the first place, by showing where they lead.

Orwell disavowed absolute pessimism in a letter about *Nineteen Eighty-Four* published shortly after the book appeared. In it he says, "I do not believe that the kind of society I describe necessarily *will* arrive, but I believe (allowing of course for the fact that the book is a satire) that something resembling it *could* arrive" (*CEJL* 4: 502). The distinction he makes here clearly suggests the possibility of prevention, and the words are carefully chosen. Yet curiously enough, when he sent this letter to Francis Henson of the United Automobile Workers, he made what he calls "a stupid slip": he apparently wrote "but I believe . . . that something resembling it *will* arrive" rather than "*could* arrive." [28] Both versions (one more optimistic, one more pessimistic) might be said to express a part of what Orwell really felt. His older faith in the efficacy of political enlightenment and his fundamental trust in people's ability to understand politics and to right social wrongs had become far more shaky by the 1940s than they had been in the previous decade. Yet he had not abandoned them entirely. The society pictured in *Nineteen Eighty-Four* is, after all, one in which *Nineteen Eighty-Four* could never have been published. The hope that totalitarianism could be avoided in the democratic countries was perhaps fragile, but it was real, and Orwell wrote to strengthen it.

Whether totalitarianism can be destroyed once it has been successfully established—especially in a society invulnerable to external threat—is much more problematical. Orwell's book seems to be quite pessimistic in its answer to this question. It begins where *Animal Farm* breaks off—with a fully consolidated totalitarian regime in which the victims are oppressed and leaderless. Both worlds are ripe for revolution; neither is likely to produce a successful one. All of Orwell's arguments for the unique power of a totalitarian regime to prevent revolution apply to the state pictured in *Nineteen Eighty-Four*—its use of modern communications systems for surveillance, its supervision of all organs of opinion, its ability to alter "human nature," its control by an aristocracy of talent unlikely to grow weak.

There are two hopes for revolution in the book—Goldstein's secret society and "the proles." Significantly, the statements about both are ambiguous or directly contradictory. It is a question of which spokesman we are to trust. Winston, in a cautious entry in his diary, writes, "If there is hope . . . it lies in the proles," but he immediately sees the statement as both "a mystical truth and a palpable absurdity" (*NEF*, p. 86). Later, he more confidently predicts the eventual triumph of a real proletarian, socialist revolution that will produce "a world of sanity. Where there is

---

28. See the MS letter to Leonard Moore, 13 July 1949, Berg Collection, New York Public Library.

equality there can be sanity. Sooner or later it would happen, strength would change into consciousness. The proles were immortal" (*NEF*, p. 226). But the passage occurs immediately before Winston and Julia are arrested and learn that all of their rebellious gestures have been observed and even temporarily encouraged by the state. And the state, as represented by O'Brien, claims that all thought of proletarian revolution is mere fantasy: "The proletarians will never revolt, not in a thousand years or a million. They cannot. I do not have to tell you the reason: you know it already. If you have ever cherished any dreams of violent insurrection, you must abandon them. There is no way in which the Party can be overthrown. The rule of the Party is for ever" (*NEF*, pp. 267–68).

To add to the ambiguity, Emmanuel Goldstein's revolutionary book predicting the triumph of the proles is only quoted in part—the part that analyzes the history and principles of the Party. Its hopeful conclusion (which would have paralleled the ending of Trotsky's *The Revolution Betrayed*) is never actually reproduced in *Nineteen Eighty-Four*; it is scornfully summarized by O'Brien, who dismisses its predictions and then even claims to have written the book himself. The same ambiguity surrounds the clandestine subversive organization of which Goldstein is the putative leader. Does it really exist? Or is he, and is his revolutionary cell, merely a convenient fiction of the regime? These questions cannot be answered without trusting one or another of the opposed characters in *Nineteen Eighty-Four*, and this the book does not permit us to do. It maintains its deliberately ambiguous poise as an accurate expression of Orwell's divided feelings.

Despite this ambiguity, *Nineteen Eighty-Four* is certainly a far darker book than its predecessor. In contrast to *Animal Farm*, its tone is unrelievedly grim. The regime of Oceania is in a crucial transitional stage: it is about to eliminate the last vestiges of revolutionary opposition, thought, and even language. Winston is among its last possible rebels because of his older, pretotalitarian cast of mind. He hates to think in Newspeak; his thoughts wander constantly back to the past; his memory is fixated in the regime's prehistory and is dominated by the old-fashioned individualism and family-feeling of his mother. He can judge the present because he can remember the past. But his kind is being replaced by a breed that not only knows no pretotalitarian history but lives entirely in a world in which the past has no real existence. Such creatures will be trained to express themselves exclusively in a language without any terms for rebellious ideas, one in which such ideas will thus be literally unthinkable.

An optimist who envisioned this kind of society would probably invent a hero and possible martyr, but Orwell deliberately denies Winston heroic stature when he allows him to betray Julia and shows him to be too weak to maintain his inner opposition to the Party. The state can triumph because it knows every potential hero's Achilles's heel and uses this knowledge to crush his rebellion. Such a vision does not grow only out of an analysis of totalitarianism or speculation on the shape of future societies, however. It seems rather to embody a conviction that human beings are creatures whose limitations make it impossible to achieve the goals they set for themselves. This is, of course, a fundamentally conservative position. Orwell's final strong attraction to it illuminates the precariousness of his optimistic socialist faith and recalls the defeated rebels of his early novels.

The strong pessimistic element in *Nineteen Eighty-Four* raises the question of whether the book can be considered in any sense a socialist document, even a strongly revisionist one. A hopeless faith is finally a contradiction in terms. Perhaps Orwell's book, like Burnham's *Managerial Revolution*, should be considered a farewell to socialism. "Ingsoc," the ideology of Oceania, once stood for English socialism, and in several significant ways the society of *Nineteen Eighty-Four* is clearly socialist: private property no longer exists and capitalism is dead. Goldstein suggests that the society is merely the logical culmination of the socialist movements of the past: "Socialism, a theory which appeared in the early nineteenth century and was the last link in a chain of thought stretching back to the slave rebellions of antiquity, was still deeply infected by the Utopianism of past ages. But in each variant of socialism that appeared from about 1900 onwards the aim of establishing liberty and equality was more and more openly abandoned" (*NEF*, p. 208). In this interpretation, socialism is a terminal case, and *Nineteen Eighty-Four* records its death rattle.

Does this mean that Orwell's native pessimism had finally swamped his socialism? In 1946, he had still been able to write, "A Socialist is not obliged to believe that human society can actually be made perfect, but almost any Socialist does believe that it could be a great deal better than it is at present, and that most of the evil that men do results from the warping effects of injustice and inequality." [29] The cause-and-effect relationship suggested in this statement is crucial: human evil is the product of social injustice; change society and "most of the evil that men do" can be eliminated. Yet the logic of *Nineteen Eighty-Four* apparently reverses these terms; social injustice in that world is the product of the obsessive need some men have for tyrannical power, a need no system of government is likely to change. Orwell describes the power drive as a fundamentally irrational force, which suggests the futility of trusting to a Dickensian "change of heart" for its elimination.

The strongly conservative flavor of this belief is unmistakable, and the fact that *Nineteen Eighty-Four* was taken up with such enthusiasm by the Right is no accident. Orwell understood that this was likely to happen and even insisted that the historical moment was ripe for the assertion of those plausible elements in conservatism which the reigning left-wing orthodoxy had conveniently denied: "Perhaps it is even a bad sign in a writer," he said in 1948, "if he is not suspected of reactionary tendencies today, just as it was a bad sign if he was not suspected of Communist sympathies twenty years ago" (*CEJL* 4: 412–13). A writer's task is to raise the embarrassing questions of his society, not to reinforce its conventional wisdom.

Behind this attitude lies Orwell's belief that socialism as a movement can be stripped of its illusions and still survive. His attempt to isolate and expose the unnecessary and even damaging accretions of the socialist movement had engaged his energies as a writer for most of his career. He had attacked its millennialism, its

29. George Orwell, "What Is Socialism?" *Manchester Evening News*, 31 January 1946, p. 2.

belief in ideological orthodoxy, its confusion with state planning, its association with industrialism, its dishonesty in refusing to face unpleasant facts, its tolerance of immoral means to reach socialist goals; he had exposed the motives of its disciples and the cult of the Soviet Union. Yet all of this criticism had been sustained by his belief in the ideals of socialism and his faith that it might one day be established. The branches might be diseased, but the roots were sound.

Yet by the end of his career, the habit of "internal criticism" had become so strong that it even threatened the roots of his belief. Perhaps, after all, too much had been exposed, too little left dark. Orwell had begun by revealing the illusions of others but ended by becoming aware of his own. It was by no means clear that his own socialist faith was founded on a bedrock of truth. Perhaps his confidence in inevitable though modest progress was false; perhaps his belief in the power of reason and objectivity as political weapons was misguided; perhaps the only kind of socialism the world was likely to produce would bring with it enough unfortunate or even intolerable side effects to make its contribution to the alleviation of human misery questionable.

In addition, he felt that the socialist movement had never managed to solve its two most crucial problems, one tactical, the other psychological. The tactic of revolution seemed doomed because in order to be successful it must abandon humane action and put power in the hands of a determined, fanatical sect unlikely ever to surrender it. The tactic of "permeation" seemed ineffectual, both because of its hopeless dependence on bourgeois cooperation, and because of its apparently inevitable tendency to compromise principle to expediency. And the psychological problem was even more insoluble. Every form of socialism had ignored certain elements in human nature that did not seem to be the products of social conditioning but were probably inherent, unchangeable. The desire to dominate others might conceivably be a biological instinct that would undermine and eventually destroy any unprotected egalitarian society. In his last years, Orwell treats the idea "that man is naturally good and is only corrupted by his environment" as one of the "distinctly questionable beliefs" that "the Left had inherited from Liberalism" (*CEJL* 4: 410).

The attitudes and beliefs Orwell called into question late in his life had all, at some point, been his own, and insofar as he could call himself a socialist, perhaps they still were. For many years he had really been unable to acknowledge how powerful his doubts had become. Yet by 1947, in the imagery of disease which he had begun to use more and more frequently, he described socialism's chances in this way:

> A Socialist today is in the position of a doctor treating an all but hopeless case. As a doctor, it is his duty to keep the patient alive, and therefore to assume that the patient has at least a chance of recovery. As a scientist, it is his duty to face the facts, and therefore to admit that the patient will probably die. Our activities as Socialists only have meaning if we assume that Socialism *can* be established, but if we stop to consider what probably *will* happen, then we must admit, I think, that the chances are against us. [*CEJL* 4: 370]

This attitude might well be described as deeply pessimistic, but it cannot be called cynical. Orwell never retreated from faith to resignation or indifference.

Yet we might well ask whether anything really remained of Orwell's euphoric affirmation of socialism by the end of the ten-year period following the Spanish Civil War. In order to answer this question, we must distinguish between his political ideals and his sense of political realities. The ideals remained those of a democratic socialist. He wished passionately for a society in which all significant distinctions of class, power, and wealth had ceased to exist, in which international cooperation and equality had replaced competition and exploitation among nations, in which an equal measure of freedom and leisure were the prerogatives of every human being. Nothing in the experience of the previous decade had altered his commitment to these goals or his willingness to work for their realization. What *had* changed, and changed decisively, was his faith that such a world might eventually come into being. He was unlike other socialists in that he finally did not believe his ideals would be, or could be, realized; and it is this fact which makes his political ideas and attitudes toward the end of his life so heterodox and accounts for their odd tangle of conservative and radical strands. This kind of hopeless commitment might be seen either as heroic tenaciousness or simply as a failure of nerve. It is a dilemma Orwell himself never had the chance to work out, a knot he could not, in the end, untie. Yet the whole thrust of his concern in the last years of his life was directed toward making readers feel that such issues could no longer be ignored: "The actual outlook, so far as I can calculate the probabilities, is very dark, and *any serious thought should start out from that fact*" (*CEJL* 4: 375; italics added). His critique of socialism is finally a plea for a new socialist dispensation that acknowledges the tragic history of the movement and tries, first of all, to account for what went wrong. It is in line with Orwell's later analytic habits of mind that he seemed finally to be calling for a form of "scientific" socialism the world had not yet produced—a post-Freudian socialism founded on the realities of human nature and on the probable behavior of men. Since his time, many socialist thinkers have addressed themselves to the tactical and psychological problems that finally seemed insoluble to him. If the realistic socialism Orwell hoped to find ever comes into being, it will be in part because he illuminated the need for its existence.

Part 2

Writing for the Cause

5

Class and Audience

In his critical essays, Orwell characteristically asks questions about the artist's audience: For whom was Kipling writing and why was he so popular? How did H. G. Wells influence the minds of the young at the beginning of the century? Or, as he asks about the audience of English boys' weeklies, "The question is, Who are these people? Who reads the *Gem* and *Magnet?*" (*CEJL* 1: 467). Even the comic art of Donald McGill is examined in these terms, and Orwell concludes that it is "aimed at the better-off working class and poorer middle class" (*CEJL* 2: 158). Orwell clearly thinks that the relationship between the artist and his audience is of crucial importance and an understanding of it one of the first tasks of intelligent commentary. It seems legitimate and important to ask the same kind of question about his work: what sort of reader did he think he was addressing?

A politically conscious writer in the later 1930s could scarcely fail to be aware of the problem of audience, and Orwell was certainly no exception. With the polarization of political attitudes during the period, the responses of various groups of readers became more and more familiar, predictable, and finally institutionalized. The Left Book Club (which commissioned *The Road to Wigan Pier*) created a very large, reliable audience for left-wing books; by 1937 it had fifty thousand members.[1] A Right Book Club was soon founded to organize the potential readers on the other side. Finding one's audience became less a happy accident than part of a systematic ritual. Certain publishers became

1. As its directors wrote, "A circulation of 50,000 of a Left Wing book, month by regular month, would have been thought the dream of a lunatic two years ago: for it must be remembered that outside the Left Book Club probably not more than two or three books a year, from all the publishers' lists, achieve a sale at this level (best-selling novels included), and in some years not a single book has sold such a number of copies." *Left News*, no. 26 (June 1938), p. 832.

associated with particular ideologies. When Orwell began to attack Soviet communism as a betrayal of socialism, for instance, he predictably had to change publishers from Gollancz to Secker and Warburg and was convinced that he could never again write anything Gollancz would publish (*CEJL* 3: 392).

One of the peculiarities of Orwell's career is that he did not fit into, or else publicly scorned, most of the potential groups with which he might plausibly have become associated. Before the publication of *Animal Farm* made him famous, his books generally sold between one and two thousand copies, although he was publishing regularly and attracting notice. On a number of occasions, publishers asked him to make crucial changes in his manuscripts or refused to publish them altogether because the material was considered dangerous to a particular cause. In one case, a journal went so far as to rip out an essay of his from all copies intended for distribution, after the entire issue had been printed and bound.[2] Far from fitting effortlessly into the contemporary literary scene, then, Orwell was engaged in a prolonged conflict with both publishers and readers. From the point of view of the left-wing political groups, he was always addressing the wrong audience, or telling the right audience the wrong things. In class terms, he refused either to abandon his middle-class allegiance or to leave that class in peace. From an orthodox Marxist point of view, this simply made no sense. The classes were at war; one had to choose. At the critical moment, Marx and Engels had said, a certain highly conscious portion of the bourgeoisie "cuts itself adrift," abandons its class, and identifies itself with the revolutionary proletariat. It then stands in an adversary relation to its caste. To examine Orwell's attitudes toward the working class and the bourgeoisie is to become aware of how impossible it is to see his case in these classic terms.

It was one of the dogmas of the radical Left in the 1930s that the socialist writer must not only address the working class but identify himself with them. Orwell's attitude toward and picture of the English working class, however, is one of the great

---

2. "Benefit of Clergy: Some Notes on Salvador Dali," *Saturday Book*, no. 4 (October 1944), pp. 255–60.

anomalies of his work. It is clear, I think, that he tried very consciously to make himself their spokesman, and that his sympathies were instinctively with them in any conflict with their hierarchical superiors. This does not mean, however, that he "identified" himself with them. In fact, his very sympathy for the working class, together with his deliberate social descent into their world in order to write works like *The Road to Wigan Pier*, made him acutely conscious of his own unalterably different class identity. It is one of the marks of Orwell's honesty that he could not allow himself to forget this distinction, although he certainly tried to annihilate it. He describes it persuasively in *Wigan*:

> For some months I lived entirely in coal-miners' houses. I ate my meals with the family, I washed at the kitchen sink, I shared bedrooms with miners, drank beer with them, played darts with them, talked to them by the hour together. But though I was among them, and I hope and trust they did not find me a nuisance, I was not one of them, and they knew it even better than I did. However much you like them, however interesting you find their conversation, there is always that accursed itch of class-difference, like the pea under the princess's mattress. It is not a question of dislike or distaste, only of *difference*, but it is enough to make real intimacy impossible. Even with miners who described themselves as Communists I found that it needed tactful manoeuvrings to prevent them from calling me "sir"; and all of them, except in moments of great animation, softened their northern accents for my benefit. I liked them and hoped they liked me; but I went among them as a foreigner, and both of us were aware of it. Whichever way you turn this curse of class-difference confronts you like a wall of stone. Or rather it is not so much like a stone wall as the plate-glass pane of an aquarium; it is so easy to pretend that it isn't there, and so impossible to get through it. [*RWP*, p. 157]

This gulf was widened by Orwell's refusal to participate in the political "reshaping" of working-class attitudes. He felt that a socialist movement must be responsive to the actual, present attitudes of the working class, not to some theory of how they should, or eventually would, feel. He was convinced, for example, that the bulk of the British working class was patriotic, distinctly unrevolutionary, and even politically indifferent. That is why, in "Inside the Whale," he could call Henry Miller a proletarian novelist: because his political passivity was close to the actual attitudes of ordinary men. Miller, unlike more "purposive writers," was "passive to experience" and for this reason had become an unwitting spokesman for the ordinary man: "For the ordinary man is also passive. Within a narrow circle (home life, and perhaps the trade union or local politics) he feels himself master of his fate, but against major events he is as helpless as against the elements. So far from endeavouring to influence the future, he simply lies down and lets things happen to him" (*CEJL* 1: 500).

A Marxist would respond by insisting that it is precisely the duty of writers like Orwell to help turn such debilitating and degrading passivity into enlightened activism. His task is to transform the working class into a conscious proletariat by encouraging it to fight against and defeat a passivity nurtured by those who would profit from it. To a Marxist, a politically unawakened class of workers is so much raw material, corrupted by capitalist ideology, suffering from a disease Marx called "false consciousness," and indifferent to its own and society's best interest. But for Orwell, as John Mander observes, "the principles of justice and liberty, the underlying ideals of Socialism, were already incarnate in the working class. It was merely a question of persuading the rest of the community to embrace these principles." [3]

For this reason, Orwell is not particularly interested in the working class of the future, but only in that of the past and the present. He has frequently (and legitimately, it seems to me) been accused of sentimentalizing working-class life. The *locus classicus* is his cozy picture of an English lower-class family with its "warm, decent, deeply human atmosphere" in *The Road to Wigan Pier*:

> I have often been struck by the peculiar easy completeness, the perfect symmetry as it were, of a working-class interior at its best. Especially on winter evenings after tea, when the fire

3. *The Writer and Commitment* (London, 1961), p. 91.

glows in the open range and dances mirrored in the steel
fender, when Father, in shirtsleeves, sits in the rocking chair
at one side of the fire reading the racing finals, and Mother
sits on the other with her sewing, and the children are happy
with a pennorth of mint humbugs, and the dog lolls roasting
himself on the rag mat—it is a good place to be in, provided
that you can be not only in it but sufficiently *of* it to be taken
for granted. [*RWP*, pp. 117–18]

The picture is shamelessly, even self-consciously, sentimental.
Orwell's wish to be "sufficiently *of* it to be taken for granted"
again reveals his awareness of class barriers. We are back with the
plate-glass pane of the aquarium, and Orwell's response recalls
Yeats's description of Keats in "Ego Dominus Tuus":

> I see a schoolboy when I think of him,
> With face and nose pressed to a sweet-shop window.

The whole fantasy of the "working-class interior" seems to me
essentially middle-class, even Dickensian. Its stress is clearly on
the warmth and completeness of family life. Orwell's picture in
this passage is not only sentimental but likely to appeal to the
middle-class sense of propriety, with its strong reliance on family,
domesticity, property, and settled order. It is clear that this
working-class family, in its very contentedness, poses no threat to
any other class. They are not only unmilitant; they might even be
said to know their place.

Orwell's pictures of working-class life are more often the
products of wish and fantasy than of his usual scrupulous
observation. They are curiously voyeuristic. One of the central
images in *Nineteen Eighty-Four* is Winston Smith's observation of
the "prole" woman singing as she hangs up her laundry. We can
see in it the same elements as in the *Wigan* description:
sentimentality, a kind of generic rendition of the scene with loss of
particularizing detail, a feeling of harmony, and a sense of the
distance between the observer and his object:

> As he fastened the belt of his overalls he strolled across to the
> window. The sun must have gone down behind the houses; it
> was not shining into the yard any longer. The flagstones were

wet as though they had just been washed, and he had the
feeling that the sky had been washed too, so fresh and pale
was the blue between the chimney pots. Tirelessly the
woman marched to and fro, corking and uncorking herself,
singing and falling silent, and pegging out more diapers, and
more and yet more. He wondered whether she took in
washing for a living, or was merely the slave of twenty or
thirty grand-children. Julia had come across to his side;
together they gazed down with a sort of fascination at the
sturdy figure below. [*NEF*, p. 225]

The effect is that of genre painting, and indeed there is something
clearly aesthetic in these twin pictures: the woman is a "figure" in
the beautifully lit landscape; the worker's "interior" has a
"perfect symmetry." As Winston continued to look at the woman,
"it struck him for the first time that she was beautiful" (*NEF*,
p. 225).

To maintain this sort of attitude, distance is essential, real
exposure destructive. In *Homage to Catalonia*, Orwell meets an
Italian militiaman in the Lenin Barracks in Barcelona. They
exchange exactly six words:

"Italiano?"
I answered in my bad Spanish: "No, Ingles. Y tu?"
"Italiano."
As we went out he stepped across the room and gripped
my hand very hard. Queer, the affection you can feel for a
stranger! It was as though his spirit and mine had momentarily succeeded in bridging the gulf of language and
tradition and meeting in utter intimacy. I hoped he liked me
as well as I liked him. But I also knew that to retain my first
impression of him I must not see him again; and needless to
say I never did see him again. [*HC*, pp. 1-2]

The militiaman becomes a symbolic figure in Orwell's book, an
idealized portrait of the real hero (and victim) of the Spanish
Civil War. But to idealize and sentimentalize such people in his
own mind, he must give them no more than the bare essentials of
independent life. For the rest, they are dependent on Orwell's

imagination, which characteristically invents an ineradicable tableau as their permanent setting. It is odd how self-conscious Orwell is about the operation of this whole process in himself: "I also knew that to retain my first impression of him I must not see him again." There is never any question, then, of Orwell's turning himself into a proletarian writer speaking to a proletarian audience. He often wrote about the working class but he seldom addressed it directly. There are, however, a few interesting exceptions to this general rule. For nearly twenty years, Orwell was a working journalist as well as a writer of books, and a number of his columns and reviews were quite clearly written in a more popular style—for example, the weekly book reviews he contributed during the war to the *Manchester Evening News*, or some of the short essays he wrote for *Tribune* in the regular series he called "As I Please." These columns were much more popular and less demanding intellectually than the serious essays he was writing at the same time for such journals as *Horizon*, *Polemic*, and *Partisan Review*.

Given Orwell's absorbing interest in language, it is not surprising that he should have been highly conscious of the different styles a writer had to use in addressing these two audiences. In an essay called "Propaganda and Demotic Speech" (1944), he explains the whole method of stylistic simplification, the intellectual's attempt to adopt "demotic speech": "The first step . . . is to find out which of the abstract words habitually used by politicians are really understood by large numbers of people. . . . Secondly, in writing one can keep the spoken word constantly in mind. . . . say to yourself, 'Could I simplify this? Could I make it more like speech?' " (*CEJL* 3: 138). Despite this earnestness, Orwell probably felt more comfortable writing in the educated style of his more serious essays than he did translating such material into "demotic speech." The reason for addressing an alien audience, as the title and date of Orwell's essay should make clear, is that England was at war and good propaganda a necessity for survival. Only on such occasions (or in a more casual, unbuttoned kind of writing) does the middle-class intellectual have any business trying to address "the people" in their own language.

Orwell made one serious attempt to write in a style other than his own—the novel *Coming Up for Air*, which was published in 1939. Its hero, George Bowling, is the only major character in Orwell's fiction significantly different in *sensibility* from his creator. He is jovial, relaxed, politically indifferent, "ordinary." The self-torture and internal conflict of the characteristic hero of Orwell's novels is notably absent from his makeup. What is more, the novel is written in the first person, which means that all its observations are filtered through the alien consciousness of Bowling. Yet it would be a mistake to think of the book as Orwell's venture into proletarian fiction. Bowling is not exactly working-class. He is a moderately successful insurance agent struggling along on a lower-middle-class income, living in a little semi-detached suburban house with his penny-pinching wife and two children. Although he says he is incapable of looking like a gentleman, most working-class people in Britain would certainly have thought him well off.

The members of Bowling's class would probably not have read Orwell's previous books. It seems probable that Orwell felt unhappy about the narrowness of the appeal of his early fiction and deliberately tried to expand his audience to include people like Bowling when he wrote *Coming Up for Air*; for the lower-middle class his hero represents was the missing link between the victims and the victimizers of British society. In a country on the brink of world war, that class could no longer be left in its state of comfortable political indifference. The vision of the future that Bowling has at a crucial point in the novel is designed to create political awareness in an apolitical audience:

> And yet it frightens me. The barbed wire! The slogans! The enormous faces! The cork-lined cellars where the executioner plugs you from behind! For that matter it frightens other chaps who are intellectually a good deal dumber than I am. But why? Because it means good-bye to this thing I've been telling you about, this special feeling inside you. Call it peace, if you like. But when I say peace I don't mean absence

of war, I mean peace, a feeling in your guts. And it's gone for ever if the rubber truncheon boys get hold of us. [*CUA*, pp. 168–69]

In contrast to this vision of the future, which is a kind of rehearsal for *Nineteen Eighty-Four*, the novel celebrates the feeling Bowling calls "peace," which was rapidly disappearing from English life. The search for it takes Orwell's hero back to the world of his youth, in a kind of nostalgic, pastoral excursion to a time that still offered the sense of privacy, a time before hysteria and urgency had established themselves as the normal style of modern life. The celebration of the values of the past is a political act. It is the product of Orwell's sense of the imminence of disaster and the need to awaken his normally passive audience. He was convinced that only the working class and the lower-middle class could fight effectively against the possible triumph of "the rubber truncheon boys." Too many of the intellectuals were committed to one or the other form of totalitarianism and even welcomed its methods, and the upper class was too blindly patriotic to understand that certain qualities of British life were not worth sacrificing no matter what the threat from a militant Germany. England's salvation, if it lay anywhere, lay with the ordinary, "decent" lower and lower-middle classes.

The immediacy of the danger encouraged Orwell to modify his natural style, to speak through Bowling rather than in his own voice. The effect of this decision is everywhere evident in the style of the book. There is something like an attempt at demotic speech here, although it is not perfectly consistent. Bowling's style is chatty direct address:

I'm fat—yes. I look like a bookie's unsuccessful brother—yes. No woman will ever go to bed with me again unless she's paid to. I know all that. But I tell you I don't care. I don't want the women, I don't even want to be young again. I only want to be alive. And I was alive that moment when I stood looking at the primroses and the red embers under the hedge. It's a feeling inside you, a kind of peaceful feeling, and yet it's like a flame. [*CUA*, p. 167]

It is a style designed as an alternative to the educated dialect—its sentences short, its grammar primitive, its vocabulary innocent of polysyllables, its metaphoric flights embarrassed, its meaning spelled out. Every hint of high-brow or "literary" inflation is immediately undercut by an apology for incipient articulateness: "There's something about it, a kind of intensity, a vibration—I can't think of the exact words" (*CUA*, p. 166).

Orwell is, however, a poor ventriloquist. We are constantly aware of his impatience with these self-imposed limitations. Bowling's values are those of his creator, but when the novel forces him to spell them out, he inevitably becomes more self-conscious, more theoretical, and more generally observant than such a character is likely to be. Orwell's experiment is always in danger of breaking down because it is constantly being pulled in two directions—the need to articulate a political warning clearly and forcefully, and the need to be true to the colloquial, impoverished vocabulary of the narrator and the audience he is designed to represent and reach. In writing the novel, Orwell must have become even more conscious of how difficult it is for a middle-class intellectual to "cross over," to write for and about a world he can only know at second hand. In a letter to an acquaintance who is apparently familiar with such material, he asks many detailed questions about what an insurance agent like Bowling would be likely to do on an ordinary working day, the extent of his territory, how much of the time he would actually be traveling, and so on (*CEJL* 1: 358). In this instance, at any rate, Orwell found it impossible to write from his own experience; he had to acquaint himself with an alien world—the world which remained behind the aquarium pane, but which the urgency of the moment forced him to try and reach.

The middle-class writer's need to reach the lower classes at all was dependent on how much he thought of himself as a propagandist and polemicist, as a man trying to coerce a social group into action. There were a few times in Orwell's career when he did indeed see his task in these terms, and the years immediately before and after the war were among them, but in general he was resigned to leaving the working class and lower-middle class alone. As we have seen, he felt that they had managed to preserve a fundamental decency in the midst of general sordidness. Characteristically, they inspire a kind of envy in Orwell's heroes. Here, for example, is Gordon Comstock in *Keep the Aspidistra Flying*:

> He wondered about the people in houses like those. They would be, for example, small clerks, shop-assistants, commercial travellers, insurance touts, tram conductors. Did *they* know that they were only puppets dancing when money pulled the strings? You bet they didn't. And if they did, what would they care? They were too busy being born, being married, begetting, working, dying. . . . The lower-middle-class people in there, behind their lace curtains, with their children and their scraps of furniture and their aspidistras— they lived by the money-code, sure enough, and yet they contrived to keep their decency. [*KAF*, p. 293]

Although these people are identified as "lower-middle-class," there are clear connections here to the passage about the prole woman and her diapers. Both lead "the lives of common men"; and this identification makes us aware that Orwell is either not conscious of, or else is deliberately obfuscating, the distinction between the working class and the lower-middle class in English society. The whole treatment of the lower classes in Orwell's work seems to dissolve traditional barriers—between the men with regular jobs and the tramps, between the lower-middle class and its immediate inferiors, between impoverished gentility and the classes among whom they are forced to live. We will see that this blurring of distinctions which are often insisted on fanatically in English society was an essential part of Orwell's political strategy.

Orwell's class analysis is partly a critique of Marxist labels. He felt that orthodox Marxist theory got in the way of a proper understanding of the class structure of a country like England. It assumes, as he says in *The Road to Wigan Pier*, a simple conflict between "the more or less mythical figure of a 'proletarian', a muscular but downtrodden man in greasy overalls" and "a 'capitalist', a fat, wicked man in a top hat and fur coat. It is tacitly assumed that there is no one in between; the truth being, of course, that in a country like England about a quarter of the

population is in between" (*RWP*, p. 225). Between the exploiters
and the exploited there was a very large group of people in an
anomalous position, a group that included the small shopkeepers,
the genteel poor, the new technological middle class, the large
group who had managed, in the course of their lives, either to rise
from poverty or to fall from affluence. Orwell claimed that he
himself was one of these people; he defines his own class, with
almost comic precision, as "the lower-upper-middle class," a
"sub-caste" attempting to live with all the outward signs of
prosperity and culture on about £400 a year (*RWP*, p. 123).

One of the troubles with the socialist movement in Western
countries was that it consistently alienated such people and
taught them to think of their own interests as opposed to those of
the working class and therefore indistinguishable from those of the
real bourgeoisie. As George Bowling describes a similar attitude in
his own "sub-caste": "We're all respectable householders—that's
to say Tories, yes-men and bum-suckers. . . . Every one of those
poor downtrodden bastards, sweating his guts out to pay twice the
proper price for a brick dolls' house that's called Belle Vue
because there's no view and the bell doesn't ring—every one of
those poor suckers would die on the field of battle to save his
country from Bolshevism" (*CUA*, pp. 16–17).

The hope of social transformation without a bloody revolution
was to win this class over to the socialist cause, since an alliance
between them and the proletariat was likely to be much more
powerful than the working class could be when its potential allies
acted as a buffer for the real enemy. The "class in-between" must
be made to see itself as fundamentally exploited rather than as
existing comfortably above the battle. In Orwell's eyes they were
no less troubled, no less insecure financially, than the working
class. As he says in *The Road to Wigan Pier*:

> The essential point here is that all people with small,
> insecure incomes are in the same boat and ought to be
> fighting on the same side. . . . It has got to be brought home
> to the clerk, the engineer, the commercial traveller, the
> middle-class man who has "come down in the world", the
> village grocer, the lower-grade civil servant and all other

doubtful cases that they *are* the proletariat, and that Socialism means a fair deal for them as well as for the navvy and
the factory-hand. . . . The people who have got to act
together are all those who cringe to the boss and all those
who shudder when they think of the rent. [*RWP*, pp. 225–26]

Here, broadly speaking, is the class Orwell most consistently
wanted to reach, though its heterogeneity made it almost
inevitable that he could not reach all parts of it by using a single
voice. Complacent or hostile to social justice as its members
frequently were, they were also capable, he felt, of compassion
and insight. They were ignorant and often deliberately sealed
themselves off from an understanding of less privileged ways of
life; but Orwell thought there was a fundamental decency in
them as well, which writers could nurture and which, once
released, could create a society of equals. The problem was that
people with "small insecure incomes" were not used to thinking of
themselves as a single class; they magnified trivial differences in
education and life style and ignored their essential economic
identity with the rest of the group. They were obsessed with what
Freud called the narcissism of small differences, and the real
bourgeoisie could exploit this dividedness among the "lower
orders" to preserve its own privileges.

It is worth noting that Orwell is interested in appealing to them
at least in part on the basis of their own interest. The socialist
movement in Britain had made hardly any attempt to understand, and address itself to, the reflex hostility of the "class
in-between." In effect, then, it wrote off the possibility of winning
over its most potentially useful allies. Orwell, however, insisted
that the class had an identity of its own, that it was capable of
being converted, and that once converted it could be loyal to the
ideals of socialism. The decade was moving toward a crisis, and
there would soon come a moment, he wrote in *Wigan*, "when
every person with any brains or any decency will know in his
bones that he ought to be on the Socialist side. But he will not
necessarily come there of his own accord; there are too many
ancient prejudices standing in the way. *He will have to be persuaded,
and by methods that imply an understanding of his viewpoint.* Socialists

cannot afford to waste any more time in preaching to the converted" (*RWP*, p. 210; italics added).

Orwell's audience and his sense of mission as a writer could hardly be described more economically. He would try to persuade the person "with any brains or any decency" of the justice of socialism rather than spending his time contributing to the family newsletter of the Left. He would begin by trying to understand how the person outside the movement feels, and what he really wants. All other forms of appeal were doomed; an insensitive, orthodox socialist lecture is useless because it does not, in the first place, take its audience seriously enough to understand its prejudices. The voice of the orthodox socialist was a monologue, or at best a monologue with supporting chorus. His own would be part of a dialogue, with the opposing voice of a skeptical audience always present in the background. In a modern, industrial democracy, the support of the class Orwell was addressing was essential for a socialist revolution. The idea of the "proletarian revolution," he explained, was formed "before the modern technical middle class came into being," and was therefore no longer relevant to modern conditions. On the other hand, the "concept of revolution as a more or less voluntary act of the majority of the people—the only kind of revolution that is conceivable under modern Western conditions—has always been regarded as heretical." [4] It was a heresy to which Orwell subscribed, and for which he was often attacked.

It is hard to decide how aware Orwell was of the difficulty of the task he had set himself. Lenin, in a more bitter vein, had called the marginal middle class "the real *agents of the bourgeoisie in the working-class* movement, the labour lieutenants of the capitalist class." [5] And many recent sociological and political studies have demonstrated how conservative the group consisting of white-collar workers, small farmers and businessmen, and skilled artisans tends to be. It is the class that characteristically supports

4. George Orwell, "Patriots and Revolutionaries," in *The Betrayal of the Left: An Examination and Refutation of Communist Policy*, ed. Victor Gollancz (London, 1941), pp. 239–40.

5. V. I. Lenin, preface to *Imperialism, The Highest Stage of Capitalism*, in *Selected Works in Three Volumes* (Moscow, 1960), 1: 717.

totalitarian demagogues, the class most likely to feel the impotent rage Scheler called "ressentiment," the class most desperate to erect a barrier of ideology and life style between itself and the group immediately below on the social ladder. In England, the nonmanual lower-middle class traditionally votes Conservative by overwhelming majorities and has a kind of negative identity: Not Working Class.[6] It often seems that Orwell, in stressing the idea that the working class and the lower-middle class have an identical economic interest, is ignoring the fact that psychological motives can be more powerful than economic ones.

From the first, however, Orwell believed that the chief obstacle the potential convert from the middle classes faces is his own ignorance of the conditions of life among the dispossessed. Many of the institutions of modern life were in effect designed to protect men of good will from understanding, or in fact having any contact with, the misery of life in the lower depths. This ignorance is not at all accidental, though it may be unconscious. The retreat into artificial stupidity is a useful way for people to protect themselves from guilt, from the disturbing sense of their own complicity in an unjust society. The *protected victimizer* was one of Orwell's chief targets. It was his intention to make it impossible for such people to use their ignorance as an excuse.

We can see this method at work in one of Orwell's first published pieces, the spare, beautifully controlled essay he called "A Hanging," a description of the execution of a Hindu prisoner. It begins:

> It was in Burma, a sodden morning of the rains. A sickly light, like yellow tinfoil, was slanting over the high walls into the jail yard. We were waiting outside the condemned cells, a row of sheds fronted with double bars, like small animal cages. Each cell measured about ten feet by ten and was quite bare within except for a plank bed and a pot of drinking water. In some of them brown silent men were

6. See Eric A. Nordlinger, *The Working-Class Tories: Authority, Deference and Stable Democracy* (Berkeley and Los Angeles, 1967); John Bonham, *The Middle Class Vote* (London, 1954); Mark Benney, A. P. Gray, and R. H. Pear, *How People Vote: A Study of Electoral Behaviour in Greenwich* (London, 1956).

squatting at the inner bars, with their blankets draped round them. These were the condemned men, due to be hanged within the next week or two. One prisoner had been brought out of his cell. He was a Hindu, a puny wisp of a man, with a shaven head and vague liquid eyes. He had a thick, sprouting moustache, absurdly too big for his body, rather like the moustache of a comic man on the films. Six tall Indian warders were guarding him and getting him ready for the gallows. Two of them stood by with rifles and fixed bayonets, while the others handcuffed him, passed a chain through his handcuffs and fixed it to their belts, and lashed his arms tight to his sides. They crowded very close about him, with their hands always on him in a careful, caressing grip, as though all the while feeling him to make sure he was there. It was like men handling a fish which is still alive and may jump back into the water. But he stood quite unresisting, yielding his arms limply to the ropes, as though he hardly noticed what was happening. [*CEJL* 1: 44]

What is remarkable about this description is its unremitting visuality. Although it is hard to imagine a more eloquent argument against capital punishment than "A Hanging," the essay begins and ends with description rather than argument. Orwell is writing a documentary, a dry, precise, highly factual account of exactly what happened. The essay is designed for people who instinctively support the institution of capital punishment because they do not have the slightest idea of what the execution of a human being is actually like. The aim is to expose the protected victimizer to his victim, to make comfortable people see and feel exactly what life in the "other world" is like. The whole passage speaks to the reader's unconscious prejudices about condemned men and the propriety of executing them: that such creatures have no individual identity, that they are formidable threats to society, that they are not quite human. These prejudices are actually reinforced by the first paragraph of the essay, with its Olympian perspective, and then begin to be exposed in an ironic light in the second, with its stress on the condemned man's sharp individuality and his almost absurd lack of force. Every detail of Orwell's description is purposive.

Orwell starts with the fact that modern oppression is indirect, that the people who make and support the laws and institutions of the modern state are protected from the knowledge of their effect by a class of hired middlemen—the policemen, the executioners, the social workers, the professional charity officials. The middlemen are there to protect the upright citizen, to protect his innocence as well as his life and property. The human conscience has been delegated. As a policeman in Burma, Orwell had once been, for a period of five years, one of those middlemen. Unlike most of the left-wing writers of the thirties, he knew what the victims of colonialism or other oppression were like; and he considered it part of his task as a writer to tear down the protective screen that prevented the middle class from confronting its victims face to face. His aim was to make the retreat into pseudostupidity, the innocence of ignorance, an impossible alternative and to force such people to make a choice—either to support oppression once it had been exposed, or to begin to transform the unjust world they had finally come to understand. The method implies, I think, a considerable faith in the ultimate decency of "the class in-between," since Orwell begins with the optimistic feeling that many of them are capable of confronting the moral squalor of a system to which they give tacit consent. The whole reformist strategy of Orwell's early work depends on this idealistic strain in his makeup.

It is an essential part of this technique of enlightenment that Orwell himself, the chief witness, begin in equal ignorance. His attitude in essays like "A Hanging" is never that of the righteous judge who sees things in their true light from the first. Rather, his own preliminary ignorance matches that of his reader. In fact, the characteristic pattern of Orwell's documentary essays and books is the movement from ignorance to enlightenment. He is anxious to record the process of his own education, which is why he characteristically begins with simple observation rather than analysis. To analyze the situation as an accomplished fact is to turn preacher before the audience has become familiar with the text. In one way or another, almost all of Orwell's books are accounts of a gradual enlightenment, whether of himself, in such books as *Down and Out in Paris and London*, *The Road to Wigan Pier*, and *Homage to Catalonia*, or of a fictional hero, in novels like *Burmese Days*, *Keep the Aspidistra Flying*, *Coming Up for Air*, and *Nineteen Eighty-Four*. He is anxious to identify himself with people who are capable of learning, whose minds are not closed, and for this reason his characteristic story is the record of an education.

It should be stressed that Orwell believed in the possibility of a radical transformation of consciousness because it had been the pattern of his own experience. It is clear from his autobiographical remarks in *The Road to Wigan Pier* and from the published reminiscences of those who knew him that he had not always been on the side of the victim. The very decision to become a British policeman in Burma after his graduation from Eton suggests at least a partial acceptance of the legitimacy of imperialism, and it is likely that this acceptance was emotional as well as intellectual. In Burma, he says he "was part of the actual machinery of despotism" (*RWP*, p. 147). Malcolm Muggeridge has suggested that "there was a Kiplingesque side to his character which made him romanticise the Raj and its mystique."[7] In "Shooting an Elephant," Orwell speaks of the rage he had felt "against the evil-spirited little beasts [the Burmese] who tried to make my job impossible" (*CEJL* 1: 236). And certainly Flory, the hero of *Burmese Days*, is hardly liberated from a sense of racial superiority over the natives. Given the paucity of information about Orwell's early life, however, all statements about the attitudes of his youth and young manhood must remain extremely speculative. What is

7. " 'Burmese Days,' " *World Review*, n.s. no. 16 (June 1950), p. 45. Peter Stansky and William Abrahams suggest that Orwell "seems to have had no understanding or premonition of what it meant to become an officer in the Indian Imperial Police, what the job would demand of him. His entire interest was directed to going out, going back, to a dreamscape of India" (*The Unknown Orwell* [New York, 1972], pp. 151–52). Their analysis of the tradition of colonial service in Orwell's family makes it clear that his decision to serve the Empire in Burma was a natural rather than anomalous one. And despite the striking transformation of Orwell's attitudes in adult life, at times the ancient habit sticks. For example, when Orwell lists the contributors to a BBC program he is arranging during the war, he politely mentions himself last—except for the sole Indian (Mulk Raj Anand), whose name follows his (*CEJL* 2: 246).

clear is Orwell's own feeling of discontinuity, a sharp break with the past that made him feel compelled to reject an earlier identity.

When the sense of revulsion from his own class and racial prejudice, and from his complicity in the machinery of oppression, finally came in Orwell's twenties, it was powerfully traumatic, as he makes clear in the *Wigan* sketch:

> For five years I had been part of an oppressive system, and it had left me with a bad conscience. Innumerable remembered faces—faces of prisoners in the dock, of men waiting in the condemned cells, of subordinates I had bullied and aged peasants I had snubbed, of servants and coolies I had hit with my fist in moments of rage (nearly everyone does these things in the East, at any rate occasionally: orientals can be very provoking)—haunted me intolerably. I was conscious of an immense weight of guilt that I had got to expiate. I suppose that sounds exaggerated; but if you do for five years a job that you thoroughly disapprove of, you will probably feel the same. [*RWP*, p. 149]

Orwell's expiation was his life task and took the form of a voluntary descent into the world of the oppressed. The descent would not be romantic but purposeful. His aim was to make the life of the oppressed classes as vivid for the protected middle-class reader as the faces of his own victims had become for him. His work became a systematic attempt to harrow and enlighten the reader. For, as he goes on to say about his colonial experience, "in the police you see the dirty work of Empire at close quarters, and there is an appreciable difference between doing dirty work and merely profiting by it. Most people approve of capital punishment, but most people wouldn't do the hangman's job" (*RWP*, p. 147). Insofar as literature can be a substitute for real experience, Orwell's books were to make this distinction impossible, were to make the "innocent" reader see, feel, hear, smell exactly what was being done by his delegates in his name, whether to the natives in the colonies, the derelicts in the casual wards, the miners in the North of England, or the peasants in Catalonia.

"Only a participant can be a profound observer," Trotsky once said. It became Orwell's task to live with (and as nearly as possible like) the victims he decided to describe. And this meant extended contact, not merely the journalist-tourist's rapid survey of lower-class life. More than any other middle-class writer of the 1930s, Orwell tried to break down the patron-client attitude that infected the bourgeois socialist or the unaffiliated do-gooder. His life in the thirties was essentially a series of anthropological field-trips, and his chosen mode, whether in fiction or in what came to be called "reportage," was the documentary. How did it feel to be a Paris dishwasher, a London tramp, a hop-picker, an unemployed worker living on the dole, a seedy bookseller's assistant, a Spanish Republican during the Civil War? He would go and find out, and report in detail.

Not all of this was artificial slumming. During the thirties Orwell lived through some of these experiences out of necessity as well as choice. He had not found—partially at least because he did not want to find—the kind of work he was qualified to do, given his training and class. But of course his story was hardly unique at a time when finding work became a serious problem even for the middle class. Orwell's "field work" was the product of several forces—necessity, opportunity, and a certain romantic determination to descend lower than he was absolutely forced to do.

That there should even be a need for such field work was clearly an indication of the unhealthiness of the society. Ideally, the writer should have better uses for his time than acting as a kind of spy on the poor, and the victimized classes of society should not have to depend on the capricious conscience of the middle-class writer. But Orwell knew—the contemporary vogue for proletarian novels notwithstanding—that one of the conditions of victimization is to be denied a voice. The victims of the world were invisible men, in part because they were denied access to the media of communication, in part because they had never learned the public vocabulary.

There is a significant connection to be made here with Orwell's essay about his childhood, "Such, Such Were the Joys." The real subject of that piece is what goes on in a child's mind: "And here one is up against the very great difficulty of knowing what a child really feels and thinks. A child which appears reasonably happy may actually be suffering horrors which it cannot or will not reveal. It lives in a sort of alien underwater world which we can only penetrate by memory or divination" (*CEJL* 4: 366). The image reminds us again of Orwell's description of class distinctions and the glass walls of the aquarium. The children in the school were in some sense class victims living in an autocracy: "At the time I could not see beyond the moral dilemma that is presented to the weak in a world governed by the strong: Break the rules, or perish. I did not see that in that case the weak have the right to make a different set of rules for themselves; because, even if such an idea had occurred to me, there was no one in my environment who could have confirmed me in it" (*CEJL* 4: 362).

It was Orwell's task to become such a confirming voice in his adult life. Although "Such, Such Were the Joys" is in no obvious sense of the word political, it has the same elements as his political pieces—victims, oppressors, a highly systematized form of tyranny. Tyranny often succeeds in the world because for one reason or another most of its victims are inarticulate. They lack a voice, or a spokesman, or even a sense of identity. Orwell's mission, as he seems to conceive it, is to give words, thoughts, and feelings to the world's silent victims. The terrified schoolchild, the beggar in Marrakech, the Italian militiaman in Spain, the victim of totalitarianism—all these have lost, or have never really had, the power to articulate their grievances. Orwell writes as their spokesman, the man determined to give their misery and sense of injustice *words*.

His first task is simply to report the facts, and his earliest published pieces are the work of a reporter whose territory is the world of the poor. In Paris in the late twenties, he was publishing descriptions of "la grande misère de l'ouvrier britannique" and of "le bourgeois aisé d'Angleterre qui ne connaît rien—et préfère ne rien connaître—de la vie des pauvres." [8] His first published pieces in the *New Statesman* upon his return to England included descriptions of the exploited Kent hop-pickers and of common

8. George Orwell, "La grande misère de l'ouvrier britannique," trans. Raoul Nicole, *Le progrès civique*, no. 489 (29 December 1928), p. 1728.

lodging-houses in London. Both essays are exposés; both try to give some picture of the intolerable conditions of life among the poor. Orwell worked these short pieces into his later books, the former into *A Clergyman's Daughter*, the latter into *Down and Out in Paris and London*. It is clear that Orwell thought of such work as considerably more important than hack journalism. One of his models was Robert Tressell, the author of a documentary novel of working-class life called *The Ragged-Trousered Philanthropists*, originally published in 1914. Tressell's book was, Orwell said, the first to get "the *facts* of working-class life . . . on to paper. . . . It recorded things that were everyday experience but which simply had not been noticed before" (*CEJL* 2: 39–40), "the actual detail of manual work and the tiny things almost unimaginable to any comfortably situated person which make life a misery when one's income drops below a certain level." [9]

Much of Orwell's work in the thirties might be summarized in precisely the same terms. He could be describing *Down and Out in Paris and London* or *The Road to Wigan Pier*, or major sections of *A Clergyman's Daughter* and *Keep the Aspidistra Flying*. The question that he tries to answer is, how does poverty feel, day by day, minute by minute? One of Orwell's essays is called "How the Poor Die." Most of his early work could be given the general title *How the Poor Live*. He ends his description of the sordid rooming house where he stayed in Wigan with the insistence that "it is a kind of duty to see and smell such places now and again, especially smell them, lest you should forget that they exist" (*RWP*, p. 19). He knows, of course, that most comfortably situated people would prefer to remain ignorant of the seamy underside of industrial civilization, about the life of a coal-miner, for instance: "Down there where coal is dug it is a sort of world apart which one can quite easily go through life without ever hearing about. Probably a majority of people would even prefer not to hear about it" (*RWP*, p. 34). But he writes in order to pierce this wall of indifference and make his audience conscious of life outside the pale.

9. George Orwell, "Legacy from a House Painter," *Manchester Evening News*, 25 April 1946, p. 2.

One of the ways in which the middle class protects itself from the "world below" is to avoid thinking of its inhabitants as human. Victims are characteristically conceived as different in *kind* from ordinary people. Orwell says of Marrakech, for example:

> When you walk through a town like this—two hundred thousand inhabitants, of whom at least twenty thousand own literally nothing except the rags they stand up in—when you see how the people live, and still more how easily they die, it is always difficult to believe that you are walking among human beings. All colonial empires are in reality founded upon that fact. The people all have brown faces—besides, there are so many of them! Are they really the same flesh as yourself? Do they even have names? Or are they merely a kind of undifferentiated brown stuff, about as individual as bees or coral insects? [*CEJL* 1: 388]

In writing about such responses, Orwell always treats himself as a guilty party, sharing in the evil he exposes. In the above passage, for example, the questions are certainly his own as well as those of his intended audience. "Marrakech" is a personal essay and records Orwell's own experience. As he says later in the same piece: "What is strange about these people is their invisibility. For several weeks, always at about the same time of day, the file of old women had hobbled past the house with their firewood, and though they had registered themselves on my eyeballs I cannot truly say that I had seen them" (*CEJL* 1: 391).

We remember Orwell's theory that the decent but reluctant middle-class person would have to be persuaded to join the socialist side "by methods that imply an understanding of his viewpoint." Essays like "Marrakech" are an example of his attempt to describe, not only the condition of the victim, but the psychological state of the victimizer. It was only by taking these two situations with equal seriousness that class hatred could conceivably be broken down. That is why Orwell spends so much time, in books like *Down and Out in Paris and London* and *The Road to Wigan Pier*, analyzing middle-class attitudes toward the poor. In *Down and Out*, for example, he is interested in the roots of the middle-class terror of "the mob," and he concludes that it springs from a "superstitious fear" that the poor are "a horde of submen, wanting only a day's liberty to loot his [an educated man's] house, burn his books, and set him to work minding a machine or sweeping out a lavatory. 'Anything,' he thinks, 'any injustice, sooner than let that mob loose' " (*DOPL*, pp. 120–21). Oppression is a form of repression, then, and to fight it without resorting to revolution, one must take the rich fantasy life of the oppressor as seriously as his actual deeds.

In politics, fantasy becomes dangerous when detached from the realm of fact; it is only by constantly confronting fantasy with fact that its potential domination over the mind can be thwarted. The sin of the English middle class was not conscious cruelty or hard-heartedness but a simple ignorance of the facts and a failure to use their sympathetic imaginations. These were the basic assumptions behind Orwell's early attempts to reach his middle-class audience. We have seen that the events of the 1940s were to make him reexamine and finally modify them significantly. Certainly *Nineteen Eighty-Four* is built on a very different foundation.

Yet there is an element of continuity in Orwell's career. The failure of imaginative sympathy also characterized the audience he tried to reach in his later works. He was writing now for people who might well be sympathetic and even knowledgeable about the English poor but whose willful ignorance became apparent in their attitude toward totalitarianism. The English intelligentsia had often acted as apologists for such regimes because they could not imagine what it would be like to live under them. The situation exactly parallels the relationship between the complacent burgher and the inarticulate poor. In both cases, in order to respond sympathetically, "one has to be able to imagine oneself as the victim" (*CEJL* 3: 235), as Orwell says in his essay on Arthur Koestler.

To be able to imagine oneself as the victim of totalitarianism was understandably difficult for an English writer living in a country where democratic process and freedom of speech were simply taken for granted. Orwell explains the curious fact that England had produced no "literature of disillusionment about the

Soviet Union" to compare with Continental works like *Darkness at Noon* and *Fontamara* by noting that "there is almost no English writer to whom it has happened to see totalitarianism from the inside" (*CEJL* 3: 235). Unlike his Continental counterpart, the English intellectual was a sort of Candide, a political innocent who could talk with indifference about events like the Moscow Trials because they evoked nothing he had ever experienced. Orwell analyzes a line from the first version of Auden's "Spain 1937" ("The conscious acceptance of guilt in the necessary murder") in these terms:

> All very edifying. But notice the phrase "necessary murder". It could only be written by a person to whom murder is at most a *word*. Personally I would not speak so lightly of murder. It so happens that I have seen the bodies of numbers of murdered men—I don't mean killed in battle, I mean murdered. Therefore I have some conception of what murder means—the terror, the hatred, the howling relatives, the post-mortems, the blood, the smells. To me, murder is something to be avoided. . . . Mr Auden's brand of amoralism is only possible if you are the kind of person who is always somewhere else when the trigger is pulled. [*CEJL* 1: 516]

In his own way, then, the English left-wing intellectual was also a protected victimizer. His complicity made totalitarian regimes less vulnerable to attack and thereby indirectly made life worse for their victims. To save Western socialism from taking the same path, it became imperative to enlighten such an audience. Orwell's most significant work in the 1940s was an attempt to explore the life of the victim of totalitarianism in the way that he had investigated the life of the poor under capitalism in the previous decade. That is, he was anxious to create a vivid sense of how such people lived—day by day, moment by moment. *Animal Farm* and *Nineteen Eighty-Four* are the logical successors to *Down and Out in Paris and London* and *The Road to Wigan Pier.*

To describe the audience of *Animal Farm* and *Nineteen Eighty-Four* in this way is to emphasize the strain of meliorism in Orwell's thought. It was certainly there, a stubborn streak that went through his whole career, from the exposés of the early thirties to his last published work, although it grew steadily weaker as his faith in human decency declined. The exposé, after all, rests on optimistic assumptions. In Orwell's last years, those assumptions must have seemed increasingly quixotic. The enemy was clearly not only the indifferent or ignorant middle class but also a creature inside himself, a voice that kept insisting his task was impossible, his meliorism naïve. To listen would have been to feel the futility of his attempt to transform the consciousness of a class to which he belonged and toward which he still felt an instinctive loyalty. Orwell is often taken to be a quintessentially cool, rational, and realistic writer. But in trying to push his own class into imaginative sympathy, his plea is that of Lear on the heath, a Lear on the verge of breakdown and vision:

> Take physic, pomp;
> Expose thyself to feel what wretches feel,
> That thou mayst shake the superflux to them,
> And show the heavens more just.

6

The Search for Form: The 1930s

One of the peculiar things about Orwell's reputation is that he has come to be admired more as a man than as a writer. There is a general feeling that a great many of his works, especially those he wrote in the 1930s, were failures. In itself, this is not a remarkable fact, of course. The apprentice years of important writers are often dismissed in this way. But in Orwell's case, the doubts often extend to the works of his maturity, and yet, in some mysterious way, manage to have no effect on the esteem in which he is generally held. He has become a "figure," and it is common to talk about him as though he were curiously independent of his works. Julian Symons, for example, says, "I have always believed that what Orwell wrote is less important than what he was"; Frederick Karl suggests that he was "better as a man than as a novelist"; and Lionel Trilling quotes with approval the reverent praise of one of his students: "He was a virtuous man." [1] Such attitudes are based, I believe, on the sense that Orwell's characteristic voice comes through in everything he wrote, no matter how imperfect it is, and on the feeling that he never found a literary *form* which would serve as the ideal vehicle for that voice.

Most writers eventually specialize; they become interested in a particular genre and so stop being "writers" and become poets, or novelists, or dramatists, or essayists. An obvious fact about Orwell's career is that this never happened to him. He was not satisfied with any of the existing literary forms, and he experimented extensively with several of them throughout his life. In the early thirties he was still writing, and occasionally publishing, verse. Later he moved on to realistic fiction and to the documentary. In the forties he turned to the long critical essay and finally

1. Julian Symons, "Orwell, a Reminiscence," *London Magazine* 3 (1963): 48; Frederick R. Karl, *A Reader's Guide to the Contemporary English Novel* (London, 1963), p. 166; Lionel Trilling, *The Opposing Self* (New York, 1959), p. 154.

to fantasy. He never became a specialist in any of these genres; rather, he remained a writer who employed the various forms available to him and discarded them when they no longer seemed useful. One sometimes feels that he thought the particular vehicles of literary expression were all equally unsatisfactory for his purposes. His deepest literary commitment was to powerful and lucid *prose*, rather than to any of the particular forms in which it was used; he was finally unwilling to choose one of them and make it his own.

The danger for such writers is that their relationship to the literary forms can become parasitic. They tend to appropriate the existing trends in the various genres rather than transforming them to suit their own needs. This is especially apparent in Orwell's attempts to write realistic fiction in the 1930s. The four novels he produced in that decade (*Burmese Days, A Clergyman's Daughter, Keep the Aspidistra Flying,* and *Coming Up for Air*) demonstrate practically no interest in extending or experimenting with the existing techniques of fiction. His single attempt to abandon the vocabulary of the realistic novel—the Trafalgar Square episode in *A Clergyman's Daughter*—is obviously based on the Circe chapter in *Ulysses*; it is an appropriation rather than an experiment, and not a particularly successful one at that.

Even Orwell's most sympathetic critics have usually been dissatisfied with these novels. George Woodcock says that they reveal "an inability to perceive or imagine deeply." Mrs. Leavis concludes that "nature didn't intend him to be a novelist." Some critics were disturbed that his fictional works were often indistinguishable from the books in which he spoke in his own voice. John Mander, for example, notes that "whole passages can be lifted from [the novels] and put alongside similar passages from the documentary writings without the reader being able to distinguish one from the other." [2]

Orwell himself was as hard on these early novels as his critics have been, though he thought of *Burmese Days* and *Coming Up for Air* as relative successes. For *A Clergyman's Daughter* and *Keep the*

---

2. George Woodcock, "George Orwell, 19th Century Liberal," *Politics* 3 (1946): 386; Q. D. Leavis, "The Literary Life Respectable," *Scrutiny* 9 (1940): 175; John Mander, *The Writer and Commitment* (London, 1961), p. 73.

Aspidistra Flying he had nothing but contempt. When Secker and Warburg decided to bring out a uniform edition of his books after the war, these two did not seem to him worth reprinting. And in arranging for the publication of his *Critical Essays* (1946), he asked his agent to include only his nonfictional work of the thirties and *Animal Farm* in the list of his previous books.[3] In a letter to George Woodcock, he dismissed some of the novels as worthless hackwork, written only because he was in financial need: "There are two or three books which I am ashamed of and have not allowed to be reprinted or translated, and that [*Keep the Aspidistra Flying*] is one of them. There is an even worse one called *A Clergyman's Daughter.* This was written simply as an exercise and I oughtn't to have published it, but I was desperate for money, ditto when I wrote *Keep the A.* At that time I simply hadn't a book in me, but I was half starved and had to turn out something to bring in £100 or so" (*CEJL* 4: 205).

Fiction was the only kind of writing that could be even moderately profitable, since novels reached a relatively large audience. Orwell was responding to what John Wain calls "the appalling imbalance of modern literary taste, which dictates that no book shall have more than a handful of readers unless it is a novel." [4] Yet Orwell wrote fiction not only because it meant solvency but because his political purposes required a larger audience. For a writer so deeply committed to effecting significant changes in his society, a wide audience meant greater influence, the chance of being taken seriously.

This does not mean Orwell's interest in fiction was merely an exploitation of a popular form for practical ends. It is worth remembering that his whole attitude toward culture was instinctively democratic rather than elitist. Most of his literary essays are about highly popular writers—Tolstoy, Shakespeare, Swift, Dickens, Wells, Kipling, P. G. Wodehouse, etc. His essential endorsement of popular culture is an important strain in his literary criticism, and he even invented a category—which he called "Good Bad Books," after Chesterton—of works that have man-

3. See the MS letters to Leonard Moore, 23 October 1946 and 1 December 1945, Berg Collection, New York Public Library.
4. "The Last of George Orwell," *Twentieth Century* 155 (1954): 71.

aged to survive despite great aesthetic imperfections: *Uncle Tom's Cabin*, for example (*CEJL* 4: 19–22). He believed literary importance was finally established by a kind of plebiscite of posterity: "Ultimately there is no test of literary merit," he says in "Lear, Tolstoy and the Fool," "except survival, which is itself merely an index to majority opinion" (*CEJL* 4: 290).

If the novel was popular, then, it was because for a variety of reasons it deserved to be so, because it had some kind of power and interest other forms could not match. In writing the realistic novels of the thirties, Orwell was deliberately associating himself with a literary tradition he regarded with respect. Some of the great writers of that tradition—Dickens, Zola, Tolstoy, Conrad, Gissing—were constantly in his mind, not exactly as literary models, but as masters who had reached levels of accomplishment to which he aspired. He invokes Zola at the beginning of a long descriptive section of *Down and Out in Paris and London*: "Then the grand turmoil of the day started—the dinner hour. I wish I could be Zola for a little while, just to describe that dinner hour" (*DOPL*, p. 64). And the terms in which he writes about Dickens suggest not only aesthetic but moral admiration: "It is the face of a man who is always fighting against something, but who fights in the open and is not frightened, the face of a man who is *generously angry*—in other words, of a nineteenth-century liberal, a free intelligence, a type hated with equal hatred by all the smelly little orthodoxies which are now contending for our souls" (*CEJL* 1: 460).

Yet if Orwell genuinely admired the masters of realistic fiction so extravagantly, why did he seem so uncertain of his own commitment to the genre? Why did he abandon it just as his apprentice years were coming to an end? To say simply that Orwell gave up the realistic novel because he realized that he had no great talent for it is, I think, to beg the question and to create a mystique of "talent" that fails to illuminate the problem.

It seems more likely that Orwell abandoned realistic fiction after 1939 because he saw a conflict between his aims as a writer and the demands of the genre. He thought of the fictional form as a vehicle created by others—as a set of awkward restrictions rather than brilliant opportunities. A remark he makes in a letter to Julian Symons is revealing: "One difficulty I have never solved," he writes, "is that one has masses of experience which one passionately wants to write about . . . and no way of using them up except by disguising them as a novel" (*CEJL* 4: 422). The statement suggests a fundamental dissatisfaction with the genre: it is a necessary but contemptible "disguise" for one's passionate feelings, and possibly even dilutes the intensity of those feelings. Fiction was suspect first of all because of its indirectness, the need to invent characters, situations, settings, the crises of a plot, when one simply wanted to record the "masses of experience" about which one felt passionately.

To combine these two needs—the desire to write fiction and the need to speak in one's own voice—would have required a revolution in the novel. In the 1930s, at any rate, Orwell did not have the fundamental commitment to the possibilities of the fictional mode to break with the devices of the past and create his own form; he attempted to make do with the traditional elements available to him. As a result, we are always aware of a conflict between the needs of the novel and the needs of its creator, with one or the other sacrificed at various points in the books themselves. As we shall see, this conflict expresses itself in a variety of ways—in a resistance to the indirectness of fictional technique, in an unwillingness to make his fictive world resonate or his characters come to life, and in his hesitation between objective and subjective fictional models.

The first sign of this conflict is Orwell's frequent confusion between himself and his major characters. In his early novels he seldom takes more than the hero seriously, and the hero often acts as a spokesman for Orwell himself. He was aware of this problem, especially as it affected his attempt to write first-person narrative, *Coming Up for Air*. Its hero, George Bowling, is a fat and jovial insurance agent. Similarities between him and his creator should be purely coincidental. Yet Orwell admits the justice of a friend's complaint that his own character constantly intrudes on that of the narrator: "I am not a real novelist anyway, and that particular vice is inherent in writing a novel in the first person, which one should never do" (*CEJL* 4: 422). This seems an odd conclusion. Surely a novelist "should never do" it only if he is impatient with the *indirect* nature of such fictional devices and has a need to express himself more directly. There is no truth in Orwell's statement that the "vice" of confusing the narrator with the author is inherent in the form. In one of the first serious essays published on Orwell, George Woodcock put his finger on the solipsistic nature of these books, on the tendency of his characters to "Orwellise in their thoughts in a way which hardly fits their external, worldly natures." [5]

An even more important conflict between the demands of fiction and Orwell's motives was the product of the political pressures of his time. In the late essay "Why I Write," Orwell suggests that "political purpose"—the desire "to alter other people's idea of the kind of society that they should strive after"—is one of the four principal motives for writing (*CEJL* 1: 4). It is interesting that he lists it fourth, after "sheer egoism," "aesthetic enthusiasm," and "historical impulse," possibly to suggest that under ordinary circumstances the writer's political purpose is seldom his dominant one. But the 1930s were not ordinary. There was no honorable—finally perhaps no practical —way for most artists to avoid political commitment: in a highly polarized society they had to take sides. The whole concept of artistic detachment and political neutrality was thoroughly discredited by the middle of the decade, and Orwell's books became more and more blatantly political. He describes this process as outside his control: "I have been forced into becoming a sort of pamphleteer" (*CEJL* 1: 4).

He soon became aware of the conflict between aesthetic and political considerations in writing fiction. The essential indirectness of the novel—its invention of a coherent, self-contained fictive world, its emphasis on character and narrative, its demand for concreteness rather than abstraction—worked against the simple and passionate declaration of political allegiances. In addition, the novelist demands more imaginative work from his readers than does the essayist. He trusts his audience in a way the essayist does not, trusts it to understand things that are not explained on the surface, his attitude toward the characters, the

5. Woodcock, "George Orwell," p. 386.

meaning of symbolic objects or scenes, and so on. Orwell's fiction seldom suggests that he was ready to accord his readers such trust. He was afraid of being misinterpreted and was convinced that without help they would not see the point.

The most obvious manifestation of this fear is the sudden intrusion of miniature essays into the narrative. The transition is often awkward, as in this passage from *Burmese Days:*

> What was at the center of all his [Flory's] thoughts now, and what poisoned everything, was the ever bitterer hatred of the atmosphere of imperialism in which he lived. For as his brain developed—you cannot stop your brain developing, and it is one of the tragedies of the half-educated that they develop late, when they are already committed to some wrong way of life—he had grasped the truth about the English and their Empire. The Indian Empire is a despotism—benevolent, no doubt, but still a despotism with theft as its final object. [*BD*, p. 68]

And then there follows a short essay on the nature of British imperialism, which more or less leaves Flory waiting in the wings until the narrative begins again. It is obvious that "the truth about the English and their Empire" is no longer Flory's truth, but Orwell's, and that he must put it down in the most abstract and authoritative terms he can invent, despite the fact that the novel constantly illustrates the thesis so baldly stated here.

Such passages, in which the narrative is temporarily suspended and the characters forgotten, occur frequently in Orwell's novels. In *A Clergyman's Daughter*, for example, there is a long section in which the heroine, Dorothy Hare, is forced to teach in a terrible private school owned and operated by a Mrs. Creevy. Orwell is anxious that the school be seen as typical of such institutions, and so at one point he allows Mrs. Creevy to explain, at great length, the fundamental assumptions under which she operates. The speech is not really in character, as Orwell realizes: "But as to what Mrs. Creevy had said about 'practical school-teaching,' it had been no more than a realistic facing of the facts. She had merely said aloud what most people in her position think but never say" (*CD*, p. 259). But it is precisely her saying it—and to a character like Dorothy, who is anything but a confidante—which is, in fictional terms, thoroughly implausible.

Up to this point in the passage, we are still following the characters in the book, at least in theory. But Orwell must have felt that his idea was not yet sufficiently clear; and so the passage continues: "There are, by the way, vast numbers of private schools in England. Second-rate, third-rate and fourth-rate (Ringwood House was a specimen of the fourth-rate school), they exist by the dozen and the score in every London suburb and every provincial town" (*CD*, p. 259). He then goes on to analyze the nature of such schools in a two-page essay, which concludes, "It was only later, and by degrees, that Dorothy discovered these facts about private schools" (*CD*, p. 261). The artlessness of such devices is readily apparent: the apologetic "by the way" with which Orwell introduces his disquisition, and the attempt to present it as a summary of insights the heroine would have at a later time and in a much more fragmentary way. The need to expose the institution he is dealing with is too great for him to trust to the relatively slow and confusing devices of fiction. One constantly feels that Orwell thought of the novel as a kind of monster which could feel but not think, and onto which he was determined to graft a brain—his own.

The same unwillingness to rely on the intelligence of the reader is evident in Orwell's use of symbolism. A symbolic object or event can become a different way of expressing meaning, with a powerful resonance of its own. Orwell's symbols can hardly be described in that way: they are purely instrumental and seldom kindle into life. And yet his novels are regularly symbolic: for example, the aspidistra in *Keep the Aspidistra Flying*, the fishing scene in *Coming Up for Air*, and Flory's birthmark in *Burmese Days*, are all of central importance in those books.

It is worth looking at one of these symbols in more detail to see how Orwell instructs the reader. The hero of *Coming Up for Air* keeps recalling a frustrated fishing trip from his youth, and we soon understand that something about the trip is associated in his mind with everything that was good in his childhood. The climactic moment of the novel comes when he revisits the scene of that adventure and finds, to his horror, that the idyllic rural retreat of his youth has been turned into a hideous fake-Tudor housing development. It would be clear enough from the description of the childhood episode and from this later scene that Orwell is treating Bowling's passion for fishing symbolically; but it might not be easy to think of a simple, abstract translation. This could be considered a defect of symbolism only by a novelist whose thematic purpose is primary and who is afraid to let the story usurp the theme. So we get the following explanatory passage, with Bowling acting as ventriloquist's dummy for Orwell:

> You'll think it damned silly, no doubt, but I've actually half a wish to go fishing even now, when I'm fat and forty-five and got two kids and a house in the suburbs. Why? Because in a manner of speaking I *am* sentimental about my childhood—not my own particular childhood, but the civilisation which I grew up in and which is now, I suppose, just about at its last kick. And fishing is somehow typical of that civilisation. As soon as you think of fishing you think of things that don't belong to the modern world. The very idea of sitting all day under a willow tree beside a quiet pool—and being able to find a quiet pool to sit beside— belongs to the time before the war, before the radio, before aeroplanes, before Hitler. There's a kind of peacefulness even in the names of English coarse fish. Roach, rudd, dace, bleak, barbel, bream, gudgeon, pike, chub, carp, tench. They're solid kind of names. The people who made them up hadn't heard of machine-guns, they didn't live in terror of the sack or spend their time eating aspirins, going to the pictures and wondering how to keep out of the concentration camp. [*CUA*, p. 76]

After reading such a passage, the reader is of course perfectly aware of the symbolic meaning of the fishing sections of the book. But this elucidation has been purchased at a price. As with the direct essayistic intrusions, the passage interrupts the narrative. In such sections, our whole attitude to reading becomes more passive, since our interpretive work is being done for us. We may nod assent or feel that Orwell's point is strained and unconvincing, but in either case we are reacting to the *point* and not to the story or the characters. The need to inform and convince has displaced the novelist's obligation to imagine and invent.

In discussing Orwell's uneasiness with the novel, I have concentrated on his impatience with its indirectness. But another kind of dissatisfaction with the methods of fiction is also evident in these early works, as well as in the narrative portions of his nonfictional documentaries of the thirties. It is a dissatisfaction with the apparent *uniqueness* of the world the novelist invents. A great novel always creates a new identity, a situation and a set of characters imagined in such rich detail that they tend to replace rather than confirm our previous notions about the way of life being described. A compelling fictive world lodges itself in our memory, not because it is perfectly familiar, but because its familiar elements have been absorbed into a vision that seems authoritative and new. A novel that recorded only the typical and recognizable would not command much attention.

It is obvious that this characteristic requirement of fiction must conflict with the desire to *illustrate* or *exemplify* some pattern of life that exists outside the limits of the particular novel, in the writer's own society. Orwell, however, felt both a need to use the fictional form illustratively and an uneasiness about employing the particular or the unique in his novels. We can see these objections as the impulse of Orwell the sociologist, just as the previous ones to the indirectness of fiction were the response of Orwell the social critic. He wanted to be certain that what he described in his novels was typical and that the reader would recognize it. He was afraid to involve the audience so deeply in his fictive world that they would forget the society of which it was supposed to be a mirror. The novel is justified in his eyes, finally, because it is an instrument acting to increase the reader's understanding of society and his desire to improve it. It must not be more than a temporary stopping place on the road that leads to social regeneration.

The effects of this attitude toward fiction are everywhere evident in Orwell's early novels. As Richard Rovere has observed, Orwell's "uniqueness lay to some degree in his almost studied avoidance of the unique. The experience he chose to deal with was the kind of experience known to large numbers of people, to whole social classes, to entire nations. He did not often concern himself with the single instance. . . . The merely anomalous, the merely phenomenal, the exotic, the bizarre—none of these attracted his interest very much." [6] The minor characters in Orwell's novels are almost always there not because they are necessary to the plot but because they typify characteristic attitudes or life styles in the particular environment Orwell is investigating. The Europeans in *Burmese Days*, for example, are clearly intended to exemplify the full range of colonial attitudes, from Ellis's violent hatred of the natives to Flory's pathetic attempts to fraternize. The first section of *A Clergyman's Daughter* could be called "Provincial Life," since it includes vignettes of all the important types one is likely to find in a small English town. In the long section of reminiscence in *Coming Up for Air*, the prewar society of Lower Binfield is recaptured in the same way.

Each of the minor characters in these novels is given just enough space to "illustrate" himself. There is never any danger that he will take over the novel, that he will change in any significant way, or that he will stick in one's memory as a unique creation in the way that even very minor characters in Dickens so often do. Orwell's unwillingness to have his characters take over the novel is evident in the way he cuts them off in the middle of a speech, as in this example from *Burmese Days*:

> Mrs. Lackersteen would sit down and continue smudging a sheet of sketching paper with a Conté crayon while Elizabeth worked.
>
> "How wonderful you are, dear. So practical! I can't think whom you inherit it from. Now with me, Art is simply *everything*. I seem to feel it like a great sea surging up inside me. It swamps everything mean and petty out of existence. Yesterday I ate my lunch off *Nash's Magazine* to save wasting time washing plates. Such a good idea! When you want a clean plate you just tear off a sheet," etc., etc., etc. [*BD*, p. 93]

6. "Introduction," *The Orwell Reader: Fiction, Essays, and Reportage* (New York, 1956), p. xii.

Clearly, this amusing sketch of bohemian pretentiousness has Dickensian possibilities, the kind of vitality, inventiveness, and detail that can make a minor character memorable. When Orwell ends the passage with "etc., etc., etc.," he protects himself against this possibility. He frequently uses this dismissive verbal formula to suggest that the rest is perfectly familiar and can be filled in by any reader. The character is not permitted to filibuster, to take up more space than Orwell was originally willing to assign him. One seldom has the feeling that his fictional material is forcing itself upon him. In other words, Orwell's sense of purpose and his commitment to types sometimes makes him a kind of repressive writer, unwilling to let the fiction take on independent life and quickly putting down spontaneous elements that threaten his firm control.

Orwell also frequently introduces characters in a way that encourages the reader to use his familiarity with the type as a substitute for detailed description of the particular example. The phrase "one of those people who" occurs frequently in his novels. From *A Clergyman's Daughter*: "He was one of those people who say 'Don't you know?' and 'What! What!' and lose themselves in the middle of their sentences." "She was one of those women who can never move anything without banging it about" (*CD*, pp. 207, 221). From *Keep the Aspidistra Flying*: "She was one of those malignant respectable women who keep lodginghouses." "They were one of those depressing families, so common among the middle-middle classes, in which *nothing ever happens*" (*KAF*, pp. 31, 50). Such passages serve to confirm rather than extend the reader's familiar perceptions, and they directly conflict with Orwell's determination—examined in the previous chapter—to enlarge and deepen the reader's understanding of alien ways of life. This emphasis on the typical sometimes extends to the major as well as the minor characters in these novels. The hero of *Coming Up for Air* describes himself in this way: "Do you know the active, hearty kind of fat man, the athletic bouncing type that's nicknamed Fatty or Tubby and is always the life and soul of the party? I'm that type. 'Fatty', they mostly call me. Fatty Bowling. George Bowling is my real name" (*CUA*, p. 8).

Orwell's reliance on familiar types is a form of abdication: his imagination refuses to take on the work usually assigned to the novelist and asks the reader to fill in the blanks. His use of the technique grows out of a fundamental distrust of the imagination rather than an inability to invent. The constant danger is that the artist's imagination, when allowed full play, will produce not the recognizable but the bizarre, the private, the incomprehensible. Such material would conflict with Orwell's political and sociological purposes and must therefore be suppressed.

Yet his suppression of these elements was not entirely successful. Despite all the emphasis on the typical and representative in these early works, they also include material that seems distinctly private and obsessional, and bears little relationship to the public sociological or political matter that dominates them. Orwell is really working with two very different fictional traditions, one more or less analytic and objective, the other lyric and highly subjective. The more subjective kind of novel is characteristically dominated not by social observation and realistic description but by an urgent, confessional quality, a concentration on feelings rather than actions, an intense, highly metaphorical style, a sense that the form can barely contain the emotions the novel records. Examples like *Wuthering Heights* and *Notes from Underground* readily come to mind. Northrop Frye has suggested that the methods used in such novels are so different from those of realistic fiction that the books belong to a completely different category, which he calls "romance." [7]

I am not arguing that Orwell wrote "romances" (in Frye's sense) rather than realistic novels, but rather that some of the peculiar qualities of both kinds of fiction are present in his work, and that the relationship between them is often strained. *Burmese Days* offers a good example in its concentration on Flory's birthmark, a hideous facial disfigurement always in his thoughts. At an early point in the novel, Flory is asked by a violently intolerant member of the English club, to sign a racist petition. Refusal would take an act of courage, which he cannot manage. Orwell explains: "Flory had been fifteen years in Burma, and in Burma one learns not to set oneself up against public opinion. But

7. *Anatomy of Criticism: Four Essays* (Princeton, 1957), pp. 304-07.

his trouble was older than that. It had begun in his mother's womb, when chance put the blue birthmark on his cheek" (*BD*, p. 64). In all the intense scenes in the novel, Flory's consciousness of the birthmark returns, usually in vivid similes: "He sat staring fixedly at the altar, his face rigid and so bloodless that the birthmark seemed to glow upon it like a streak of blue paint." "He almost cringed from her, and the birthmark stood on his yellow face like a splash of ink" (*BD*, pp. 274, 154). There are times in the novel when the birthmark explains what is happening much more satisfactorily than Orwell's insights about imperialism or the colonial mind. When this happens, we seem to be entering another realm, one dominated by expressive content, by a kind of chaotic, uncensored quality rather than by meticulous observation and control.

Dorothy Hare's morbid fear of sex in *A Clergyman's Daughter* creates the same effect. Orwell's description of her reaction to a passionate kiss recalls the intense, metaphorical passages about Flory's birthmark:

> It was not until she had quite rubbed out the imaginary stain which his lips had left there that she walked on again. . . . Even now her heart was knocking and fluttering uncomfortably. I can't *bear* that kind of thing! she repeated to herself several times over. And unfortunately this was no more than the literal truth; she really could not bear it. To be kissed or fondled by a man—to feel heavy male arms about her and thick male lips bearing down upon her own—was terrifying and repulsive to her. Even in memory or imagination it made her wince. It was her especial secret, the especial, incurable disability that she carried through life. [*CD*, p. 91]

The idea of an "incurable disability" that is not the product of society but of chance or private history clearly moves us into the realm of individual psychology, to the "merely anomalous, the merely phenomenal, the exotic, the bizarre," which, as we have seen, Rovere claims did not often concern Orwell.

It is quite possible, I think, that Orwell would have found his early novels more satisfactory if such elements had actually intruded on them less frequently than they did. One often feels that these highly charged and untypical passages have forced themselves into an alien atmosphere. It is difficult to decide what relationship they have to Orwell himself; any guess is likely to be highly speculative. It is however worth noting that the "incurable disabilities" of Flory and Dorothy Hare turn them into fringe members of their society. The same thing might be said of Gordon Comstock's poverty in *Keep the Aspidistra Flying*, a condition both curable and social in origin, but which in its effects is comparable to the disabilities of the other characters.

A considerable portion of these three books is given over to the intense expression of the feelings of futility, alienation, inadequacy, and shame; Orwell was certainly using the novels in part as vehicles for those emotions. His three main characters become outcasts of, rather than participants in, the society they describe. This condition could serve the sociological novelist well enough, since the outcast's perspective on his society often makes him a sharp and sensitive social critic. In these novels, however, we are too conscious of the neurotic nature of the three characters to trust them as commentators on the social scene. They are too thoroughly trapped by their own disabilities to speak with authority, and so we find ourselves looking curiously *at* them rather than through their eyes. This is certainly true of Dorothy Hare and Flory, true to a great extent even of Gordon Comstock.

It is only in *Coming Up for Air*, in which Orwell tried to invent a character very different from himself, that we feel we can trust the observations of the hero. Yet even in that book, we sense that Orwell often writes in a lyrical, expressive way. The whole section describing the world of Bowling's childhood, rural England before World War I, is an extraordinarily evocative piece of nostalgia. Here is a typical passage:

A Sunday afternoon—summer, of course, always summer—a smell of roast pork and greens still floating in the air, and Mother on one side of the fireplace, starting off to read the latest murder but gradually falling asleep with her mouth open, and Father on the other, in slippers and spectacles, working his way slowly through yards of smudgy print. And the soft feeling of summer all round you, the geranium in the

window, a starling cooing somewhere, and myself under the
table with the *B.O.P.*, making believe that the tablecloth is a
tent. [*CUA*, p. 47]

The lyrical, imaginative transformation of the real world in this
passage—in which a typical scene becomes an archetypal one—
exists essentially to record a deeply felt emotion, not to describe or
comment on something external to the observer. Although the
passage is not neurotic or obsessive, it is certainly highly
subjective, the product of a relaxation of the will and a surrender
to reverie.[8] So that even in the novel of the thirties in which
Orwell most obviously separates himself from the main character,
he is using the form to record intense emotions from which he had
no wish to separate himself. We recall his complaint to Symons
that "one has masses of experience which one passionately wants
to write about . . . and no way of using them up except by
disguising them as a novel" (*CEJL* 4: 422). The very phrase
"using them up" suggests that subjective material exerts a kind of
pressure on the writer until it is released in literary expression.
The novel has become a vehicle for the expression of intense
emotion.

It should be clear, then, that two very different fictional modes
are to be found in these early books—the realistic, sociological
one, which deals in familiar types and abstract ideas, and the
lyrical, expressive one, which exists to record urgent, individual
emotions. I am not, of course, suggesting that these two strains are
usually found in the pure state, or that the novelist has to make an
absolute choice between them. There are many great novels in
which they are more or less successfully combined—*Middlemarch*,
for example, or *Ulysses*—although even in those books we often
sense a tension between the two modes. It is also possible,
however, that the two forces can interfere with rather than
reinforce each other, and it seems to me that this happens
consistently in Orwell's early novels.

Too often the expressive and the sociological elements in these
books are working at cross-purposes and nearly cancel each other

8. It is also remarkably similar to Orwell's sentimental picture of working-class
life in the passage from *The Road to Wigan Pier* quoted above, pp. 120–21.

out. In *Keep the Aspidistra Flying*, for example, Orwell seems to be
attacking the materialism of his society, particularly the way in
which all human values in it are measured in financial terms. The
book apparently demonstrates how every form of idealism, all the
so-called higher pursuits—love, friendship, culture, artistic creation—are absolutely dependent on money. It has all the marks of
a thesis novel. Yet it is difficult to be sure, because the thesis is
reiterated exclusively by its poverty-stricken hero, Gordon Comstock, and part way through the book his tirades begin to seem
compulsive and exaggerated rather than authoritative. In a
crucial passage, Orwell seems to cut the ground out from under
him:

> He [Gordon] perceived that it is quite impossible to explain
> to any rich person, even to anyone so decent as Ravelston,
> the essential bloodiness of poverty. For this reason it became
> all the more important to explain it. He said suddenly:
> "Have you read Chaucer's *Man of Lawe's Tale?*"
> "The *Man of Lawe's Tale?* Not that I remember. What's it
> about?"
> "I forget. I was thinking of the first six stanzas. Where he
> talks about poverty. The way it gives everyone the right to
> stamp on you! The way everyone *wants* to stamp on you! It
> makes people *hate* you, to know that you've no money. They
> insult you just for the pleasure of insulting you and knowing
> that you can't hit back."
> Ravelston was pained. "Oh, no, surely not! People aren't
> so bad as all that."
> "Ah, but you don't know the things that happen!"
> Gordon did not want to be told that "people aren't so
> bad." He clung with a sort of painful joy to the notion that
> because he was poor everyone must *want* to insult him. It
> fitted in with his philosophy of life. [*KAF*, pp. 114–15]

It seems to me that the passage suggests a fundamental
uncertainty in Orwell's attitude toward his main character. His
speech is introduced in the first place by a phrase ("perceived that
it is quite impossible to explain to any rich person . . . the
essential bloodiness of poverty") which suggests that he is in

possession of a truth a benighted world cannot understand. When, however, we get to his explanation, its terms suggest blind rage rather than truth ("The way everyone *wants* to stamp on you! It makes people *hate* you"). It is also revealing that Gordon completely ignores Chaucer's ironic perspective on the Man of Lawe's words. Yet Ravelston's denial is certainly too weak and inconclusive to suggest authority ("Oh, no, surely not! People aren't so bad as all that"). The issue is apparently resolved by the narrator's suggestion, in the final paragraph, that Gordon is obsessed and deluded. But the resolution is temporary, for in the rest of the novel the narrator hardly ever interferes again, and Gordon's voice, attacking the society in ways that seem alternately convincing and insane, remains both unchallenged and unconfirmed.

The two possible interpretations of the book work against each other. If *Keep the Aspidistra Flying* is to be read as a sociopolitical novel exposing the corruptions of its society, Gordon's attacks must be taken at face value; he must be seen as Orwell's spokesman. If, on the other hand, the book is primarily an attempt to record the hysterical feelings of failure and alienation the condition of poverty creates, almost nothing that Gordon says about his society can be taken as true. His words must be looked at clinically, as the rant of a man driven to the wall by despair. The expressive content of the book thus seems to be in direct conflict with its political purpose. This confusion is, I believe, the product of Orwell's own ambiguous attitude toward the character he has created. It can be demonstrated that a similar ambiguity exists in the other three novels of the thirties, and that it grows directly out of Orwell's need to use fiction in two ways that are, at the least, very difficult to combine.

To add to his problems, he was writing in a time and for an audience not very sympathetic to the novel as a form. Among left-wing writers, there was widespread distrust of—even contempt for—imaginative writing of any kind. "Fiction" meant falsifying the truth of existing conditions. The reader became as interested in the character and responses of the writer as in the world the novel described. The feeling that imaginative literature was simply too frivolous and personal a vehicle for the recording of reality was common in left-wing circles. There was a demand that it be replaced by literary works modeled on the sociological study and the documentary film. The novelist Storm Jameson, for example, insisted that the writer interested in poverty go on a pilgrimage to the poor and come back with a precise knowledge of, say, the feelings of a family on the dole: "He must go for the sake of *the fact*, as a medical student carries out a dissection, and to equip himself, not to satisfy his conscience or to see what effect it has on him. His mind must remain cool; he must be able to give an objective report, neither superficial nor slickly dramatic." [9]

Many other left-wing intellectuals of the period echoed this antifictional prejudice and proposed the alternative of a documentary literature. The influential Left Book Club, for example, hardly ever selected a fictional work; and when it did so, it went through quite extraordinary formal apologies to its members. When the Club picked two novels as a monthly offering in 1936, the publisher, Victor Gollancz, wrote in the Club's newsletter: "It seemed to us that fiction of this kind [André Malraux's *Days of Contempt* and Hillel Bernstein's *Choose a Bright Morning*], if chosen with the greatest care and on rare occasions—probably only once a year, and particularly in a holiday month—would be welcome to members." And two years later, when the Club offered Belfrage's novel, *Promised Land*, Gollancz again apologized: "It is in fictional form, but the disguise is a very thin one." [10]

As the political picture darkened in the late thirties, fiction came to seem more and more of a luxury. In 1938, Stephen Spender announced, in a journal appropriately named *Fact*, that the magazine would no longer review novels, "unless they derive from a basis of factual material such as might form a number of FACT itself." A prediction made by a reviewer in another left-wing journal was accurate: "there will be an increasing division of literature into two polar categories, the purely factual and the purely imaginative." The purely factual literature was called "reportage," "documentary," or "descriptive writing," and Mon-

9. "Documents," *Fact*, no. 4 (1937), p. 12.
10. *Left Book News*, no. 3 (1936), p. 35; *Left News*, no. 22 (1938), p. 681.

tagu Slater, writing in the *Left Review*, assured his readers that it could be both "a scientific and literary discipline" and "one of the most effective means of changing an enemy's mind." [11]

The most peculiar expression of this new documentary urge was probably "Mass-Observation," an organization founded in 1936 in order to study human behavior by the technique of group observation. Its model was clinical research: "the main function of the Observer is to *describe* the components of social behaviour in an objective, scientific fashion. This is, to paraphrase Pavlov, 'an attempt to elucidate the activities of complex structures in their fullest range directly.' " Such a technique turns the writer into "a recording instrument of the facts," whose aim is to avoid *"atmosphere"* and the "air of artifice" and to create "unalloyed objectivity." The effect is to "de-value considerably the status of the 'poet,' " and to "raise" his work from subjectivity to objectivity.[12] The insistence on the superiority of documentary to imaginative literature had brought the "poet" to a strange pass, forcing him to put his title in quotation marks and become a Pavlovian clinician in order to legitimize his calling.

Orwell's three book-length documentaries—*Down and Out in Paris and London* (1933), *The Road to Wigan Pier* (1937), and *Homage to Catalonia* (1938)—were products of a similar distrust of fiction. Some of his critics feel that it was here, rather than in the novels, that he finally discovered his vocation and produced distinguished works. John Mander, for example, writes that these books, and shorter documentary essays like "Shooting an Elephant" and "A Hanging," "enabled Orwell to bring his real gifts into play, while excusing him from further psychological development of his characters." They represent, he says, "his most satisfactory achievement; the kernel of his creative work as a writer." [13] Certainly some of the problems Orwell faced in using the fictional vehicle—the inclusion of abstract essays, the interest in the generic rather than the unique, the desire to make his point

11. *Fact*, no. 20 (1938), p. 75; D. S. Savage, "Writing in Revolt," *Plan* 4 (1937): 32; Montagu Slater, "The Purpose of a Left Review," *Left Review* 1 (1935): 365.

12. C. M., "Oxford Collective Poem," *New Verse*, no. 25 (1937), p. 16; "Poetic Description and Mass-Observation," *New Verse*, no. 24 (1937), pp. 2–3.

13. Mander, *The Writer and Commitment*, p. 80.

absolutely clear—simply disappeared in the documentary, in which abstraction, typicality, and perfect clarity were virtues. There was also no need to invent imaginary situations and characters that only seemed to deflect the reader's interest from the conditions of real life. It might very well seem, then, that in the documentary Orwell had found a more congenial form than fiction had been.

The matter is not so simple, however. Although documentary writing could accommodate some of Orwell's needs, its insistence on the writer's complete objectivity, the reduction of his role to that of scientific observer, was to prove intolerable. The critical statements about the form all make this demand. Subjective elements of any kind were considered an intrusion: the writer was merely an observing machine. Orwell has been criticized for breaking these "rules." "The ideal narrator of documentary," Mander writes, "is like Defoe's hero in *A Journal of the Plague Year*, a physically mobile but psychologically passive character, whose mind we know well, but who does not obtrude his opinions on us too strongly. Documentary is concerned with the outward world, and the ordering of its apparent chaos. And, in this sense, it is a serious criticism of Orwell that we can say of his *Homage to Catalonia* (though not, I think, of *Down and Out*) that it tells us more about Orwell than about the Spanish civil war." [14]

Our analysis of the expressive content of Orwell's novels should have made it clear that he would have found such restrictions intolerable. Whenever he did limit himself to public issues and to an objective recording of the facts, he felt deeply that he had betrayed a part of himself as a writer. In a letter to Stephen Spender, he expresses some of his impatience with public subject matter: "I hate writing that kind of stuff and am much more interested in my own experiences, but unfortunately in this bloody period we are living in one's only experiences *are* being mixed up in controversies, intrigues etc. I sometimes feel as if I hadn't been properly alive since abt the beginning of 1937" (*CEJL* 1: 311). As he poses the problem here, it is insoluble—a choice between equally unsatisfactory forms of writing, one dehumanizing, the

14. Ibid., p. 108.

other self-indulgent and irrelevant. The real problem, as Orwell realized in a later essay, was not to choose between these alternatives but to find some way of combining them: "So long as I remain alive and well I shall continue to feel strongly about prose style, to love the surface of the earth, and to take pleasure in solid objects and scraps of useless information. It is no use trying to suppress that side of myself. The job is to reconcile my ingrained likes and dislikes with the essentially public, non-individual activities that this age forces on all of us" (*CEJL* 1: 6).

The reconciliation did not come easily. In fact the first of Orwell's book-length documentaries, *Down and Out in Paris and London*, seems to be an attempt to write the genre by the rules. There is a curious impersonality about it, even though it is written in the first person and records experiences that are generally taken to be autobiographical in their main outline. Its original readers must have been extremely puzzled by the book. Here was an unknown writer, writing under a pseudonym, clearly well-educated and decidedly middle-class in upbringing, recounting the story of several months spent first as a poverty-stricken dishwasher in Paris and then as a penniless vagrant in England. Who was he? What was he doing? Why couldn't he find work more suitable to his obvious qualifications? Why wasn't he helped by the relations or friends in the world he must have left to go "down and out"? Almost all of these questions remain unanswered. We find out nothing about the narrator's personal history; we have no idea what he is doing in Paris in the first place and why he is without work or money. We gather he occasionally writes, but we find out little more than that bare fact.

In the middle of the book, we are suddenly informed that he has written a letter to "my friend B. in London asking him if he could get me a job" (*DOPL*, p. 112). The mysterious "B."—who is never otherwise identified—does in fact get him a job, sends him some money for the journey from Paris, and then on his arrival informs him that he will have to wait a month to assume his new post, since his employers have gone abroad. Orwell (or "the narrator"—one hardly knows what to call this faceless creature) decides that rather than confess to "B." that he is destitute, he will depend on the charitable institutions for the next few weeks. His explanation is curiously unconvincing: "Sooner or later I should have to go to B. for more money, but it seemed hardly decent to do so yet, and in the meantime I must exist in some hole-and-corner way" (*DOPL*, p. 127).

The whole section that follows this decision—in which Orwell leads the life of a tramp, familiarizing himself with the agencies of public and private charity and exposing their evils—can lead only to the deus ex machina conclusion, the application to "B." for another loan. This fact gives a strange air of unreality to the entire intervening "down and out" narrative. It ends in a completely anticlimactic sentence: "B. lent me a final two pounds, and, as I had only another eight days to hold out, that was the end of my troubles" (*DOPL*, pp. 212–13). But if his "troubles" can be ended in such an offhand, arbitrary manner, one feels cheated into having been asked to take them seriously in the first place. There is clearly something missing: the sense of whom we are listening to in this book and what he is really doing.

Moreover, it is not simply that the "I" of the book has no personal history. His lack of identity also extends to his vision of what he describes. There is no ideological consistency to the point of view in the book. One never, I think, feels that the man who is writing this narrative has a real grasp of the meaning of the situations he describes. At times his attitude seems fatalistic, at times naïvely meliorist, at times angry, at times sentimental and celebratory. What is absent is an authoritative sense of the nature of poverty and destitution, some theoretical base that would make the "I" less of an aimless observer and more of a reliable (or even misguided) interpreter. The absence of such a point of view explains the book's extreme looseness of structure. Its arrangement is chronological, with interpolated additional narratives and bits of local color as well as informative essays on such subjects as the way hotel kitchens function or the argot of London low life. There is an obvious artlessness in all this, a suggestion that the writer is at the mercy of his material rather than in control of it. At the heart of the book there is a mysterious void.

Orwell's next work of reportage, *The Road to Wigan Pier*, almost seems to have been written out of a sense of the failure of the first. In any case, it clearly rejects the "rule" of documentary writing which insists that the narrator remain neutral and allow the observed material to speak for itself. Here, the reader can scarcely ignore Orwell's presence, and no one would be likely to mistake the book for a clinical document. *The Road to Wigan Pier* is a study of the conditions of life among working-class people, both employed and unemployed, in a northern industrial town; but at the same time, it is a study of the responses to these conditions by a middle-class London writer. Neither of these subjects can properly be called mere background for the other. Yet though they are both foreground, they are very imperfectly fused. The book is divided into two distinct parts, the first a documentary account of life among the Wigan working class, the second a long autobiographical and interpretive essay. The second part, which contains a good deal of quite personal material, is probably Orwell's most important piece of autobiographical writing. In it he talks about his family, his middle-class prejudices, his experiences in Burma, his growing disgust with British imperialism there, his acceptance of socialism. There is certainly no feeling that we are dealing with a mysterious, faceless narrator here.

Some of the book's first readers were shocked by this breach of decorum, both by the "impertinence" of the observer in thinking himself comparable in importance to the Wigan workers, and by some of his thoroughly unorthodox attitudes, for example, the admission that as a child he had been taught that the lower classes had a disagreeable smell. *The Road to Wigan Pier* was a selection of the Left Book Club, probably the most controversial one in its history. In an extraordinary preface to the Club edition, Gollancz felt obliged to justify its selection in a tortured and highly apologetic manner. Much of what he says is an attack on Orwell's ideas and attitudes in the second part of the book. It is clear that the whole section made him intensely uncomfortable, and he confessed that he had "marked well over a hundred minor passages about which I thought I should like to argue with Mr. Orwell." [15] The Club in fact prepared for mass distribution at one shilling a copy an abbreviated version of the book omitting the

15. Victor Gollancz, Foreword to George Orwell, *The Road to Wigan Pier* (London: Left Book Club Edition, 1937), p. xiv.

second part entirely and printing only the relatively objective description of Wigan: censorship masquerading as economy.[16]

There are indications in the book itself that Orwell was not breaking with the conventions of the documentary without misgivings. He feels called upon, at the beginning of the second part, to apologize for the personal nature of what follows. It is interesting that he justifies its inclusion by stressing its typicality, an impulse we have also seen in the fiction: "Here I shall have to digress and explain how my own attitude towards the class question was developed. Obviously this involves writing a certain amount of autobiography, and I would not do it if I did not think that I am sufficiently typical of my class, or rather sub-caste, to have a certain symptomatic importance" (*RWP*, p. 123). And he goes on to categorize his position in school as "the common experience of boys of the lower-upper-middle class," and its effects on him as "probably the usual ones" (*RWP*, p. 139). The justification is highly unconvincing, however, for Orwell includes a great deal of material—particularly about his deep disgust with the role he had played as a policeman in Burma—that seems quintessentially private, and certainly atypical of people in similar circumstances.

He wanted to write a documentary report on the condition of the poor in industrial England; he wanted to write a kind of spiritual autobiography. In *The Road to Wigan Pier*, the two are yoked by violence together. The result is a rich and interesting work, which nevertheless has serious structural flaws. It is not merely that Orwell has written two separate books, each of which could be regarded as a coherent unit. One has a sense of fragmentation within the sections as well, of starts and stops, mysterious shifts from description to narration, from narration to tangentially relevant analytic essays, from essays to confession, from confession to exhortation. The very multiplicity of elements compounds the problem of coherence that already defeated Orwell in the much simpler *Down and Out in Paris and London*. There was certainly a guiding intelligence here, a narrator who did not simply disappear behind the mask of his objectivity; but

16. See *Left News*, no. 11 (1937), p. 247.

he had only been permitted to come in by the back door, and with profuse apologies. He was not yet in full control of the proceedings.

By the time he came to write *Homage to Catalonia*, Orwell no longer felt obliged to pretend that any part of his book was purely objective reporting. His account of the Spanish Civil War is also consistently and unapologetically a personal narrative, a history of Orwell's responses to the events he describes. The two subjects are not artificially separated, as they were in *The Road to Wigan Pier*, but are kept continuously present. The very title suggests the importance of the subjective element: "homage" rather than description; Catalonia, where Orwell was actually stationed, rather than Spain as a whole. In the book itself, Orwell twice warns the reader to take into account the author's bias: "I have tried to write objectively about the Barcelona fighting, though, obviously, no one can be completely objective on a question of this kind. One is practically obliged to take sides, and it must be clear enough which side I am on. . . . I warn everyone against my bias, and I warn everyone against my mistakes" (*HC*, p. 170). And again in the final pages, he says, "beware of my partisanship, my mistakes of fact and the distortion inevitably caused by my having seen only one corner of events" (*HC*, p. 247).

Homage to Catalonia thus has two narrative strands, one concerned with external events, the other with internal ones. The first records what happened in Catalonia between December 1936 and the middle of 1937 and argues that in these crucial months the genuine socialist revolution which had taken place there was betrayed. The second—the internal narrative—records the process of Orwell's own education, from the naïve idealist of the early pages to the hard-headed realist of the last. These two strands are constantly related in the book. It is impossible to separate them because the external events directly contribute to Orwell's education, which in turn leads him to see a pattern in those events rather than merely recording them as meaningless facts. At one point in the book he worries about whether he has been able to suggest enough of the *internal* meaning of what he describes: "I suppose I have failed to convey more than a little of what those months in Spain mean to me. I have recorded some of the outward events, but I cannot record the feeling they have left me with" (*HC*, p. 246).

Despite this apology, the book constantly and very movingly describes Orwell's personal responses. Here, for example, is part of the description of his first sight of Barcelona:

> Waiters and shop-walkers looked you in the face and treated you as an equal. Servile and even ceremonial forms of speech had temporarily disappeared. . . . The revolutionary posters were everywhere, flaming from the walls in clean reds and blues that made the few remaining advertisements look like daubs of mud. Down the Ramblas, the wide central artery of the town where crowds of people streamed constantly to and fro, the loud-speakers were bellowing revolutionary songs all day and far into the night. And it was the aspect of the crowds that was the queerest thing of all. In outward appearance it was a town in which the wealthy classes had practically ceased to exist. Except for a small number of women and foreigners there were no 'well-dressed' people at all. Practically everyone wore rough working-class clothes, or blue overalls or some variant of the militia uniform. All this was queer and moving. There was much in it that I did not understand, in some ways I did not even like it, but I recognized it immediately as a state of affairs worth fighting for. [*HC*, p. 3]

The transition in this passage from meticulous objective description to subjective response is effortless and natural. Orwell's feelings are introduced without apology and without trying to make them appear representative. After the abortive experiments of *Down and Out in Paris and London* and *The Road to Wigan Pier*, Orwell had found a way of making the documentary both a descriptive and an expressive form. In doing so, he had revolutionized the genre in a way that had seemed impossible when he was working with realistic fiction.

Yet if *Homage to Catalonia* was the best of Orwell's documentaries, it was also the last, and this fact demands explanation. He certainly had a sense of the book's quality; he wrote to his agent in 1945 that it was "about the best I have written" (*CEJL* 3: 392).

Why then did he not go on, in the last dozen years of his life, writing in the form he had so triumphantly molded to his needs? His most important works in the 1940s were either essays or fantasies. With one exception, "How the Poor Die," the major essays published after 1939 are theoretical rather than documentary; and even "How the Poor Die," which was first published in 1946, is about experiences Orwell had in 1929. The two book-length works of the 1940s, *Animal Farm* and *Nineteen Eighty-Four*, are radical departures from the realistic fiction and reportage of the previous decade.

The fact is that Orwell was nearly as dissatisfied with the documentary form as he had been with the novel. We have seen that he originally turned toward fiction partly because it might bring him a large readership. Although *The Road to Wigan Pier* was a Left Book Club selection and consequently widely read (or at least owned), the documentary form was in general not likely to bring a writer to the attention of a large audience. *Homage to Catalonia*, for example, sold about nine hundred copies from the time of its publication to Orwell's death, and it was only published in America after his last two books had made him world-famous.[17] The factual could not compete in its appeal with the imaginary world of fiction. Of course, it might have been possible to transform the documentary into a highly charged, passionate form, but this Orwell was unwilling to do. He had made the documentary into a personal vehicle, but he could not turn it into an irrational one. In these books, he constantly passes up opportunities for emotional writing in favor of cool observation. When a sniper's bullet goes clean through his neck in Spain, he begins his description of the incident with the deadpan sentence, "The whole experience of being hit by a bullet is very interesting and I think it is worth describing in detail" (*HC*, p. 198).

The attempt to convey horror in such objective terms, Orwell eventually came to feel, was doomed. The documentary form, with its facts and statistics, its subject matter so exotic to a

17. Christopher Hollis, *A Study of George Orwell: The Man and His Works* (London, 1956), p. 107.

comfortable middle-class audience, and its dry intellectual base, seemed to leave an essential part of the reader's psyche untouched. In an essay in *Tribune* that begins as a review of Gollancz's *In Darkest Germany*, a documentary report of conditions in the British zone of occupation after the war, Orwell raises the whole problem of the failure of the genre:

> [*In Darkest Germany*] is not a literary book, but a piece of brilliant journalism intended to shock the public of this country into some kind of consciousness of the hunger, disease, chaos and lunatic mismanagement prevailing in the British Zone. This business of making people *conscious* of what is happening outside their own small circle is one of the major problems of our time, and a new literary technique will have to be evolved to meet it. Considering that the people of this country are not having a very comfortable time, you can't, perhaps, blame them for being somewhat callous about suffering elsewhere, but the remarkable thing is the extent to which they manage to remain unaware of it. Tales of starvation, ruined cities, concentration camps, mass deportations, homeless refugees, persecuted Jews—all this is received with a sort of incurious surprise, as though such things had never been heard of before but at the same time were not particularly interesting. The now-familiar photographs of skeleton-like children make very little impression. As time goes on and the horrors pile up, the mind seems to secrete a sort of self-protecting ignorance which needs a harder and harder shock to pierce it, just as the body will become immunised to a drug and require bigger and bigger doses. [*CEJL* 4: 270]

The documentary seemed unable to awaken the mind out of its torpor. Its fundamental assumptions made it unfit for this task. As Orwell sees, "a new literary technique" had to be evolved to break through the wall of indifference the horrors of the last decade had built up.

Writers had taken to the documentary form in the first place out of a sense of urgency. Some intolerable human condition was being allowed to persist because of people's ignorance; it de-

manded to be exposed, and reportage was taken to be the
indispensable tool for this purpose. Orwell's doubts about the
form grew out of a conviction that it was not doing its work, that
it was in fact the wrong tool for the job. If this was true, his
sacrifices in using it were wasted. Those sacrifices had been heavy:
the demands of reportage constantly conflicted with Orwell's
aesthetic instincts. The urgency and immediacy of the issues often
dictated the form and content of the final work, rather than
permitting the writer freedom in choosing his materials. Orwell
describes how this happened even in *Homage to Catalonia*:

> My book about the Spanish civil war, *Homage to Catalonia*, is,
> of course, a frankly political book, but in the main it is
> written with a certain detachment and regard for form. I did
> try very hard in it to tell the whole truth without violating
> my literary instincts. But among other things it contains a
> long chapter, full of newspaper quotations and the like,
> defending the Trotskyists who were accused of plotting with
> Franco. Clearly such a chapter, which after a year or two
> would lose its interest for any ordinary reader, must ruin the
> book. A critic whom I respect read me a lecture about it.
> "Why did you put in all that stuff?" he said. "You've turned
> what might have been a good book into journalism." What
> he said was true, but I could not have done otherwise. I
> happened to know, what very few people in England had
> been allowed to know, that innocent men were being falsely
> accused. If I had not been angry about that I should never
> have written the book. [*CEJL* 1: 6]

The conflict Orwell describes is the classic one for the writer of
documentaries: on the one hand there is the artist's need to shape
his work, to be in complete control of its subject matter, language,
structure, and tone; on the other there is the raw material of the
book, which seems to demand attention for its own sake and often
forces the writer to ignore aesthetic considerations. The artist's
need for detachment and concern for form are constantly
threatened by the chaos of the actual materials; but he ignores
that chaos at his peril, for at its heart lies his impulse to write.
Although there is always a conflict between raw material and

form in the creation of a literary work, it is greater in documentary writing than in fiction, simply because facts (especially historically important facts, known to one's audience from other sources) exert a pressure, and seem to form a pattern, of their own. There is a kind of tyranny here, the tyranny of subject matter which it has become impossible to control. Orwell realized that the writers of the thirties had largely surrendered aesthetic detachment because "what books were *about* seemed so urgently important that the way they were written seemed almost insignificant" (*CEJL* 2: 126).

The urgency of the issues created another problem for the writer with an artistic conscience, that of dealing with strictly contemporary subject matter. The conditions described in documentary literature changed from day to day; it was part of the task of such literature to assist in that change, to exert pressure in a certain direction. The inevitable effect was to turn these works into journalistic writing that would seem hopelessly dated a few months after publication. The last chapters of *The Road to Wigan Pier*, for example, are almost impossible to take seriously today; their absurd prophecies of the coming of fascism to Britain and their tone of hysteria are typical of the excesses of the political writing of the period. They are written out of the moment—and inevitably for the moment. Reading them more than three decades later, we are conscious primarily of their strained rhetoric.

Orwell was deeply preoccupied with the danger of using contemporary subject matter in works that made any claim to permanence. He saw it, finally, as an impossibility. In a letter written near the end of his life to T. R. Fyvel, who had succeeded him as literary editor of *Tribune*, he complained: "You are always attacking novelists for not writing about the contemporary scene. But can you think of a novel that ever was written about the strictly contemporary scene? It is very unlikely that any novel, i.e. worth reading, would ever be set back less than three years at least. If you tried, *in* 1949, to write a novel about 1949 it would simply be 'reportage' and probably would seem out of date and silly before you could get it into print" (*CEJL* 4: 496–97). This contemptuous dismissal of the whole genre of "reportage" suggests

how alien some of Orwell's most significant work of the thirties
had become to him by the next decade.

He was not alone in this feeling. By 1940, most of the important
left-wing writers in England had had their fill of crisis literature
and the primacy of the political purpose. The statement of policy
of the most influential literary journal of the forties, *Horizon*, put
the matter succinctly: "Our standards are aesthetic, and our
politics are in abeyance." [18] Its editor, Cyril Connolly, wrote a
book in the early forties that begins: "The more books we read,
the clearer it becomes that the true function of a writer is to
produce a masterpiece and that no other task is of any consequence. . . . Every excursion into journalism, broadcasting,
propaganda and writing for the films, however grandiose, will be
doomed to disappointment. To put our best into these is another
folly, since thereby we condemn good ideas as well as bad to
oblivion. It is in the nature of such work not to last, and it should
never be undertaken." [19]

Orwell would have been sympathetic to this impatience with
ephemeral writing, especially by the middle of the war, after ten
years of journalism, commissioned reportage, and exposé fiction.
Much of what he had produced had been written out of a sense of
imminent catastrophe or a need for money. By the end of the
thirties he realized that he must begin to write with as much
loyalty to the work itself as to any political cause. But it is just
here that his attitude must be differentiated from that of the
disillusioned left-wing writers of the decade. For Orwell could
never say that his politics were in abeyance and his standards
purely aesthetic. It was precisely when he wrote without a
political purpose that he "was betrayed into purple passages,
sentences without meaning, decorative adjectives and humbug
generally," as he says in "Why I Write" (*CEJL* 1: 7).

The real problem was to see one's political purpose in a context
less confining than the immediate present. Every local abuse,
every temporary crisis could make both political and human sense
only when seen as the product of forces that were always present.

18. "Comment," *Horizon* 1 (1940): 5.
19. Palinurus [pseud.], *The Unquiet Grave* (London, 1952), p. 1.

And to see it in these terms meant approaching a kind of aesthetic detachment. In 1946, Orwell wrote that what he had most wanted to do throughout the past ten years was "to make political writing into an art" (*CEJL* 1: 6). In that attempt, he abandoned the genres in which he had specialized in the thirties—the realistic novel and the documentary—and began to write in two forms that promised him greater freedom: the essay and fantasy.

7

The Search for Form: The 1940s

Most of Orwell's important work in the 1940s grows out of a determination to put some distance between himself and the demands of the moment. That he could do so is particularly remarkable given the hysterical pressure of the war, which forced people to think in short-range terms: today's headline, tomorrow's danger. Orwell was certainly not detached from day-to-day events, as the wartime diary he kept clearly shows. Yet despite his complaints in the early years of the war that serious writing was impossible under such circumstances, that "only the mentally dead are capable of sitting down and writing novels while this nightmare is going on" (*CEJL* 2: 54), he managed to produce a remarkable number of works immediately before and during the war years that have lasted: *Animal Farm* (written November 1943–February 1944) as well as major essays like "Charles Dickens," "Boys' Weeklies," "Inside the Whale," "The Art of Donald McGill," "Looking Back on the Spanish War," and "Notes on Nationalism."

There is a sense of contemplative detachment in these and later works of the forties that differs markedly from the tone of his work in the thirties. The journalist becomes a historian: time becomes comprehensible in its larger patterns. The past is revisited, the future imagined. In order to see contemporary life from such a perspective, Orwell needed different literary forms. The documentary and the realistic novel began to strike him as myopic genres that forced the writer to concentrate excessively on the world immediately before his eyes. He needed forms that would permit his mind to range and to imagine at will, and he found them in the essay and in fantasy. Almost all of Orwell's longer essays, as well as his two departures from realistic fiction, were published in the 1940s. Even when these essays turned into miniature documentaries (as in "How the Poor Die" and "Such,

Such Were the Joys"), they were reminiscences about the past rather than reports from the present. A need for historical perspective, for breathing space, is everywhere apparent in the works of Orwell's last ten years. The essayistic intrusions in the novels and documentaries of the thirties make it clear that Orwell's interest in the essay as a form of expression was a constant element of his career. I have suggested that his need to write essays—that is, to explain his ideas directly rather than in fictional disguise—interrupts the natural flow of his narratives. And we have seen that Orwell himself thought the essay in defense of the Trotskyists in *Homage to Catalonia* worked against the "detachment and regard for form" of the book as a whole (*CEJL* 1: 6). But it was only toward the end of the thirties that he began to think seriously about the essay as an independent, expressive form. He was drawn to it because it finally gave him the opportunity to abandon the strained ventriloquism of his novels and to speak in his own voice. The hero of the early novels is consistently less perceptive than his creator, yet he is always the center of consciousness. Flory, Dorothy Hare, Gordon Comstock, George Bowling (even, later on, Winston Smith) are all treated with fundamental sympathy. In each case, however, we sense a disparity between their level of understanding and Orwell's own. Yet their helpless confusion must be taken seriously in the books themselves because Orwell is interested in tracing the gradual process by which these people begin to make sense of their circumstances.

Such a subject demands great self-control on the part of the writer, and it is clear that it did not come easily to Orwell. Occasionally, his annoyance with the character's limited understanding breaks through in an impatient aside, as in this sentence from *A Clergyman's Daughter* about Dorothy's reaction to Warburton: "For all his vices he was distinctly likeable, and the shoddy brilliance of his conversation—Oscar Wilde seven times watered —*which she was too inexperienced to see through*, fascinated while it shocked her" (*CD*, pp. 49–50; italics added). More frequently, however, the novel will plod along with the character step by step through all the stages of his confusion without insisting on his limited insight. This is particularly true of *Coming Up for Air*, in which, as we have seen, Orwell attempts to eliminate his own voice altogether and turns the novel over to his hero-narrator. Such fictional techniques are a form of self-denial. They are clearly connected with the occasional short essays in these books, in which the impatient author is allowed to take over from his characters for a few moments before he surrenders his novel to them once again.

As his experience became more extensive and his analytic intelligence sharper, Orwell must have felt the need to expand these passages in his novels and documentaries into full-scale essays. More and more in the last ten years of his life, he wanted to express his ideas directly, in his own voice and at his own level of insight. This need is related to Orwell's attacks on the English intelligentsia, which were based on the conviction that they had abused their trust and betrayed their own intelligence. Marx had said, "The philosophers have only *interpreted* the world, in various ways; the point, however, is to *change* it." [1] But in their impatience to change the world, the new left-wing intellectuals had largely given up the task of interpreting it accurately and clear-sightedly in the first place. Orwell felt that their writings were more often the product of unconscious wish and conscious deception than of observation.

In such a situation, there was a need for "a free intelligence" willing to observe and interpret without ideological bias, and with the honesty to reveal all the contradictions that came to light without fear of betraying his cause. Orwell soon saw this need as his calling and his opportunity. The depth, intellectual seriousness, and sense of personal witness revealed in the essays of the forties are all products of his sense of mission. He was no longer merely an observer. There were certain truths he seemed capable of seeing, to which his contemporaries remained blind. The long essay became the instrument of his vision.

There is an obvious paradox here. The kind of essay Orwell chose to write—whether it is classified as literary criticism, sociological analysis, or political commentary—seems to offer few

1. "Theses on Feuerbach," in Karl Marx and Frederick Engels, *Selected Works in Two Volumes* (Moscow, 1962), 2: 405.

opportunities for "self-expression." Each has a manifest subject to which Orwell must address himself: the work of Dickens or of Swift, the phenomenon of literary censorship or of anti-Semitism, the political theory of James Burnham or of Gandhi, and so on. Many of these essays begin with a journalistic occasion of some kind—the publication of a book, or an event in the news. Orwell is obliged to address himself to that occasion, or in any case to the task of saying plausible things about the subject before him. The ability to turn these restrictions into opportunities is one of the marks of a great essayist. He treats the *occasion* of the essay as a given which nevertheless allows him considerable interpretive freedom. The only necessity is that he care deeply about the problem under investigation: that it be pressing rather than merely "interesting." Under such conditions, the essay—literary, sociological, or political—can become a work of art.

Of course such work presupposes a considerable freedom from journalistic restrictions. Most of Orwell's nonfictional prose of the previous decade had been determined by the formulas of the journals for which he wrote. He produced these pieces to support himself, and this meant accepting the conditions of literary journalism: the endless batches of new books to review, whether he was in fact interested in them or not, the specified length (usually much too short to develop his ideas adequately), the popular style, the need to introduce and summarize the subject. By the 1940s, however, his growing reputation allowed him to make his own conditions. Many of the journals to which he began to contribute at this time were anxious to publish his work no matter what its ostensible subject matter. He could review the books he found interesting and develop his ideas at length. He could write for an audience "where he had no need to explain his references as he went along." [2] He could even write essays that

2. Sonia Orwell, Introduction, *CEJL* 1: xvii. Orwell knew that such essays were different in kind from his journalism and that they were likely to last. He wrote to his agent, "I think sooner or later a book of reprinted critical articles mightn't be a bad idea, but I don't think it's worth reprinting anything shorter than 2000 words. Books made up of short reviews always seem to me to have a hurried scrappy appearance. We must wait till I have 10 or 20 long articles in pickle" (MS letter to Leonard Moore, 6 December 1943, Berg Collection, New York Public Library).

had no connection with a current occasion. The freedom that journals like *Horizon*, *Polemic*, and *Partisan Review* allowed him made it possible for Orwell to use the essay as an expressive form. To read through the posthumously published *Collected Essays* is to become aware of the persistence of certain themes, particularly the relationship between literature and politics, the nature of popular culture, and the threat of totalitarianism. No matter what the occasion of the essay, Orwell returns again and again to these problems. The presence of such obsessive subject matter is a sign that Orwell is using these essays as a way of working through problems that have a personal urgency for him. We find him, for example, using many of the essays of the forties to investigate a phenomenon that we have seen disturbed him deeply: the lust for power. The essays in which this subject becomes important are remarkable for the variety of their ostensible subjects: "Raffles and Miss Blandish" is about detective fiction; "Wells, Hitler and the World State" and "Lear, Tolstoy and the Fool" discuss important literary figures; "James Burnham and the Managerial Revolution" analyzes certain political ideas; "Such, Such Were the Joys" recalls Orwell's school days. Yet each of these essays deals at some point with the desire for power over others, and these passages are often the most interesting part of the essay.

The section in "Lear, Tolstoy and the Fool" on Tolstoy's intellectual brutality, his need to coerce others into thinking as he did, may take the essay away from its original subject, yet it clearly stimulates Orwell's imagination. He has found a subject he cannot treat with mere clinical detachment and polite interest. His desire to talk about it is a powerful, private need. It is worth quoting a long passage from this essay to demonstrate how Orwell moves from his "occasion" to his true subject:

> Tolstoy renounced wealth, fame and privilege; he abjured violence in all its forms and was ready to suffer for doing so; but it is not so easy to believe that he abjured the principle of coercion, or at least the *desire* to coerce others. There are families in which the father will say to his child, "You'll get a thick ear if you do that again," while the mother, her eyes brimming over with tears, will take the child in her arms and

murmur lovingly, "Now, darling, *is* it kind to Mummy to do that?" And who would maintain that the second method is less tyrannous than the first? The distinction that really matters is not between violence and non-violence, but between having and not having the appetite for power. There are people who are convinced of the wickedness both of armies and of police forces, but who are nevertheless much more intolerant and inquisitorial in outlook than the normal person who believes that it is necessary to use violence in certain circumstances. They will not say to somebody else, "Do this, that and the other or you will go to prison," but they will, if they can, get inside his brain and dictate his thoughts for him in the minutest particulars. [*CEJL* 4: 301]

Such passages combine two distinct traditions of the essay: the formal and the familiar. The familiar essay has its roots in Montaigne, whose great merit, according to Hazlitt, was that he was "the first who had the courage to say as an author what he felt as a man." [3] The vogue of the familiar essay in the nineteenth century exploited this license to reveal oneself. In doing so, however, it seemed to make it difficult for the essayist to deal with the important issues of the day and divorced him from the tradition of the formal periodical essays of the previous century. In the words of one literary historian, "the ulterior purpose of the eighteenth-century essay—to hold the mirror up to nature and reform society of its foibles if not its vices—is at variance with the spirit of the familiar essay." [4] This antithesis would have struck Orwell as unfortunate. He tried to perfect a kind of essay that would combine the desire to analyze and reform society with the need to say as an author what one felt as a man. His best essays are personally expressive and yet illuminate the world outside the self. The subjective and objective components in them seem perfectly balanced.

Although he may not have thought of his own contribution in

3. William Hazlitt, "On the Periodical Essayists," *Lectures on the English Comic Writers* (London: Everyman, n.d.), p. 92.

4. Melvin R. Watson, "The *Spectator* Tradition and the Development of the Familiar Essay," *ELH* 13 (1946): 192.

such long-range historical terms, there is no doubt that in the
forties Orwell became quite self-conscious about the essay as a
form, particularly when it was used for political subjects. This was
part of his determination since the mid-thirties "to make political
writing into an art." Around 1935, Orwell began to put together
an extensive collection of pamphlets on political and social
questions. With Reginald Reynolds, he later edited an interesting
anthology called British Pamphleteers, which was intended to
illustrate the evolution of the genre. In the introduction to that
edition, Orwell argues that such works are examples of "a special
literary form which has persisted without radical change for
hundreds of years, though it has had its good periods and its bad
ones." And he hopes that people will "once again become aware
of the possibilities of the pamphlet as a method of influencing
opinion, and as a literary form: in other words, that the prestige of
the pamphlet should be restored." [5]

Orwell's study of the history of the political essay revealed that
the form had degenerated markedly in the twentieth century. The
earlier pamphlets in his anthology had a kind of vitality that
revealed the presence of an individual voice, even when they were
written for a party or a clearly identifiable cause. The contemporary examples seemed to have been written by committees. The
ideological orthodoxy of modern political movements, Orwell
says, robs these essays of their individuality and life: "A modern
political hack, boosting some doubtful cause, would be very
unlikely to show the same humour and ingenuity, because he
could never allow his imagination to range so freely. Party
orthodoxy would not only take all the colour out of his
vocabulary, but would dictate the main lines of his argument in
advance." [6] The ideal of orthodox political writing was impersonality—the elimination of the writer as an important presence in
the essay. Clearly this conflicted with Orwell's determination to
combine political and social analysis with absolute sincerity of
statement.

5. George Orwell, Introduction, British Pamphleteers, ed. George Orwell and
Reginald Reynolds (London, 1948), 1: 7, 16. Orwell's extensive collection of
modern political pamphlets is now in the British Museum.

6. Ibid., p. 14.

This problem is related to Orwell's well-known study of modern prose style, "Politics and the English Language." Most of the appalling examples in that piece come from political or literary essays; all illustrate what has happened to nonfictional prose in the twentieth century. Orwell concludes that the most important cause of the degeneration he records is that the writers he quotes do not have the courage to say what they really think: "The great enemy of clear language is insincerity. When there is a gap between one's real and one's declared aims, one turns as it were instinctively to long words and exhausted idioms, like a cuttlefish squirting out ink" (*CEJL* 4: 137).

This kind of analysis of the writer's language, his most basic tool, is clearly connected with Orwell's desire to revitalize the essay as a literary form. He argues that the essay demands conscious craftsmanship as well as passion and sincerity, and that its words must be as carefully chosen as those of a poem. By the mid-forties, Orwell must have known that the essay had become an indispensable medium for him as a writer, and he was anxious for readers to treat it as a genre worthy of serious attention from both a political and an aesthetic point of view. "Politics and the English Language" is a self-conscious attempt to formulate a viable theory of nonfictional prose style. It rests on the assumption of the potential dignity and importance of the essay form.

The political essay had degenerated in recent times because it had become propagandistic in intent. Propaganda was considered a necessity of war, yet one of the entries in Orwell's wartime diary shows that he was not at all resigned to its omnipresence:

> We are all drowning in filth. When I talk to anyone or read the writings of anyone who has an axe to grind, I feel that intellectual honesty and balanced judgement have simply disappeared from the face of the earth. Everyone's thought is forensic, everyone is simply putting a "case" with deliberate suppression of his opponent's point of view, and, what is more, with complete insensitiveness to any sufferings except those of himself and his friends. . . . But is there no one who has both firm opinions and a balanced outlook? Actually there are plenty, but they are powerless. All power is in the hands of paranoiacs. [*CEJL* 2: 423]

If the essay was to be saved as a literary form, and if the political world was to be rescued from paranoid habits of mind, this trend had to be reversed. The characteristic coolness and fairness of Orwell's essays is a calculated response to the hysteria of the world around him.

In his own essays on political subjects, Orwell consistently tries to substitute analysis for propaganda. He deliberately treats highly controversial subject matter with a kind of scrupulous detachment. This tendency soon becomes a hallmark of his style. He is always asking the question *why* instead of apportioning praise or blame. A good example is the essay on Salvador Dali, "Benefit of Clergy." Dali's work had been violently attacked and defended, yet neither position had cast much light on his achievement. Orwell tries to shift the emphasis: "The question is not so much *what* he is as *why* he is like that. . . . The important thing is not to denounce him as a cad who ought to be horse-whipped or to defend him as a genius who ought not to be questioned, but to find out *why* he exhibits that particular set of aberrations" (*CEJL* 3: 161).

Similarly, he is impatient with the irrational protests that greeted P. G. Wodehouse's broadcasts on the German radio during the war. Wodehouse's countrymen responded by banning his books and accusing him of fascism, but Orwell insists that his actions "do not convict Wodehouse of anything worse than stupidity. The really interesting question is how and why he could be so stupid" (*CEJL* 3: 344). Once again, "the really interesting question" becomes an occasion for analysis rather than for apportioning praise or blame. Orwell's attitude toward intellectual disagreement turns steadily more clinical in the 1940s, and his later essays demonstrate considerable psychological insight as he becomes interested in the pathology of political belief.

This does not mean, however, that his political and moral convictions are suppressed or forgotten. His allegiances remain firm, but he is determined not to close his mind to the nature of the enemy. The propagandist characteristically refuses to allow the rival point of view a hearing. In rescuing the essay from this kind of thinking, Orwell regularly defends the pariah of the Left and criticizes its current hero. He knows and directly addresses his audience's easy prejudices. When Kipling and Wodehouse are out of favor, he insists on presenting the case for them. When Gandhi is hailed as a saint, Orwell begins his essay about him with a serious paradox: "Saints should always be judged guilty until they are proved innocent" (*CEJL* 4: 463). Yet neither does he succumb to the temptations of counterpropaganda. The essay on Gandhi, for example, ends with this highly ambiguous sentence, its ambiguity an index of the complexity of Orwell's mind:

> One may feel, as I do, a sort of aesthetic distaste for Gandhi, one may reject the claims of sainthood made on his behalf (he never made any such claim himself, by the way), one may also reject sainthood as an ideal and therefore feel that Gandhi's basic aims were anti-human and reactionary: but regarded simply as a politician, and compared with the other leading political figures of our time, how clean a smell he has managed to leave behind! [*CEJL* 4: 470]

The habits of mind that had made English political essays seem unreadable except to the disciples of the cause for which they were written had had an equally disastrous effect on literary criticism. It is impossible to separate Orwell's political from his literary essays. He not only addresses himself to the same problems in both but constantly explores the areas of intersection between the two provinces. His literary essays are best read as an attempt to use the assumptions of Marxist criticism in a legitimate way. Orwell accepts certain basic elements of Marxist aesthetics: the interest in "tendency" and in the writer's audience, the conviction that all literature is, at least unconsciously, propagandistic, the belief that culture is a superstructure largely determined by economic causes. What appalled him was the way in which these ideas had been used as the basis for the *evaluation* rather than simply the understanding of literature. In the hands of committed intellectuals and political bureaucrats, the artist's "tendency" and class loyalty became a reliable guide to assessing his achievement. In the thirties, literary discussion had become more and more blatantly coercive, its ultimate aim to turn literature into conscious propaganda for the "right" side.

It is important to realize, however, that Orwell's dislike of this trend in left-wing literary criticism was not based on the argument that such issues were irrelevant and that all standards of judgment should be aesthetic. He clearly had little interest in literary discussion that concerned itself only with technique and ignored the writer's fundamental values. Nevertheless, his "Marxist" criticism was very unfashionable. He was in effect reaching back past the literary policies of Lenin, Stalin, and Zhdanov, to the aesthetic attitudes of Marx, Engels, and Plekhanov. For the founders of Marxism had no policy toward the arts and did not hesitate to recognize the genius of writers whose underlying political assumptions they found distasteful. Engels's attitude toward Balzac is a good example, and it reminds us of the fundamental complexity of mind we saw in Orwell's essay on Gandhi:

> Balzac was politically a legitimist; his great work is a constant elegy on the irreparable decay of good society; his sympathies are with the class that is doomed to extinction. But for all that, his satire is never keener, his irony never more bitter, than when he sets in motion the very men and women with whom he sympathizes most deeply—the nobles.[7]

Such generosity and subtlety of mind had all but disappeared among politically conscious literary critics in the thirties. Conservative or reactionary writers were treated as aesthetically defective. Critics had succumbed to the temptation "to claim that any book whose tendency one disagrees with must be a bad book from a *literary* point of view" (*CEJL* 3: 365). In order to bring the criticism of the Left back from this simplistic world, Orwell first of all had to insist on the elementary but seemingly forgotten principle that a great work could be written for the "wrong" side. His essays on Yeats, Kipling, and Swift are all based on this assumption. The point of view is consistently generous, even when Orwell is obviously repelled by the writer's political loyalties. He acknowledges that "by and large the best writers of our time have been reactionary in tendency." As in the more strictly political

7. Karl Marx and Frederick Engels, *Literature and Art: Selections from Their Writings* (New York, 1947), p. 43.

essays, this fact arouses his curiosity, not his anger: "The relationship between Fascism and the literary intelligentsia badly needs investigating, and Yeats might well be the starting-point." And he concludes that such questions are best answered by a critic who "knows that a writer's political and religious beliefs are not excrescences to be laughed away, but something that will leave their mark even on the smallest detail of his work" (*CEJL* 2: 276).

This is Orwell's own fundamental interest as a literary critic—to uncover a writer's largely unconscious political beliefs and then to show how they "leave their mark even on the smallest detail of his work." The finest example of this method is his important essay on Dickens. It is apparent there that his deviation from Marxist literary criticism was not simply a matter of substituting analysis for polemic but also an expression of his impatience with the crude categories often used in such discussion. A writer's class loyalty could be a highly complex matter, and great artists are not easily pigeonholed. Orwell recalls Gilbert Murray's rueful anecdote about lecturing on Shakespeare to a socialist debating society: "At the end he called for questions in the usual way, to receive as the sole question asked: 'Was Shakespeare a capitalist?' " (*CEJL* 2: 294).

The Dickens essay can be read as an attack on the simplemindedness of such thinking. Orwell addresses himself throughout to the question of whether Dickens could be considered a writer with radical political sympathies. He argues that Dickens's class loyalties are much more complex than any of the standard Marxist labels would suggest. For one thing, his picture of the lower classes is very unrepresentative: Dickens's criminals and servants can hardly be made to stand for the proletariat. And his feelings about industrialists, shopkeepers, and people who are merely respectably well off are so different that they cannot be lumped together to suggest a single attitude toward the bourgeoisie. Orwell criticizes Marxist literary terminology as a blunt instrument, insensitive to shades and to the vital internal distinctions and contradictions in a literary work. Yet his criticism accepts the legitimacy of the fundamental questions that Marxist (unlike purely aesthetic) literary criticism poses; the essay on

Dickens is a serious attempt to understand Dickens's social and political attitudes. Once again, Orwell writes as an internal critic of the Left, as a man trying to reform the abuses of his own camp. What he once said about the work of Edmund Wilson applies equally well to his own literary essays: Wilson "is one of the few literary critics of our day who give the impression . . . of having digested Marx's teachings instead of merely rejecting them or swallowing them whole." [8]

Orwell's literary essays are a critique not only of the excesses of Marxist criticism but of the assumptions of the rival camp—the apolitical, purely aesthetic literary experts. He disliked the unconscious elitism of the latter group, which found expression in their coterie methods and their indifference to popular culture. Orwell's own critical essays are remarkably untechnical and unprofessional, and the scholar in any of the fields he writes about will have no difficulty finding a number of distortions of fact or perversions of judgment. Yet Lionel Trilling's defense of Orwell's political writings applies equally to his literary criticism. Orwell, he says, "frees us from the need for the inside dope. He implies that our job is not to be intellectual, certainly not to be intellectual in this fashion or that, but merely to be intelligent according to our lights." [9] Despite their implicit critique of the cult of the expert, nevertheless, the best of Orwell's literary essays suggest that he has immersed himself in the subject. The generalizations in such essays as "Charles Dickens" and "Boys' Weeklies," for example, seem to grow out of a lifelong familiarity with the material. As Mrs. Leavis wrote in her review of Orwell's first volume of literary criticism, "because what he knows is live information, not card-index rubbish, his knowledge functions." [10]

More important than his method is his subject matter. Orwell was one of the first writers with a literary sensibility to take popular culture seriously and to show that the attempt to understand it could be an absorbing and revealing discipline. He was thoroughly aware of what he was doing. He says of his own

8. George Orwell, "An American Critic," *Observer*, 10 May 1942, p. 3.
9. *The Opposing Self* (New York, 1959), p. 158.
10. Q. D. Leavis, "The Literary Life Respectable," *Scrutiny* 9 (1940): 174.

Critical Essays, for example, that they are "instructive more from the sociological than from the literary point of view." [11] In practice, this means that Orwell is less interested in the work itself than in what it reveals about the sensibility of its author or the fundamental values of its audience. His essays treat individual works and literary trends as *symptoms* rather than as final facts. For example, he says of the literature on sale in a small newsagent's shop that it "is the best available indication of what the mass of the English people really feels and thinks" (*CEJL* 1: 461). And though he knows that Rupert Brooke's once popular poem "Grantchester" is "something worse than worthless" from an aesthetic point of view, "as an illustration of what the thinking middle-class young of that period *felt* it is a valuable document" (*CEJL* 1: 503). He consistently uses popular literature as a tool of sociological investigation. His analysis of two detective novels in "Raffles and Miss Blandish," for instance, focuses on "the immense difference in moral atmosphere between the two books, and the change in the popular attitude that this probably implies" (*CEJL* 3: 212).

This interest in popular taste is not evident merely in "Boys' Weeklies," "The Art of Donald McGill," and "Raffles and Miss Blandish." Almost all of Orwell's essays on more respectable literary figures deal with writers who have wide popular appeal. His literary taste grows out of his egalitarianism. His interest in "good bad books" and "good bad poetry" is an endorsement of the vitality if not the discrimination of popular taste and a demonstration of the "emotional overlap between the intellectual and the ordinary man" that writers ignore at their peril (*CEJL* 2: 195). To ignore it means, in effect, that the writer can no longer influence human events, that he takes himself out of the mainstream of his culture. Although Orwell could hold a difficult writer like Joyce in great esteem, it was clearly the achievement of a Dickens that he envied.

11. George Orwell, "Author's Preface to the Ukrainian Edition of *Animal Farm*," in I. R. Willison, "George Orwell: Some Materials for a Bibliography" (University of London thesis in Librarianship, 1953), p. 222. The version of the preface published in *CEJL* 3: 402–06 is incomplete and does not include this quotation.

It should be evident that these aesthetic attitudes are an integral part of Orwell's political beliefs. His instinctive faith in equality made it impossible for him to like (though he could admire) literature or literary criticism written for a clique. He was as anxious to break down the barriers between audiences as those between social classes. He relied on a highly skeptical aesthetic in which the only reliable test of literary quality was survival—continuing popularity. All other standards, including his own, were suspect. The easy dismissal of theoretical problems in such an attitude shows us that we are up against one of Orwell's absolutes. Yet in his refusal to ignore or dismiss popular culture, in his willingness to read the wrong books and look at the wrong pictures, his influence was certainly liberating, and indirectly revealed the unsuspected limitations of more fastidious taste and more rigorous aesthetic doctrine.

In some sense, all of Orwell's essays grow out of his quarrel with doctrinal thinking. Dogmatic principles and unexamined tenets of faith are his consistent targets. His interest in popular culture is an attempt to go beyond certain widely accepted class myths— both the Marxist and the bourgeois myths of what the working class is like, for example. The analysis of popular culture is a form of field work, as revealing as the more orthodox sociological research of *The Road to Wigan Pier*. Orwell is after *reality*, felt life; he uses it to show up the class myths he finds accepted everywhere around him. He is interested in the literature of the Right for the same reason: in order to substitute an accurate picture of the adversary for the ludicrous caricature that had come to be accepted in his own camp.

The documentary essays ("A Hanging," "Shooting an Elephant," "Marrakech," "How the Poor Die," and "Such, Such Were the Joys") often have a similar aim. They begin with a commonly accepted myth—the "joys of childhood," for example, or the brutal efficiency of colonial administrators. Orwell uses his own detailed experience—his sense of *fact*—to reveal the distortion of the accepted myth. Clearly all of these purposes intersect with the basic impulse of his more strictly political essays: to create a political faith rooted in his own experience and observation rather than in ideology.

Orwell's distrust of political orthodoxy grows out of his faith in inductive rather than deductive reasoning. He begins with particulars and then works his way slowly toward general ideas. This is not only a philosophic principle with him but a literary technique. His essays are all closely reasoned, but they seldom begin with ideas. It is instructive to quote a few of his first sentences: "It was in Burma, a sodden morning of the rains" ("A Hanging"); "First of all the physical memories, the sounds, the smells and the surfaces of things" ("Looking Back on the Spanish War"); "You never walk far through any poor quarter in any big town without coming upon a small newsagent's shop" ("Boys' Weeklies"); "Soon after I arrived at St Cyprian's (not immediately, but after a week or two, just when I seemed to be settling into the routine of school life) I began wetting my bed" ("Such, Such Were the Joys"). If Orwell the novelist constantly needed the techniques of the essay, Orwell the essayist just as surely appropriated the language of fiction. From such beginnings, the essays work slowly, and often haltingly, toward general statement. One frequently has the feeling that abstract ideas and inevitable conclusions are deliberately delayed, then qualified by counterexamples as soon as stated. In any conflict between fact and theory, fact must be trusted, theory modified or discarded.

The essays are the work of a man who trusts the mind to make sense of experience as long as it works in a scientific way and struggles to divest itself of myth and dogma, or at least recognizes and makes allowances for its individual and predictable distortions. Although each of these essays has its roots in Orwell's outrage or delight, his guilt or fear or admiration, the final product is rational, and the ultimate appeal of his controlled consecutive thinking is to human reason. This is both their great strength and their inevitable limitation. For the most part, his longer essays were published in high-brow periodicals and made a reputation for him among intellectuals.

Orwell must have been aware of the irony of writing about popular culture in journals that would never find their way into working-class homes. Yet it was entirely appropriate that the quarrel with the intelligentsia should be carried on in their own organs of opinion. He never stopped writing such essays as he had stopped writing realistic novels and book-length documentaries. Although its audience was limited, the genre had become indispensable to him. And possibly he could justify such coterie work by knowing that simultaneously he was turning to a different form that would make him one of the most widely read writers of the twentieth century; for the decade of the forties not only saw the publication of most of Orwell's important essays, it also produced *Animal Farm* and *Nineteen Eighty-Four*.

The turn to fantasy[12] in the 1940s was the most important shift in Orwell's career. Although most of the longer essays he wrote were also the product of his last decade, there was a clear continuity between them and the essays and book reviews of the thirties. *Animal Farm* and *Nineteen Eighty-Four*, on the other hand, were radical departures from Orwell's previous work in that they *replaced* the realistic fiction and book-length documentaries in which he had previously specialized. It is unusual for a writer to give up a literary method he has mastered in order to adopt an entirely different mode. This significant turn in Orwell's career raises a number of questions that have not yet been answered: Why did he abandon realism and documentary? What attracted him to fantasy and how did he plan to use it as a vehicle for his political commitments? How well did he succeed in solving the inherent problems of the form?

In his attempt to make political writing into an art, Orwell had used the documentary and the realistic novel to expose the evils of his society; yet as we have seen, he had gradually come to feel that neither form was doing its job. Both were fundamentally rational and depended on the writer's ability to observe and record the events and characters of the real world with accuracy. Possibly the appeal to reason failed to convey a sense of urgency; and perhaps the accuracy of external observation merely made

12. I use the general term *fantasy* to point to an important connection between *Animal Farm* and *Nineteen Eighty-Four*, despite the many differences between the two books. They are, of course, related to a variety of traditional literary forms: animal fable, allegory, utopia and anti-utopia, satire, and science fiction. The essential similarity among these various genres, and between Orwell's last two books, is that all permit the writer unusual imaginative freedom and present even his most extravagant inventions as legitimate possibilities.

readers treat such works as travel books, as topographical descriptions of an exotic landscape. In any case, it was clear that both documentary and realistic novel had failed to make the audience care sufficiently about the abuses they exposed.

The history of the 1930s and 1940s added to this sense of the bankruptcy of realism and documentary for the politically committed writer. Could totalitarianism, genocide, the resurgence of dictatorship and fanatic nationalism, the revival of torture and political imprisonment be explained adequately in documentary fashion? The world had become profoundly irrational since Orwell's young manhood, and he felt that its blatant insanity could only be understood by venturing beyond the boundaries of reason. In the essay "Wells, Hitler and the World State," he argues that the sensible humanitarian optimist can no longer grasp contemporary reality. Recent history had been dominated by primitive passions, which benevolent rationalists like Wells (the Wells of the later prophecies and tracts, not the early fantasies) seemed incapable of understanding: "The energy that actually shapes the world springs from emotions—racial pride, leader-worship, religious belief, love of war—which liberal intellectuals mechanically write off as anachronisms, and which they have usually destroyed so completely in themselves as to have lost all power of action. . . . Wells is too sane to understand the modern world" (*CEJL* 2: 141, 145).

Orwell hoped to find, in the fantastic works of the 1940s, a literary vehicle for exposing readers directly to the irrational forces that seemed to control the world. Clearly, he needed a form that would give him great freedom to invent, one that would rely on the power of his imagination rather than the accuracy of his observation. He wanted a mode of expression that acted on some deeper and more primitive level of consciousness than realism or documentary had done. Yet he must have made this decision with considerable reluctance. Fantasy is an unpredictable force and not at all easy to manipulate in order to express preconceived purposes. It can become powerful only if the artist relaxes his absolute rational control and frees his imagination. That such relaxation of purpose did not come easily to Orwell is suggested by the difference between his earlier and later experiments in fantasy. *Animal Farm* and *Nineteen Eighty-Four* are both about some of the irrational forces that dominate the modern world, and both use elements of fantasy; yet the first book is obviously much more rigidly and logically controlled than the second.

Orwell was moving toward an interest in and a need for myth, and this need was largely created by his sense of recent history. The triumph of unreason was evident not only in the actions of nations but in most forms of political behavior, and Orwell concludes in one of his *Tribune* pieces that "the world is suffering from some kind of mental disease which must be diagnosed before it can be cured" (*CEJL* 4: 249). The most disturbing symptoms to reveal themselves in the previous decade were the worship of power and the extraordinary appeal of political myths. These two forces are in fact related, for the myths were necessary to protect committed people from the knowledge that the universal hunger for power threatened every political system, no matter how idealistically conceived. The myths of the perfect society, of the inevitability of human improvement, and of the possibility of achieving genuine equality, were all necessary to hide the new *facts* of tyranny, the return to barbarism, and the entrenchment of social privilege.

All these myths came together for Westerners in the myth of the Soviet Union—the ideal socialist commonwealth. The exposes of the late 1930s were largely forgotten during the war, when Russia became the ally of Britain and America. The doubts about Stalinist autocracy were conveniently buried, to be replaced once again by the romantic fiction of the workers' state. The size of the British Communist Party, for example, more than tripled during the war years.[13] Such signs disturbed Orwell profoundly, for they seemed to present a clear threat to democratic socialism. The exposure of Stalinist Russia in the essays and documentaries of the previous decade had obviously not worked if all they had taught could be so easily forgotten or ignored. Myth was more powerful than fact in most people's lives: the writer must start with this basic assumption. Orwell felt that the image of a socialist Russia worked directly against the hopes of Western socialists like

13. Neal Wood, *Communism and British Intellectuals* (New York, 1959), p. 23.

himself: "Nothing has contributed so much to the corruption of the original idea of Socialism as the belief that Russia is a Socialist country and that every act of its rulers must be excused, if not imitated," he wrote in a preface to *Animal Farm*. "And so for the past ten years I have been convinced that the destruction of the Soviet myth was essential if we wanted a revival of the Socialist movement" (*CEJL* 3: 405).

Fire can fight fire; countermyths can defeat myths. Orwell set himself the task of exposing the illusion that the Soviet Union was an egalitarian society along with the widely accepted idea that state ownership guarantees the end of privilege. He knew that he would have to find a countermyth that would take hold of the reader's mind by replacing its rival, and that to do this his tale would have to appeal to his audience's most basic feelings. The idealization of the Soviet Union as a utopian society grew out of people's need to believe their highest hopes could be fulfilled. Orwell's fables in *Animal Farm* and *Nineteen Eighty-Four* exploit an equally powerful emotion: the fear that one's worst nightmares might come true. To deal with such elemental subject matter, he had to resort to fantasy; realistic fiction was simply unequal to the task. Only an anti-utopia could displace a utopian vision; only the fear of hell was as powerful as the need for heaven. In *Animal Farm*, one sees Orwell moving rather hesitantly toward this strategy, for though the book has managed (like its predecessor and model *Gulliver's Travels*) to achieve the status of an independent myth, it was conceived only as antimyth—as an attempt to fight fire with water, not fire.

If Orwell's fantasies are to work as cautionary tales, they must make such a deep impression that they continue to exist in the back of the mind, ready to be recalled whenever something in the actual world threatens to make them come true. In *Nineteen Eighty-Four*, for instance, Orwell tried to make an audience with little direct experience of totalitarianism sensitive to how living in a society of constant surveillance and control might feel. Only in this way will such people be able to recognize and resist its first encroachments. That much of the vocabulary of the book has passed into common speech suggests he has been remarkably successful in achieving his goal. "Big Brother is watching you," for example, has become a familiar slogan used whenever the state, or any other form of authority, attempts to invade human privacy. This must have been exactly the response Orwell hoped for. He wanted his audience to remember *Nineteen Eighty-Four* not so much as a *book* (with plot, characters, and the rest of the machinery of fiction) but rather as a *Gestalt*, as a coherent world whose entire outline immediately comes to mind whenever one of its elements is observed in the real world. For this reason the political system in *Nineteen Eighty-Four* "is endowed with a coherence that no system in the real world has ever had," as one critic has argued.[14] The paranoid intensity of Orwell's book is a product of his feeling that the modern world can no longer be understood by the sane man of good will. Yet in adopting such methods of persuasion, Orwell at last abandons his faith in rational process and reluctantly ratifies Sorel's theory of the indispensability of political myths (see above, pp. 56–57). On the deepest level, his use of exaggeration and distortion is a defeat.

Orwell was drawn to fantasy not only because of its appropriateness for presenting the madness of contemporary life but also because it seemed to make him the undisputed master over his own fictional world. Despite its dependence on the imagination, fantasy can be turned into an essentially idea-dominated form. The fabulist has much more complete control over the content of his work than the writer of realistic fiction or documentary. His freedom of choice is unlimited, while theirs is hemmed in by the demand for mimesis or for fact. In the fantastic fable, Orwell had discovered the inevitable genre for someone drawn both to the implicit method of fiction and the explicit statement of the essay. It was a form controlled by thematic urgency yet expressing itself in images, a form that directed the reader's attention to meaning rather than to plot.

Orwell's account of the genesis of *Animal Farm*, for example, suggests that his political purpose entirely determined the form of his narrative. As he explains in the prefatory note to the book, he began with the conviction that the Soviet myth must be destroyed. And then:

> On my return from Spain I thought of exposing the Soviet
> myth in a story that could be easily understood by almost

14. George Kateb, "The Road to 1984," *Political Science Quarterly* 81 (1966): 577.

anyone and which could be easily translated into other languages. However the actual details of the story did not come to me for some time until one day (I was then living in a small village) I saw a little boy, perhaps ten years old, driving a huge cart-horse along a narrow path, whipping it whenever it tried to turn. It struck me that if only such animals became aware of their strength we should have no power over them, and that men exploit animals in much the same way as the rich exploit the proletariat.

I proceeded to analyse Marx's theory from the animals' point of view. To them it was clear that the concept of a class struggle between humans was pure illusion, since whenever it was necessary to exploit animals, all humans united against them: the true struggle is between animals and humans. From this point of departure, it was not difficult to elaborate the story. [*CEJL* 3: 405–06]

If this beguiling account is to be trusted, it suggests one of the dangers of fantasy as a vehicle. Orwell's political purpose precedes his inspiration: the germ of his story is first seen as an illustration of an idea he has already formulated, and the story is then elaborated to demonstrate the idea. The mechanical nature of this process is likely to be evident in the final work. As the *Oxford English Dictionary* notes, the predominant sense of "fantasy" is "caprice, whim, fanciful invention." Such narratives often give us the feeling of mere ingenuity and contrivance, and the reader responds to them by admiring the author's cleverness but refusing to trust his vision. The feeling of the writer's absolute freedom blends too easily with a sense of his fundamental irresponsibility and arbitrariness. This is a problem that any serious fantasy must overcome.

Orwell tried to overcome it by deliberately keeping his fantastic invention close to real events. The revolution in *Animal Farm* is of course carefully modeled on the Russian Revolution, and the methods of the police state in *Nineteen Eighty-Four* would have been familiar to an audience that had recently fought against Nazi Germany. He worked hard to make the literal level of his fables recognizable. *Nineteen Eighty-Four* takes place in London, for example, not in some new fantasy-city of the future. Its buildings, neighborhoods, and way of life are clearly drawn from the familiar present. Only the telescreens and posters of Big Brother differentiate Victory Mansions, where Winston Smith lives, from a decaying block of flats in the 1940s. Orwell would never have been tempted to imagine the world of 802,701 A.D. as Wells had done in *The Time Machine*. His use of fantasy is deliberately rationed, and within the fantastic framework there is a good deal of realistic observation. *Animal Farm* could only have been written by someone who knew a good deal about farms and farm animals. There are no unicorns in Orwell's bestiary; his imaginative excursions never left the familiar world far behind. As E. M. Forster said of *Nineteen Eighty-Four*, "There is not a monster in that hateful apocalypse which does not exist in embryo today." [15]

Orwell knew that if he wanted to avoid giving the sense of arbitrary invention, he would also have to give his fantasies a paradoxical emotional plausibility. We must be able to feel that the reactions of a Winston Smith, a Julia, an O'Brien, are conceivable human responses *given the conditions in which they find themselves.* This would seem to be one of the laws of serious fantasy, that its imaginary world must nevertheless have the inner consistency of reality. The events, the agents, the settings of, say, "The Ancient Mariner" or Kafka's "Metamorphosis" can be absurd or impossible, but the emotions of the characters must strike us as plausible responses to their situations. This necessity explains, for example, some of the unexpected shifts of tone in *Animal Farm*, in which the flat characters suddenly turn round. When Boxer is taken off to his death, his friend Benjamin, who makes a specialty of ironic detachment, is suddenly but convincingly transformed into a violent and distracted creature: "They were astonished to see Benjamin come galloping from the direction of the farm buildings, braying at the top of his voice. It was the first time that they had ever seen Benjamin excited—indeed, it was the first time that anyone had ever seen him gallop" (*AF*, p. 94). And in the scene that parallels the Stalinist purge trials, the whole tone of Orwell's cool and witty narrative changes

15. *Two Cheers for Democracy* (London, 1951), p. 72.

to match the events: "And so the tale of confessions and executions went on, until there was a pile of corpses lying before Napoleon's feet and the air was heavy with the smell of blood" (*AF*, p. 67).

Such internal plausibility is a form of realism, but its complexity is likely to come into conflict with the working out of the author's political purpose, which usually demands a more rigidly schematized fictional world. We can see this schematization in the last parts of *Nineteen Eighty-Four*, after the capture of Winston and Julia. There is a general sense of stridency in this section, a feeling that a willed reality is replacing a plausible one. Orwell himself blamed his illness for these excesses, but the problem would have faced him in any case. As he wrote to Julian Symons in explanation of the "vulgarity" of the torture scenes, "I didn't know another way of getting somewhere near the effect I wanted" (*CEJL* 4: 503).

Orwell's didactic intent here conflicts with his awareness of the reality of human behavior. The particular exaggerations (O'Brien's superhuman insight and naked commitment to power, Winston's continuous naïveté and final abject surrender) are there because the thesis of the book requires them. Winston must break down completely and be left utterly without dignity; otherwise the totalitarian system Orwell warns us of would not seem threatening enough. O'Brien must know all of Winston's thoughts and manifest an incomprehensible power-hunger; otherwise the prospect of such men in control would not be sufficiently frightening. Yet this sacrifice of complexity and emotional plausibility finally works against Orwell's purposes because it undercuts the reader's involvement and trust. "We hate poetry that has a palpable design upon us," as Keats said.

The danger of fantasy as a vehicle for a serious writer, as I have suggested, is that it will give us just such a sense of contrivance rather than of inevitability and truth. Yet if some parts of *Nineteen Eighty-Four* seem mechanical, the book as a whole often seems just the opposite—obsessive and unwilled. The tight control and parsimonious release of imaginative energy so evident in *Animal Farm* do not characterize the later work. Orwell transformed the genre into a semiconfessional mode that expresses his own deepest conflicts and fears. To read his letters, essays, and journals of the 1940s is to become aware of how concerned he was with the issues raised in *Nineteen Eighty-Four*; but the parallels are not limited to ideas. He allowed himself to use even idiosyncratic personal fantasies in imagining the world of Oceania and the mind of Winston Smith. Orwell's lyrical feeling for the English country-side, his love of the naturalness of working-class life, and his nostalgia for the world of the recent past are all transferred to his fictional character.

So are some of his fears. It is worth recalling, for instance, that Orwell could think of nothing more terrifying than "a rat running over me in the darkness" (*HC*, p. 87), as he confesses in *Homage to Catalonia*. This fear becomes the basis of the torture scene in *Nineteen Eighty-Four*; for Winston too rats are "the worst thing in the world" (*NEF*, p. 290). In *The Road to Wigan Pier*, Orwell records that he is haunted by the memory of "servants and coolies I had hit with my fist in moments of rage" in Burma (*RWP*, p. 149). Winston has similar sadistic fantasies: "Vivid, beautiful hallucinations flashed through his mind. He would flog her to death with a rubber truncheon" (*NEF*, p. 19).

These extreme examples suggest that Orwell has unbound the fetters of fantasy, and that the newly freed imagination threatens to break away from all rational control. As one critic has said, *Nineteen Eighty-Four* is "a utopian 'De Profundis'." [16] Its horror is not manufactured but experienced; its urgency and sense of witness are unmistakable. This has not always been treated as a virtue, however. In his study of utopian fantasy, Richard Gerber insists that the genre cannot sustain Orwell's passionate despera-tion: "A utopia cannot bear such tragedy. A utopian tragedy tends to be hysterical or sentimental. Being seriously crushed by a utopian hypothesis is the sign of a morbidly brooding mind." [17] And Anthony West has argued that Orwell unconsciously con-structed the whole world of Oceania as an expression of his own paranoia, that his childhood sense of inferiority (described in "Such, Such Were the Joys") is projected onto society as a whole:

16. Richard Gerber, *Utopian Fantasy: A Study of English Utopian Fiction since the End of the Nineteenth Century* (London, 1955), p. 129.
17. Ibid.

"*Nineteen Eighty-Four* is not a rational attempt to imagine a probable future; it is an aggregate of 'all the things you've got at the back of your mind, the things you're terrified of'. Most of these, in *Nineteen Eighty-Four*, are of an infantile character, and they clearly derive from the experience described in *Such, Such Were the Joys*." [18]

To deny a writer the power of his obsessions is to idealize the cool and rational element in literature at the expense of some of the darker forces that also go into its making. A distorted, "unreal" fictional world can have extraordinary imaginative depth and compulsive energy, as writers like Swift, Kafka, or Lawrence make clear. Once released, however, the obsessive fantasies of a writer are not so easily controlled. Like the powers summoned by the sorcerer's apprentice, they begin by doing the master's bidding but often end by engulfing him. And yet despite this danger, Orwell's use of childhood fantasy remains largely purposive in *Nineteen Eighty-Four*. He is writing, after all, for an audience that has not experienced totalitarianism but *has*, presumably, experienced childhood terror. He is not engaged in "a rational attempt to imagine a probable future" but in trying to give his readers an inkling of how it feels to live in a totalitarian state.

Orwell's point is that such regimes do not treat their citizens as adults but wish to keep them in a state of childish dependence. All significant decisions are made for them by "Big Brother"; all independent actions are treated as threats to the authority of the state. Oceanic society is like an enormous family with the dictatorial parents in complete control. Orwell's plot records the unsuccessful rebellion of a prodigal son, a "stubborn, self-willed exile from the loving breast" (*NEF*, p. 304). Perhaps he recalls that Hitler attempted to impose the pattern of the patriarchal family on a whole culture: "Ein Volk, ein Reich, ein Führer." The "infantile character" of Winston's fears is central to Orwell's conception of how totalitarianism works.

Not all of the compulsive material reinforces the original political purpose of the book, however. It seems likely that Orwell

18. *Principles and Persuasions* (London, 1958), p. 156.

did not intend *Nineteen Eighty-Four* to be as remorselessly pessimistic as it turned out. His important essay on James Burnham, for instance, dismisses the prediction that an unconquerable state like the one pictured in the book will inevitably come into being: "The huge, invincible, everlasting slave empire of which Burnham appears to dream will not be established, or, if established, will not endure, because slavery is no longer a stable basis for human society" (*CEJL* 4: 180).

Yet *Nineteen Eighty-Four* permits no such easy optimism; its slave empire seems both established and secure, and the hopes for its overthrow (Winston's rebellion, the actions of the proles, or even Emmanuel Goldstein's revolution) are treated either as failures or as " 'opeless fancies." If the purpose of Orwell's book is to make people able to resist totalitarianism by exposing its nature and methods, the utter defeat of his hero in challenging authority is hardly apt to strengthen their resolve. It seems likely that his attack on Burnham is an attempted exorcism, for, as we have seen, the instinctive pessimism he argued against so vigorously had always lived within his own psyche. It is worth recalling that every novel Orwell wrote is essentially about a failed revolution—the unsuccessful attempt of a character to break out of the restricting way of life in which he finds himself and to alter his condition. Orwell's pessimism was a reflex imaginative act for him; by comparison, his optimism was merely an idea.

The fantasy elements of *Nineteen Eighty-Four* thus reinforce only a part of Orwell's political purpose: that of exposing the audience to the nature of totalitarianism. The more hopeful side of his political faith, however, is left without imaginative support, and the book inexorably moves in a direction far from its original goal. This does not mean that the release of Orwell's imagination has destroyed his book, though it may have altered his preliminary intention beyond recognition. The expressive component of his fantasy world must be judged not by whether it serves his socialist commitment, nor by whether it violates the traditional assumptions of a genre, nor even by whether his obsessions are "morbid." Nor does the persuasiveness of such a work depend on how closely its vision corresponds to reality. The essential question is whether the writer's imagination expresses something absolutely idiosyncratic, or whether his extreme distortions are recognizable to many readers and in some sense acknowledged as their own. The extraordinary popularity of *Nineteen Eighty-Four*—the fact that almost every serious reader knows the book—offers indisputable testimony that Orwell's obsession is shared. His vision may be selective and intense, but it is hardly unrecognizable.

Orwell himself speculated about this kind of universality in his essay on Swift, in which he argues that Swift's remorseless pessimism, though "diseased," nevertheless affects us powerfully because we have all at some time known his mood: "Swift falsifies his picture of the whole world by refusing to see anything in human life except dirt, folly and wickedness, but the part which he abstracts from the whole does exist, and it is something which we all know about while shrinking from mentioning it" (*CEJL* 4: 222). And Orwell's analysis of why *Gulliver's Travels* has endured could be used to explain the success of *Nineteen Eighty-Four*:

> The views that a writer holds must be compatible with sanity, in the medical sense, and with the power of continuous thought: beyond that what we ask of him is talent, which is probably another name for conviction. Swift did not possess ordinary wisdom, but he did possess a terrible intensity of vision, capable of picking out a single hidden truth and then magnifying it and distorting it. The durability of *Gulliver's Travels* goes to show that, if the force of belief is behind it, a world-view which only just passes the test of sanity is sufficient to produce a great work of art. [*CEJL* 4: 223]

Whether *Animal Farm* and *Nineteen Eighty-Four* are "great works of art" depends not only on the intensity of Orwell's vision, however, but also on how successfully he managed to solve some of the inherent problems of writing didactic fantasy. To say that talent is merely another name for conviction certainly oversimplifies the matter. The greatest difficulty facing the writer of fable has always been to make both the literal and symbolic levels— both the tale and the idea behind it—come alive without sacrificing one to the other. To treat the literal level as a mere distraction or a necessary evil may make the writer's purpose more apparent, but it also transforms his story into the fraudulent picture-language that Coleridge contemptuously dismissed as allegory. Whatever label one chooses to apply to such works, it is clear that they do not work through the reader's imagination and intuitive understanding; rather, they are essays in thin fictional disguise. At the other extreme, the writer of fable can surrender himself so completely to his fantasy world that his didactic purpose is lost in incomprehensible literal detail. His problem in writing didactic fantasy, in short, is to make his meaning clear without making it obtrusive.

A writer with a strong political commitment may be unwilling to trust the essential indirectness of fiction. The fear that the reader will not understand encourages him to incorporate miniature interpretive essays into his narrative. This tradition goes back to the Aesopian fable, which usually ends with an explicit moral lesson. La Fontaine, while acknowledging Aesop as his master, made his own moral tags cryptic, witty, and demanding. He occasionally dispenses with the moral altogether, "but only," as he says, "where I could not bring it in gracefully, and the reader could easily supply it." [19] Yet if the reader can "easily supply" the lesson, he probably does not need to be taught it. This suggests that the more implicit kind of fable is limited to reinforcing traditional wisdom and is not equipped to deal with unfamiliar ideas.

That Orwell's political truths were not those of the audience for which he wrote should make his uneasiness with indirect fable more understandable. He had certainly known the experience of being misinterpreted. When the Dial Press rejected *Animal Farm* in 1944, for example, they did so on the grounds that "it was impossible to sell animal stories in the USA," and Orwell wrote to his agent that they had probably "taken it for a bona fide animal story. So I suppose it might be worth indicating on the dust-jacket of the American edition what the book is about" (*CEJL* 4: 110–11). To spell out the "moral" on the dust-jacket is perhaps one step removed from tacking it onto the tale itself, but the principle—and the anxiety behind it—is exactly the same. It is as

19. Jean de La Fontaine, *Fables*, trans. Edward Marsh (London, 1952), p. xiii.

though Hawthorne had heeded Poe's impatient advice to "get a bottle of visible ink." [20] Orwell expressed a similar concern for the dust-jacket description of *Nineteen Eighty-Four*. The draft the editor had sent, he says, "makes the book sound as though it were a thriller mixed up with a love story, & I didn't intend it to be primarily that." His first concern is rather with "the intellectual implications of totalitarianism," and the audience must be made aware of this from the start (*CEJL* 4: 460).

In these two examples, Orwell is afraid that his readers will not be able to see beyond the literal level to his political purpose. He was much more seriously worried about the reader's freedom to make of his story whatever he wished, and he was particularly disturbed by the way both his final books were misinterpreted. Although he did not want to comment on *Animal Farm* ("if it does not speak for itself, it is a failure"), he could not refrain from pointing out the error of one common misreading: "A number of readers may finish the book with the impression that it ends in the complete reconciliation of the pigs and the humans. That was not my intention; on the contrary I meant it to end on a loud note of discord" (*CEJL* 3: 406).

Much more disturbing was the interpretation of *Nineteen Eighty-Four* as an attack on the Labour Party, or even on the ideals of socialism. Although Orwell realized that his last two books—intended as leftist internal criticism—were likely to be used by conservative and reactionary forces, he was unprepared for the confusion they aroused on his own side. In a public statement printed in *Life* and the *New York Times Book Review*, he was forced to spell out his purposes: "My recent novel is NOT intended as an attack on Socialism or on the British Labour Party (of which I am a supporter) but as a show-up of the perversions to which a centralised economy is liable and which have already been partly realised in Communism and Fascism" (*CEJL* 4: 502).

All of these explanatory statements, it must be remembered, are taken from prefaces and letters, not from the works themselves. This respect for the integrity of the fictional creation is much

20. *The Complete Works of Edgar Allan Poe*, ed. James A. Harrison (New York, 1902), 13: 155.

more severely strained in *Nineteen Eighty-Four* than in *Animal Farm*, however. In the later book, Orwell once again finds a way of incorporating the interpretive essay into his fiction through the device of including passages from Emmanuel Goldstein's "The Theory and Practice of Oligarchical Collectivism," a work that analyzes the theoretical foundations of the state Orwell describes so graphically. The selections from this book appear in the story like so many lumps in the porridge, and though they are brilliantly written, they can hardly help distracting the reader's attention from the narrative and diluting its force. This is particularly apparent when the climactic and moving scene of Winston's conversion to love of Big Brother is followed by the appendix called "The Principles of Newspeak." As in the early novels, such passages attempt to solve one of the perennial problems of Orwell's fiction: his deliberate use of central characters whose awareness is more limited than his own. The disparity between the mind of the author and the consciousness of his major character is, in effect, distilled to form the essays. Orwell gives up the attempt to make emotional and intellectual sense simultaneously and relegates the two aspects of his book to separate sections. He was aware of the price of such a split yet could find no more satisfactory solution to this inherent problem of didactic fantasy.

Orwell's decision to provide such explicit interpretive help may have been based on the confusion created by *Animal Farm*. He must have felt that too many intelligent readers had failed to grasp his didactic purpose. Despite the idiosyncratic interpretation of *Nineteen Eighty-Four* as an attack on the Labour Party, it created far less critical confusion than the earlier work. This was due not only to the incorporation of an acute interpreter (Goldstein) into the book itself, but by the decision not to base the literal level of the story so exclusively on the factual details of a real state.

The society of *Nineteen Eighty-Four* is more of an amalgam of different totalitarian and proto-totalitarian regimes. Its invention is, I think, a much more independent imaginative act than the working out of the story line of *Animal Farm*. The incidents of *Animal Farm* are largely selected from Soviet history and then translated into the terms of Orwell's story. Like a work of history, the book records a considerable period of time in strict chronological order. By comparison, the society of *Nineteen Eighty-Four* begins and ends as an accomplished fact, and its particular history is far from being the book's central concern. Furthermore, the relative freedom from precise historical parallels makes the later book less of a coterie work. Although it may not be necessary to know Soviet history to understand *Animal Farm*, one of the pleasures of reading it certainly lies in the prepared reader's recognition of Orwell's ingenious transformation of fact into fiction. It is more likely to appeal to a knowledgeable and sophisticated reader than to someone who is ignorant of the events to which the book constantly refers. This is much less true of *Nineteen Eighty-Four* and helps to explain its wider audience and greater influence.

Animal Farm is short because it is essentially allusive. It depends on outside knowledge to give its fictive world resonance. In deciding not to rely on his audience's preparedness, Orwell was obliged to create a total world in *Nineteen Eighty-Four*, every detail of which he would have to illustrate. This is clearly a much more difficult imaginative undertaking, and one he accomplished with remarkable success. He made it an even harder task by refusing to rely on the exotic or bizarre. Many of his predecessors in the art of inventing future societies had concentrated on scientific advances. A major portion of Wells's *The Sleeper Awakes*, for example, is taken up with descriptions of the technology of the future. The reader who is not scientifically versed is obliged to take all this on faith and cannot connect it with elements of his own experience. By comparison, Orwell's descriptions of the future placed very little stress on technological changes, and his external world remains largely recognizable. What has been transformed is human behavior and institutions—subjects on which every man is an expert. His job is to convince the reader that the whole pattern of life in his imagined world is simultaneously new and recognizable, and that it coheres.

He accomplishes this task by thrusting the reader into his world directly, without introduction. The fictive device of Wells's Time Traveller or Sleeper, as well as all the other methods utopia writers have used to bridge the gap between the present and the future—to ease the reader into the new society and give his temporary confusion a spokesman—are ruthlessly abandoned. The whole world of *Nineteen Eighty-Four* is treated as a given from the opening sentence of the book, and the unprepared reader is forced to make sense of it as he goes along. Much will at first seem incomprehensible to him. The society of the future is initially presented as an emotional reality in the consciousness of the book's major character, who is a citizen of that society. The train of thought we are asked to follow is small-scale and experiential rather than historical and theoretical. Both history and theory are there as well, but they come later in the reader's apprehension of the book.

It should be clear that this method is highly uncharacteristic of didactic writing, and that for all of Orwell's anxiety to control the interpretation of his work, he is ready enough to rely on the reader's blind response at crucial points in his narrative. He is willing to use a technique of literature that does *not* have a "palpable design upon us"—the slow unfolding of the author's purposes rather than their direct presentation. Orwell was in fact torn between these two literary methods—implicit and explicit, mysterious and schematic. Although he was tempted by propaganda, he knew that no propagandistic work was likely to last, no matter how powerfully it might affect its first audience. And he understood that to exert the kind of influence which interested him by this stage in his career, he would have to work through the imagination and the emotions of his readers. To change their minds was an easier task than to shape their feelings; but the second was the more significant (and permanent) transformation. Despite all his doubts about the efficacy of fiction for political purposes, Orwell came to realize that he would have to trust its slow and unpredictable power. He did so to the limits of his ability, and he hoped that the dense, literal reality he had permitted himself to imagine in *Nineteen Eighty-Four* would sink into the consciousness of his readers whether or not they perfectly understood the book's theoretical implications.

It is tempting to see Orwell's achievement in writing didactic fantasy as the successful conclusion of his lifelong search for form.

He says that *Animal Farm* was the first book in which he tried "to fuse political purpose and artistic purpose into one whole" (*CEJL* I: 7); yet it is clear that the attempt to resolve the conflict between these two forces informs his whole career. The same can be said of Orwell's struggle to turn relatively "objective" literary genres into forms that would also witness the author's presence and express his deepest feelings. The factual documentaries and realistic novels of the thirties constantly demonstrate the conflict between objective and subjective components. The literary and political essays of the next decade are remarkable in part for their combination of objectivity and sincerity. Again and again Orwell has been accused, in effect, of turning impersonal literary forms into personal vehicles or of forgetting the iron rules of a genre. There is no doubt that these attempts have created puzzling shifts of tone in his work, along with some serious problems of structure. The more intense passages of *Animal Farm*, for example, seem out of place in an animal fable, at least if one recalls the perfect ironic composure of the narrator of Aesop's or La Fontaine's fables or of Chaucer's "Nun's Priest's Tale."

This kind of stretching of traditional forms characterizes most of Orwell's mature work. Given the multiplicity of his interests and the complexity of his own makeup, it is hardly surprising that few—if any—of his books strike us as seamless. The difficulty of the task he set himself—to find a literary vehicle that could accommodate confession, realistic observation, intellectual analysis, and political persuasion—was surely bound to defeat him, and helps to explain why so many of his works later struck him as failures. Nearly everything he wrote gives us the sense of a troubled consciousness attempting to find a means of expression that would serve all of his complex needs as an artist, as a political thinker, and as a human being. It is perhaps our sense of the ambitiousness and inherent difficulty of this attempt that makes us discount some of the obvious imperfections of Orwell's work and see the career itself as more successful and impressive than the individual works it produced.

It is worth reiterating that Orwell's need to include all these seemingly conflicting elements in his work was the product of his political convictions. His distrust of ideology motivated him to test all theories against his own feelings and experience, and against the reality of other people's lives. His dislike of social transformations engineered by an intellectual elite made it necessary to use literary methods that would assure a wide popular audience. His hatred of any form of deception in politics encouraged his search for a form of expression rooted in absolute honesty of statement. Through all of these often unsuccessful experiments in literary form, one senses an impatience with the compromises and shortcuts that more propagandistically oriented writers of his time had adopted. That Orwell never really felt comfortable with the choices his age seemed to offer the writer working for political change has made it possible for his work to survive its own historical moment and to influence a generation of readers who face a new and different set of political hopes and disappointments.

Index